Praise for

Extraordinary

"I am living proof that no matter where you have come from or what you have been through, God desires to do *extraordinary* things through you and for you. John has chosen a timely subject because if we are going to accomplish all that God has planned for this generation, we need to know that God desires so much more for us. Let John's incredible knowledge of Scripture guide you through discovering the *extraordinary* life that God has for you!"

　—JOYCE MEYER, Bible teacher and best-selling author

"In *Extraordinary*, John Bevere does a wonderful job of showing what God created us for and how that applies to all areas of our lives. As a professional athlete, I am constantly dealing with the balance of being extraordinary for God, as well as in my career. This book has shown me that there is no separation between our spiritual lives and our everyday lives. God has called us to live extraordinarily, every minute of every day. This book is a must read for those who are looking to live fully immersed in the greatness of Jesus!"

　—KURT WARNER, NFL quarterback and two-time league MVP

"John Bevere is one of the most passionate people I know, and I believe he has truly grasped the meaning of John 10:10: 'I came that they may have life, and have it abundantly.' In *Extraordinary* he digs into the Word to show what it looks like to please God and use the talents He has given us. John pushes believers to the edge to get them to launch out into the deep. He lives life to the fullest and, through these pages, will inspire you to experience the joy of serving Christ with passion."

　—JAMES ROBISON, LIFE Outreach International

"This is a one-of-a-kind hero message! In his unprecedented approach, John Bevere has delivered a book that will unlock the extraordinary within you. I pray your heart is open and ready to receive *Extraordinary.*"

　—DARLENE ZSCHECH

"John Bevere's penetrating and practical insight into 'what makes life work' shines again from these pages. In a day when twittering quick-fixes are sought for life-solutions and sound-bite remarks are dubbed as wisdom, there's a need for this kind of honesty about the requirements for substance to build a life. John shows that extraordinary living is within every person's reach, but not on ordinary terms."

　—DR. JACK W. HAYFORD, chancellor, The King's Seminary and founding pastor,
　　The Church On The Way

"*Extraordinary* points us to that spot on the horizon—the place that could be ours to live. In his book, John gives us a glimpse of what God has for us in that place so that we will chase after it and allow God's Spirit to take us there."

　—CHRIS TOMLIN, lead worshiper, Passion City Church, Atlanta, and sixstepsrecords'
　　recording artist

"John Bevere gives a unique peek into our natural human desires for an extraordinary life and provides a frank, candid, and probing discussion of why—when we crave to soar like the mighty eagle—we often accept walking among the chickens as our ultimate fate in life. John's book shows us how to reach that extraordinary individual that resides in all of us."
— BISHOP T. D. JAKES, senior pastor, the Potter's House of Dallas, Inc.

"In *Extraordinary*, my friend John Bevere guides readers on a journey toward discovering a life of *more*—more understanding, more success, more excitement. And he shows us exactly what it takes to move beyond an ordinary existence and to take hold of an extraordinary life!"
— ED YOUNG, senior pastor, Fellowship Church and author of *Outrageous, Contagious Joy*

"My favorite thing about John Bevere's books is they're all loaded with Scripture, challenging you to grow deeper in your walk with Jesus, and *Extraordinary* is no different. John walks through the Bible and opens your eyes to God's passion of getting you away from 'the ordinary' and into 'the extraordinary.' Prepare to be challenged and changed as you read."
— AARON BADDELEY, PGA golfer, Scottsdale, AZ

"With both *grace* and *guts*, John Bevere challenges us to live a bigger life in God—the life we were always meant to live. In this powerful new book, John shows us how the grace of God can become the springboard to a 'life less ordinary.'"
— MATT REDMAN, songwriter

"John Bevere shows from the Word that everyone who wants it can live a life with impact. This book hits hard with truth. No more boring, watered-down, weak spiritual life for the body of Christ. Let's do it! We can all release God's power and do the extraordinary!"
— SHAUN ALEXANDER, former NFL MVP

"In *Extraordinary*, John Bevere examines and inspires the heart to realize God has called us all to abundant life. Each of us knows we are meant for more. This book will help you leave mediocrity behind and enjoy the great adventures God has for you."
— TOMMY BARNETT, pastor, Phoenix First Assembly and Dream Centers: Phoenix, Los Angeles, New York

"Teens and adults today spend too much time aimlessly looking for value or something worth working for. In this book John Bevere challenges us all with the simple answer to questions about meaning in life. Only those ready to make changes need apply!"
— RON LUCE, president and founder, Teen Mania Ministries

"John Bevere speaks and writes with an unmatched passion to see people become everything God intends for them to be. *Extraordinary* is another powerful step in that process, calling us all to greatness that allows us to max out our Christ-life potential and live a life that pleases the One who gave it to us in the first place."
— LOUIE GIGLIO, Passion Conferences/Passion City Church

JOHN BEVERE

Extraordinary

The Life You're Meant to Live

WaterBrook
PRESS

EXTRAORDINARY
PUBLISHED BY WATERBROOK PRESS
12265 Oracle Boulevard, Suite 200
Colorado Springs, Colorado 80921

All Scripture quotations, unless otherwise indicated, are taken from the New King James Version®. Copyright © 1982 by Thomas Nelson Inc. Used by permission. All rights reserved. Scripture quotations marked (AMP) are taken from The Amplified® Bible. Copyright © 1954, 1958, 1962, 1964, 1965, 1987 by The Lockman Foundation. Used by permission. (www.Lockman.org). Scripture quotations marked (CEV) are taken from the Contemporary English Version. Copyright © 1991, 1992, 1995 by American Bible Society. Used by permission. Scripture quotations marked (KJV) are taken from the King James Version. Scripture quotations marked (MSG) are taken from The Message by Eugene H. Peterson. Copyright © 1993, 1994, 1995, 1996, 2000, 2001, 2002. Used by permission of NavPress Publishing Group. All rights reserved. Scripture quotations marked (NIV) are taken from the Holy Bible, New International Version®. NIV®. Copyright © 1973, 1978, 1984 by International Bible Society. Used by permission of Zondervan Publishing House. All rights reserved. Scripture quotations marked (NLT) are taken from the Holy Bible, New Living Translation, copyright © 1996. Used by permission of Tyndale House Publishers Inc., Wheaton, Illinois 60189. All rights reserved. Scripture quotations marked (TEV) are from the Good News Translation (Today's English Version)—Second Edition. Copyright © 1992 by American Bible Society. Used by permission. Scripture quotations marked (TLB) are taken from The Living Bible, copyright © 1971. Used by permission of Tyndale House Publishers, Inc., Wheaton, Illinois 60189. All rights reserved. Scripture quotations marked (Weymouth) are from The New Testament in Modern Speech by Richard Francis Weymouth.

Italics in Scripture quotations reflect the author's added emphasis. Brackets in all Scripture versions except those marked (AMP) are the author's parenthetical insertions.

ISBN 978-0-307-45773-8
ISBN 978-0-307-45774-5 (electronic)

Published in the United States by WaterBrook Multnomah, an imprint of the Crown Publishing Group, a division of Random House Inc., New York.

WATERBROOK and its deer colophon are registered trademarks of Random House Inc.

The Library of Congress cataloged the hard cover edition as follows:
Bevere, John.
    Extraordinary : the life you're meant to live / John Bevere.—1st ed.
        p. cm.
    ISBN 978-0-307-45772-1—ISBN 978-0-307-45774-5 (electronic) 1. Christian life. I. Title.
    BV4501.3.B4825 2009
    248.4—dc22

                                        2009017143

Printed in the United States of America
2013—Trade Paperback Edition

10 9 8

SPECIAL SALES
Most WaterBrook Multnomah books are available at special quantity discounts when purchased in bulk by corporations, organizations, and special-interest groups. Custom imprinting or excerpting can also be done to fit special needs. For information, please e-mail SpecialMarkets@WaterBrookMultnomah.com or call 1-800-603-7051.

I dedicate this book to my son...
Austin Michael Bevere

❖

God has blessed you.
You're reliable, faithful, and sincere.
You're strong, witty, and ingenious.
You've been a delight to raise.
It's a joy to watch your extraordinary life unfold.
I'll love you forever, son...

Contents

Acknowledgments

My deepest appreciation to…

Lisa. To my gorgeous wife, best friend, lover, amazing mother, most faithful supporter, and co-laborer in the ministry. You are truly God's gift to me and His beloved church. I love, value, and treasure you.

My four sons. Addison, Austin, Alexander, and Arden. Each of you brings such great delight to my life. You are each a special treasure. Thank you for not only your encouragement but also your participation. Your reward is great!

The staff and board members of Messenger International. Thank you for your unwavering support and faithfulness. It's a pleasure to work with each of you and an honor to serve God together. Lisa and I love every one of you.

Our many ministerial friends all over the world. Space doesn't permit me to write all of your names. Thanks for the invitations and the honor of speaking and ministering at your churches and conferences. I love you pastors and ministers who serve God faithfully.

Tom Winters and Steve Cobb. Thanks for your encouragement and belief in the message God has burned in my heart.

Bruce Nygren. Thank you for your editing skills on this project. But most of all, thanks for your support.

All the staff at WaterBrook Multnomah. Thanks for supporting this message and for your professional and kind help. You are a great group to work with.

Most important, my sincere gratitude to my Lord. How can words adequately acknowledge all You have done for me and for Your people? I love You deeply and more than words can express.

1

Extraordinary

"No eye has seen, no ear has heard, and no mind has imagined what God has prepared for those who love him" (1 Corinthians 2:9, NLT).

These words paint a picture of an unimaginable and extraordinary existence, one far beyond what any mere mortal has known or experienced. You may have heard these words before and related them only to heaven's glory. But in actuality, they were penned for the here and now! For the writer, the apostle Paul, continues, "But we know these things because God has revealed them to us by his Spirit" (verse 10, NLT).

Paul, who lived during the church's inception, was divinely moved to bring into the open what had been previously hidden to our eyes, ears, and imagination. He also wrote the following to describe the mandate of his life:

> My task is to bring out in the open and make plain what God, who created all this in the first place, has been doing in secret and behind the scenes all along. Through followers of Jesus like yourselves gathered in churches, this *extraordinary* plan of God is becoming known and talked about even among the angels! (Ephesians 3:9–10, MSG)

There's One Person above all others who desires an extraordinary life for you. He is a Father who delights, like any good father, in the achievements and happiness of His children. His name is God! And nothing will please Him more than seeing you reach your highest potential.

God's extraordinary plan is revealed when we live extraordinarily. Together let's give the angels something to talk about!

EXTRAORDINARY

Extraordinary. Just hearing this amazing word arouses the desire to surpass the norm, to break away from the status quo. Its definition is "beyond what is usual, exceptional, exceeding the common measure." One-word synonyms include *remarkable, amazing, marvelous,* and *unimaginable.* To better understand the full meaning of this inspiring word, consider its antonyms: *common, normal,* and *usual.*

Ponder this a moment: the opposite of extraordinary is *normal!* If we're honest, I think we all want our lives to mean more or be more than what we've known and seen. Unless it's suppressed, there is an innate desire in each of us to rise above commonness. We yearn for the extraordinary.

The most loved popular films that have captured the hearts and attention of the public involve extraordinary powers. There's *Spider-Man, Superman, The Incredible Hulk,* the Star Wars saga, the Lord of the Rings trilogy, *The Chronicles of Narnia, The Matrix, Fantastic Four, The Incredibles, X-Men, Harry Potter, Pirates of the Caribbean,* and that's not all of them. Add to this mix the movies with extraordinary heroes who do remarkable feats and live exceptional lives, characters such as Batman, Iron Man, Indiana Jones, Zorro, William Wallace, Robin Hood, Spartacus, Sergeant York, just to name a few. In fact, as of 2009, seventeen of the top twenty-five all-time blockbuster movies fall under these categories. That's almost 70 percent, and the percentage varies only slightly if you extend the poll to the top fifty.

How intriguing that the bulk of the most popular movies of all time are not love stories, murder mysteries, espionage thrillers, war movies, true life accounts, sports flicks, westerns, police stories, or dramas of friendship, family, or life in general. No, the top box office draws are films that center on extraordinary characters doing remarkable feats, with a good number of them possessing beyond-human abilities or powers. Why? Because "extraordinary" is how we were created to live. It was God's plan from the beginning.

CHRISTIANITY'S IMAGE

Unfortunately, God's plan and man's execution of the plan are often not the same. One of the main reasons I avoided Christianity for years was its portrayal. I, like so many others, saw men of God as Bible-thumping critics who were quick to judge the flaws of others. Or they were passive, backward, and ignorant. The idea that Christians were pioneers who lived and thought outside the box, behaving in extraordinary ways, never crossed my mind. And the idea of Christian women? Well, it was even worse. I perceived that they had no say in important matters, dressed unfashionably, and neglected their appearance. It was frowned upon for a godly woman to venture beyond her domestic duties and certainly unheard of for her to lead in any way. As a young man, I didn't want my wife forbidden to think and restricted from joining me in life's ventures. I didn't want a woman who was suppressed—I wanted one full of life!

I viewed Christianity as lifeless. Becoming a believer would mean losing my individuality and forgoing creativity, excellence, passion, and the ability to succeed in the marketplace, sports, politics, education, and other arenas of life. I didn't know it then, but my views were the opposite of how God created us to live, because He is the One who breathed into us the desire for the extraordinary. Listen to God Himself:

> God spoke: "Let us make human beings in our image, make them
>   reflecting our nature
> So they can be responsible for the fish in the sea,
>   the birds in the air, the cattle,
> And, yes, Earth itself,
>   and every animal that moves on the face of Earth."
> God created human beings;
>   he created them godlike,
> Reflecting God's nature.

He created them male and female.

God blessed them:

"Prosper! Reproduce! Fill Earth! Take charge!" (Genesis 1:26–28, MSG)

We were made to reflect God's nature. He spoke both to men and women, saying, "Prosper! Reproduce! Fill Earth! Take charge!" Adam, the first man, named every species of animal on the earth (I'm sure his wife would have been involved, but she hadn't been created yet!). God brought the animals to Adam and gave him the responsibility of naming them. There are over one million species of animals on earth. Not only did Adam have the creativity to name them all, but he also had the capacity to remember each one. That was an extraordinary man doing a remarkable feat!

You may ask, "But since Adam fell, weren't those abilities lost due to his dis-obedience?" No, Jesus flipped the mess Adam created for humankind. Paul wrote, "Here it is in a nutshell: Just as one person did it wrong and got us in all this trou-ble with sin and death, another person did it right and got us out of it. But more than just getting us out of trouble, he got us into *life*!" (Romans 5:18, MSG). The word *life* doesn't merely describe the way we'll live in heaven; it also means the "here and now." Jesus not only recovered what Adam lost, but He also provided so much more—the potential of an extraordinary life!

The truth is, *God not only desires you to live extraordinarily but also has equipped you to do so.* Don't ever forget these words. Etch them on the tablet of your heart. A remarkable, amazing, extraordinary life is not restricted to certain individuals or professions. It doesn't matter who you are or how you serve in life. If you're a schoolteacher, businessperson, government leader, stay-at-home mom, athlete, factory worker, hairstylist, student, pastor (the list is endless), it doesn't matter, because you were created for extraordinary achievements in that role. The power to accomplish remarkable feats and live an exceptional life is not tied to an occu-pation but to a disposition of the heart. This is not only God's will but also His great pleasure.

Hollywood, religious people, and our culture had painted for me a warped and limited image of God's people. Why did I have this distortion? God, you, and

I have a common enemy named Satan, who is called "the ruler of this world," "the prince of the power of the air," and "the god of this world." He controls the world's systems and influences the minds of those who do not belong to God. He has billions of fallen angels and demons to carry out his grand strategy. The sad fact is that too often the church has limited Satan's chief strategy to certain behaviors, like trying to get people to drink alcohol or watch dirty sex scenes in movies. He's much more crafty than that and uses a wide variety of snares and diversions. We've missed his primary purpose. Because what he fears most is Christians discovering who God's made them to be—extraordinary people with abilities to carry out remarkable and unusual feats. This should be the image society has of Christians.

In contrast to the present reputation of Christians, one of the great struggles the early church encountered was convincing people that believers were not superheroes or gods. Cornelius, an officer in the most powerful army in the world, bowed down to worship Peter and his companions. Stunned, Peter immediately replied, "Stand up; I myself am also a man" (Acts 10:26).

In a city named Lystra, the mob "went wild, calling out in their Lyconian dialect, 'The gods have come down! These men are gods!'" Paul sharply corrected them: "What do you think you're doing! We're not gods!" (Acts 14:11, 14, MSG). When Paul was on Malta collecting firewood, a poisonous snake bit him. He shook it off, and the inhabitants anticipated his death. "But when it was obvious he wasn't going to, they jumped to the conclusion that he was a god!" (28:6, MSG).

Unbelievers said of the early church, "These who have turned the world upside down have come here too" (17:6). Christians were held in high esteem by their society. It's recorded the entire city of Jerusalem's attitude toward the church was that "everyone had high regard for them" (5:13, NLT). In our generation may we each live in such a way to recover that kind of respect for the church.

A JOURNEY

In the pages that follow, we will embark on a journey to fully understand the extraordinary way God wants us to live. I urge you not to skim through material or skip around because each chapter builds on the last.

I don't want you to experience what I did a number of times when I was growing up. Periodically I would come in late to a movie my entire family had been watching. One evening I walked into our TV room just as *West Side Story* was ending. The lead male character was dying and saying his last, climactic words. My mother, dad, sisters, and I had witnessed this scene together, but the impact it had on me was completely different. I couldn't understand why my mother and sisters were crying. Even my dad was somber and saddened. But because I had come in late, I thought, *What's the big deal?* The same scene that riveted my parents and sisters had no effect on me because I hadn't journeyed with them through the entire movie.

I don't want the same thing to happen for you with the message of this book. It's a progressive revelation that has the potential to ruin you forever for the ordinary. I speak from experience, because as I sought God, researched, wrote, and prayed over this book, I was changed forever!

As you make this journey with me, you'll not only know that you were created for the extraordinary, but you'll actually understand how to live it. Before we begin, let's pray together for God to reveal His desire and quicken yours.

Dear God, I ask as I read this book that Your Holy Spirit will teach me. I pray that I will come to know what is the richness and enormity of the calling You've placed upon my life. I also want to know the power You've placed within me to accomplish this calling and to bring glory to Your name and joy to Your heart. You've placed me here for such a time as this. I pray this message would equip me to fulfill all the wonderful works You've planned for me to accomplish on this earth. It's in the name of Jesus Christ that I make this request. Amen.

2

You Are Loved

My wife, Lisa, and I have four sons who at the time of this writing range from fourteen to twenty-two years of age. A few years ago, while we were enjoying a meal together, I made this statement: "Guys, you can't do anything to make your mother or me love you any more than we already love you. And conversely, you can't do a thing to make your mother and me love you any less than we love you."

I could see how my words made them glad and solidified their feelings of security. Who doesn't want to feel loved by their mom and dad? What I said next, though, caught them off guard. "However, boys, you are in charge of how pleased your mom and I are with you." Their smiles were replaced by more sober expressions. They realized that our pleasure in them was not unconditional, like our love, but was based on their behavior.

I know this may come as something of a shock, but the same is true of our relationship with God. We can't do one thing to make God love us any more than He already does, and conversely, we can't do anything to make Him love us any less. But how much pleasure will He feel from us? That's another story.

In recent years we have heard a lot about the unconditional love of God—a very helpful and necessary discussion. However, many people have subconsciously concluded that since God loves them, He's also pleased with them. This simply is not true.

So what's involved in pleasing God? I believe that we all long to please God, in the same way that typical children are eager to please their parents. For decades I have prayed passionately, "Father, I want to please You the best way a man can please You!" This prayer coincides with what the apostle Paul wrote to every believer:

"Therefore we make it our aim, whether present or absent, to be well pleasing to Him" (2 Corinthians 5:9).

The key phrase is "well pleasing." How are we not just "pleasing" but "well pleasing" to God? And how does He respond when we please Him in that way?

I will spend much of this book explaining the answer. But first let's make sure we understand the staggering depth of God's love for us.

I'll explain.

GOD'S UNCONDITIONAL LOVE FOR EACH OF US

God's love for us is unconditional and unchanging. This is clearly seen in the words of Jesus' prayer the night before His crucifixion: "Then the world will know that you [God the Father] sent me [Jesus Christ] and will understand that you love them as much as you love me" (John 17:23, NLT).

Did you catch that? God loves you *as much as* He loves Jesus! That's almost too much to comprehend.

Maybe you're thinking, *Jesus must have only meant the disciples who were seated around the table at the Last Supper since, after all, they spread the gospel to the known world and all but one were martyred for their faith.* If you're thinking that, you're using someone's behavior as a basis for God's love. That's not true. His love for us is separate from what we do for Him.

Another objection to this depth of love might be stated this way: *This was a group of special men chosen by God and placed on earth at that time for Him to love more than the rest of the human race.* That is definitely not true because in the same prayer Jesus also said, "I am praying not only for these disciples but also for all who will ever believe in me because of their testimony" (John 17:20, NLT). If you believe in Jesus Christ, you do so either directly or indirectly because of the testimony of these disciples. These men penned the very words of the New Testament, which you have read yourself or heard repeated by someone who shared the gospel with you. You would not be a believer in Jesus Christ without their testimony.

Another common objection to the magnitude of this love goes like this: *Yes, I can possibly believe that God may once have loved me in that unconditional way, but*

I've messed up so terribly since then that He certainly can't love me now as He did at first.

Another lie! Scripture records that God's love "is ever ready to believe the best of every person, its hopes are fadeless under all circumstances, and it endures everything [without weakening]. Love never fails [never fades out or becomes obsolete or comes to an end]" (1 Corinthians 13:7–8, AMP). His love for you can never weaken or become obsolete. It is impossible, for His love for you isn't based on your behavior but on His character of faithfulness.

God's love for us is so all-encompassing that we simply cannot comprehend its scope. Let's document some facts about His love. He sent Jesus to die for us when we were still His enemies (see Romans 5:10). John the apostle writes, "For God so loved the world [you and me] that He gave His only begotten Son, that whoever believes in Him should not perish but have everlasting life" (John 3:16). Why did God *give* Jesus? The answer is simple: to purchase us back. Our forefather Adam gave up himself and consequently all his offspring (including you and me) to a new lord when he heeded Satan's words in the Garden of Eden. Adam blatantly disobeyed God and separated himself and his descendants from their Creator.

But since God loved humankind so much, He wasn't willing to assign us the same fate as Satan and his angels (hell or the eternal lake of fire). God needed a creative plan to purchase our freedom. He did this by sending Jesus Christ, the second person of the Godhead, who was fathered by the Holy Spirit and born of a virgin. Jesus was all man and all God and lived a perfect life (the only man ever to walk the earth without sin). He went to the cross and paid the price for our disobedience to God. He took our judgment so that we wouldn't have to.

Nothing else could have purchased us, for God says, "Those who trust in their wealth and boast in the multitude of their riches, none of them can by any means redeem his brother, nor give to God a ransom for him—for the redemption of their souls is costly" (Psalm 49:6–8). The price of our soul is so expensive that nothing else could have bought us back besides Jesus Himself. Scripture states, "God bought you with a high price" (1 Corinthians 6:20, NLT). Then again it's recorded that the Father "is so rich in kindness that he purchased our freedom through the blood of his Son" (Ephesians 1:7, NLT).

No person or thing is more valuable to God than Jesus. Yet God saw our value equal to that of what He prized most. Now here is the amazing fact: If you and I had been worth one cent less to God than the value of Jesus, He would not have purchased us, because God would never make an unprofitable deal. God does not make bad purchases (Recall the above scripture, "God bought you with a high price.") A bad purchase is when you give something of more value for something of less value. In God's eyes, Jesus' value is the same as yours!

Do you see how important you are to God? This is why Jesus prays, "You love them as much as you love me" (John 17:23, NLT). That's extraordinary love!

JESUS' LOVE FOR YOU

Not long after I gave my life to Christ, I had a surprising and riveting dialogue with the Lord. I heard no audible voice but was overwhelmed by a message that surfaced in my heart: *Do you know that I esteem you better than Myself?*

You can imagine how these words alarmed me. Was this the Enemy trying to sow a blasphemous or prideful thought in my mind? How could the One who made the universe and all that is within it tell me, a peon, that He considered me more valuable than Himself? I almost said, "Get behind me, Satan. You are an offense to me!" But somehow deep in my spirit I knew this was the voice of Jesus. But I still had to be sure, for even as a new believer I knew that the Word of God commands us to "test the spirits" (1 John 4:1).

In thinking this through, I replied, "Lord, I just cannot believe this unless You give me three scriptures of confirming evidence from the New Testament." Saying this to God made me tremble, but I knew it was the right thing to do. And I soon sensed in my heart that the Lord had no problem with my request. In fact, I felt His pleasure with me for asking.

Almost immediately He responded, *What does Philippians 2:3 say?*

I knew this verse by heart, so I recited it back to Him, "Let nothing be done through selfish ambition or conceit, but in lowliness of mind let each esteem others better than himself."

There is your first scripture, the Lord informed me.

I quickly countered, "No, Lord, Paul wasn't speaking of You! He was instructing the Philippian believers to esteem each other better than themselves. He wasn't discussing how You treat and esteem me."

The answer came immediately: *I don't tell My children to do anything that I don't do Myself.*

Whoa. I was taken aback. The Lord had more.

That's the difficulty with so many families, the Lord continued. *The parents tell their children to do things they themselves don't do, or they tell them to not do things they do. Many parents tell their children not to fight, yet they regularly fight before them. Then the parents wonder why their children fight. I don't do this. I do what I tell My children to do.*

I was still a little leery, so I said, "That is only one. I still need two others!"

I then heard Him ask in my heart, *Who hung on the cross, you or Me?*

I was stunned.

I hung on that cross, bearing your sins, sickness, disease, poverty, and judgment and finally died because I esteemed you better than Myself.

Peter's words came to me: "Who Himself bore our sins in His own body on the tree" (1 Peter 2:24). I now realized I had surely heard from the Lord. He did esteem me more than Himself. Otherwise He would not have taken my judgment and died in my place.

I knew the final confirmation was on the way, and without having to ask I heard in my heart, *The third scripture is, "Be kindly affectionate to one another with brotherly love, in honor* giving preference *to one another" (Romans 12:10). I am the firstborn of many brothers* [see Romans 8:29], *and I prefer in love my brothers and sisters better than Myself,* the Lord concluded.

Of course, this information I received applies to every child of God, so it's all true for you too. He literally esteems each of us higher than Himself! That's extraordinary love that is almost too wonderful to comprehend. So not only does God the Father love you as much as He loves Jesus, but Jesus loves you as much as and, yes, even more than Himself!

THE HOLY SPIRIT

The third person of the Godhead, the Holy Spirit, loves you with the same love as well, for He's the One who poured out the love of God in your heart when you gave your life to Jesus Christ (see Romans 5:5). This is why Paul says, "Now I beg you, brethren, through the Lord Jesus Christ, and through the love of the Spirit" (15:30). Notice that the Holy Spirit's love for us is identified in this scripture. This is why He will abide with us forever. It is His love for us that causes Him to remain. He is the Spirit of Love, for God is love.

God's love for you and me is indeed unconditional, unchanging, and will last forever. He loves each of us individually as much as He loves Jesus Christ. That is almost too wonderful to comprehend, but it's true, for God cannot lie. Anytime you feel unloved, identify the feeling or thought as a lie, reject it, and remind yourself of the supreme price paid to bring you back into your Father's arms. He longs for you with a never-ending love.

I don't want you to ever forget or doubt the love God has for you. It is not conditional—based on your performance or how good you've been. It's a constant love that never fades or ends. It should be the foundation of your life in Christ.

Reflections for an Extraordinary Journey
Do you really believe that God loves you unconditionally? Why or why not?

If you don't, is your belief based on feelings or on what God has spoken? If it's based on your feelings, do you believe that they can be inaccurate?

Make a firm decision to believe God's Word over what you feel. Praise and thank God now for His remarkable love!

3

Pleasing God

With the love of God as a foundation, let's move forward and discuss pleasing Him. To reiterate what I wrote earlier, we can't do one thing to make God love us any more than He already loves us, and conversely, we can't do anything to make Him love us any less. However, just as I stated to my four sons, *we are responsible for how pleased God is with us.* His pleasure in us is based on our choices in life. This is why Paul writes in no uncertain terms, "We make it our aim…to be *well pleasing* to Him" (2 Corinthians 5:9).

Let's examine Paul's words closely. The word *aim* simply means "goal." In fact, the New International Version reads exactly this way: "So we make it our goal…" Our life goal as children of God should be to thrill our Dad!

The word *pleasing* comes from the Greek word *euarestos.* Strong's Concordance defines this word precisely as it is translated: "well pleasing." The word Paul uses doesn't mean just *pleasing* but *well pleasing.* "Average" should not be our targeted goal in bringing delight to God. We should be passionate in our pursuit to be fully pleasing to Him.

Let's examine Paul's statement from The Message: "Cheerfully pleasing God is the main thing, and that's what we aim to do, regardless of our conditions." I love the words *main thing.* This should be the driving motivation in the life of every one of us. Nothing else should take preeminence over this purpose. If we live with this supreme goal as our life standard, then two things will occur: *abounding joy* and *complete fulfillment.*

As human beings we have an inborn desire to please our father and mother. This is a mere reflection of our truest desire, which is to please our heavenly Father. Our primary motive for pleasing God is driven by our love for Him. We adore

Him because He first loved us and filled our hearts with His love! As a true child of God, your greatest satisfaction comes when you know *God is pleased with me.* If we walk in this knowledge, nothing can overpower that joy.

The second benefit of pursuing this supreme goal is that we'll be rewarded greatly. Does that sound questionable to you—perhaps selfish? Earning a great reward, however, is the exact reason Paul exhorts us to please God, and he elaborates on this in the next verse. But before examining it, let's first back up to the previous verse so we know to whom Paul is writing:

> Yes, we are fully confident, and we would rather be away from these bodies,
> for then we will be at home with the Lord. (2 Corinthians 5:8, NLT)

We know from this scripture that Paul is not speaking to all of humanity but only to believers in Jesus Christ, because when a person who's not committed to the lordship of Jesus Christ departs this world in physical death, he or she is *not* in the presence of the Lord but in hell. God's Word makes it very clear: there are only two places a person can be after leaving the body—heaven or hell. There is no paradise of virgins, purgatory, limbo, reincarnation, higher state, or the like. There is only a very real heaven and a very real hell.

In saying this I'm not meaning to be harsh or judgmental, but I am reporting the facts. We must remember that Jesus said, "For God did not send His Son into the world to condemn the world, but that the world through Him might be saved," because the world was "condemned already" (John 3:17–18). Thank God! Jesus saved us out of what we had condemned ourselves into.

I know that many people are troubled by the question, "Why would a loving God send men and women to hell?" There are several facets to the answer. First, keep in mind that hell was not created for men and women but instead for Satan and his cohorts. Jesus made this clear when He said to those who didn't live for Him, "Begone from Me, you cursed, into the eternal fire *prepared for* the devil and his angels!" (Matthew 25:41, AMP). This important fact makes it clear why God had to purchase us back. God indeed is love, but He is also just. He never lies or bends the rules, so to speak. If He did, He would no longer be God, for God "cannot lie" (Titus 1:2).

Man was legally condemned to hell because he turned himself over to the lord of sin, Satan, in the Garden of Eden. Once he did, he became a slave to sin and was doomed to its consequences—the same fate of his new master. If God were to lighten the punishment for sin on man's behalf, then He would not be just or fair to Satan. Satan could then rightly accuse God of bending the rules for humankind, thus behaving in an unjust manner. God cannot be partial in judgment because His character is the foundation of who He is. As a result, humankind had to receive the exact same judgment as Satan and his angels.

For this reason, God had to come up with a plan to save humankind from what they brought on themselves and their descendants. This is why Jesus had to die for us. Jesus was born 100 percent God, thus He was free from the curse of sin. But because He was also born 100 percent man, He could pay the price of man's great sin against God. Only another human could get us out of the judgment we had brought on ourselves. For this reason, when Jesus became sin on the cross for our sake, He cried out, "My God, My God, why have You forsaken Me?" (Matthew 27:46). He took our punishment. He took our place in regard to judgment.

So it was by one man, Adam, that sin came on all humankind, but it was by one Man, Jesus Christ, that salvation from that death became available to all. Scripture makes this clear:

> Here it is in a nutshell: Just as one person did it wrong and got us in all this trouble with sin and death, another person did it right and got us out of it. But more than just getting us out of trouble, he got us into life! (Romans 5:18, MSG)

So when men and women give their hearts and lives to the lordship of Jesus, the legal ownership of Satan is broken, and the judgment held against them by God is completely satisfied. God the Father can justly grant us entrance into His kingdom and not violate His integrity. What an extraordinary plan prepared by our amazing God!

Have you committed your life to Jesus Christ as Lord? If not and you desire to do so at this time, please turn now to page 229 for instructions on how to make this decision—the most important commitment you'll ever make.

THE BELIEVER'S JUDGMENT

Let's now return to the discussion of why we are told to be well pleasing to God. We know from Paul's words that he is addressing those who are children of God through faith in Jesus Christ, not all of humanity. He writes:

> Therefore we make it our aim, whether present or absent, to be well pleasing to Him. For we must all appear before the judgment seat of Christ, that each one may receive the things done in the body, according to what he has done, whether good or bad. (2 Corinthians 5:9–10)

We are advised to please God because someday He will judge us. You may ask, "But I thought Jesus had saved me from that?" Yes, if you have received Him as Lord, He is your Savior, but one day you'll stand before Him as Judge.

Many are unaware that on some future day every believer will stand individually before Christ's judgment seat and rewards will be given based on what was done in our short time on earth. Today's English Version states, "We will each receive what we deserve" (verse 10).

Our sins will not be judged, for the blood of Jesus eradicated the eternal punishment ascribed to sin. Rather, we will be rewarded, or suffer loss, for our labor as believers in Jesus Christ. Paul makes this clear in his first letter to the Corinthian church: "For no other foundation can anyone lay than that which is [already] laid, which is Jesus Christ" (1 Corinthians 3:11, AMP). Again, he's speaking only to those who are God's children, for the entire foundation of a believer's life is Jesus Christ. Paul writes in another letter, "Since you have accepted Christ Jesus as Lord, live in union with him. Keep your roots [or foundation] deep in him, *build* your lives on him" (Colossians 2:6–7, TEV). We are to *build* our lives on Jesus.

With this in mind, keep reading:

But if anyone *builds* upon the Foundation, whether it be with gold, silver, precious stones, wood, hay, straw... (1 Corinthians 3:12, AMP)

The gold, silver, and precious stones represent things of eternal value. The wood, hay, and straw represent things that are temporal or won't last. You have a choice day by day, hour by hour, moment by moment: you can either *build* your life on the eternal or *build* it on the temporal; it's up to you. This passage continues:

The work of each [one] will become [plainly, openly] known (shown for what it is); for the day [of Christ] will disclose *and* declare it, because it will be revealed with fire, and the fire will test *and* critically appraise the character *and* worth of the work each person has done. (verse 13, AMP)

When you put fire under wood, hay, or straw, they are devoured and no longer exist. But if you put fire under gold, silver, or precious stones, they are purified and will endure. There's more:

If the work which any person has *built* on this Foundation [any product of his efforts whatever] survives [this test], he will get his *reward.* But if any person's work is burned up [under the test], he will suffer the *loss* [of it all, losing his reward], though he himself will be saved, but only as [one who has passed] through fire. (verses 14–15, AMP)

Notice the words *reward* and *loss.* I remember the first time I read these scriptures. I was shocked. They didn't coincide with what others had related to me. I was under the impression that we would all go to heaven and be equally rewarded because of what Jesus did for us. I had not heard that a believer's rewards were based on performance.

I grew up in a denomination where many thought our good works saved us. After giving my life to Jesus, I was so delighted to learn that I wouldn't have to go to a purgatory to pay for my sins. I was saved only because of Jesus' shed blood. Salvation was God's gift and not based on my works or on keeping His laws.

However, I had confused salvation with eternal rewards or losses. I'd lumped both together when the Scriptures show something very different. Notice that Paul writes there will be people who are truly saved by the grace of God because they received Jesus Christ as their Lord and Savior, yet they'll get to the judgment seat and lose all the rewards God desired for them. These saints will not lose heaven, but they will lose their rewards. Why? Scripture's answer is that *they simply didn't do what pleased God.*

Scripture also shows that there are those who will be rewarded greatly because of how they built their lives on Jesus Christ and did what pleased God. These will be compensated even to the point of reigning beside Jesus Christ forever and ever. Amazing!

The decisions Jesus will render over our lives on judgment day are called "*eternal* judgments" (see Hebrews 6:1–2), which means there will never be any revisions, alterations, amendments, or changes to them. His decisions will stand forever! Stop and ponder this: *The simple and truthful conclusion is that* what *we do with the cross determines* where *we'll spend eternity. However, the* way *we live as believers determines* how *we'll spend it.*

In speaking to churches all over the world, I am amazed—especially in Western cultures—at how many Christians are ignorant of these truths. This knowledge is described as an "elementary" teaching of Christ (see Hebrews 6:1–2).

Pause and consider the word *elementary.* It is defined as "involving or encompassing only the most simple and basic facts or principles." Another definition the dictionary gives is "relating to an elementary school." What do you get in elementary school? The foundation for the rest of your education, such as how to read, write, add, subtract, and so forth. Can you imagine trying to build your high school or college education without knowing how to read, write, or add and subtract? It would be impossible. Yet far too many believers attempt to build their Christian life without this elementary or foundational knowledge of Christ. No wonder the church's appearance today is far from the one we observe in the book of Acts. No wonder we aren't living extraordinarily.

REWARDING OUR CHILDREN

I've discovered that many believers possess a false humility in regard to eternal rewards. Their attitude is one of gratefulness for being saved, which is good and right, but the idea of laboring for a reward from God seems presumptuous. This is far from the truth. Read what the apostle John said on the topic—keeping in mind that God is speaking through him to us: "Look to yourselves, that we do not lose those things we worked for, but that we may receive a full reward" (2 John 1:8).

And it's not just a reward God desires us to possess, but a "full reward"! Lisa and I have put challenges before our four sons with the promise of nice rewards for their labor. It delights me when they rise to the occasion and fulfill my request. Then I'm thrilled to reward them for their labor. At times, though, I've been disappointed because they didn't do what I asked and therefore I couldn't reward their work. I wanted to but couldn't, because a parent who rewards children when they don't deserve or earn it takes away incentive, and incentive is a good thing.

My oldest son, Addison, graduated high school with honors and was accepted to one of America's best universities. He shocked me a few weeks before leaving for school by asking me, "Dad, do I have to go to college next month?"

I really didn't know what to say other than, "Why would you not want to go?"

"Dad, I really want to work for the ministry full time and help you and Mom get out the Word that God has entrusted to you," he responded.

What could I say? "Sure, son," I replied.

Addison took an entry-level job, and about six months later our director of staff called me and requested that Addison be promoted to manager of an important department.

I was a bit dubious. "Is he capable, or are you doing this just because he's our son?"

"John, your son is a leader," he replied.

After Addison took over the department, he started coming up with new ways to motivate his team and to increase the effectiveness of their outreach. One day in January he cornered me in the office and asked, "Dad, what would you do if we doubled our productivity from last year?"

I almost laughed at his idealistic thinking but fortunately restrained myself. The year before, this department had done a fabulous job, so Addison's hopes were very high, which I admired, but his goal seemed wildly unrealistic. Since his request was "unattainable," I blurted out a significant reward I knew I wouldn't have to follow through with. "Son," I said confidently, "if you make this goal, I'll take you and your entire team on a seven-day cruise."

Addison smiled. "Great dad," he said and walked away.

What I didn't realize was that his vision and faith in this area exceeded mine. That year he called me frequently to request prayer that his staff would accomplish certain monthly goals. So he and I prayed together, and I also noticed his department mushrooming. After six months I realized they might do it. I was shocked (how sad on my part).

When all was said and done, twelve months later the efforts of Addison's department had produced results almost *three* times greater than the previous year. I was in awe of what God had done. Their performance was extraordinary.

Lisa and I took his entire team on a cruise at year's end. It gave me such joy to reward Addison and each member of his department for their fervent labors. It was a win-win-win situation. The first and most important win was that hundreds of thousands more people heard the Word of God. How many lives were saved, marriages restored, churches strengthened, and people healed that wouldn't have been touched by God's Word and power if Addison and his team had not gone after the goal? The second win was that Addison and the team got to enjoy the satisfaction that their efforts contributed to godly change and eternal fruit in many lives. They also benefited from a great time as a group since the cruise was fun, full of laughs, and a definite memory builder. The third win was that I had the pleasure of rewarding them. Lisa and I found so much joy in watching them enjoy the fruits of their labor. The team kept saying to each other, "Do you realize how many more people heard the Word of God because we believed and went for it?" I was amazed by their maturity. They enjoyed the cruise but didn't lose focus on what it all was about.

Now, a few years later, they haven't lost their passion and are still asking me for high goals and going after them with all their hearts. They know that the more success they have, the more lives are changed eternally. To all of us that is the greatest reward.

GOD'S GOALS FOR YOUR LIFE

How does this apply to our relationship with our heavenly Father? God has set goals for each of our lives. In fact, He recorded them in a book before time began. David writes:

> You saw me before I was born.
> > Every day of my life was recorded in your book.
> Every moment was laid out
> > before a single day had passed. (Psalm 139:16, NLT)

That is phenomenal! Did you know a book was written about you? It's not just famous people who are featured in biographies. Your story is in a book, too, and the Author is none other than God. He wrote that book before you were conceived in your mother's womb. What a staggering thought—every day of your life is recorded in that book. And even more overwhelming is the truth that it's not just each day but every moment.

Just as my oldest son pursued a specific assignment I approved, so God has designed accomplishments for you in your book. Yes, God has set goals for you. The apostle Paul also reveals how our intended labor was recorded in advance:

> For we are God's [own] handiwork (His workmanship), recreated in Christ
> Jesus, [born anew] that we may do those good works which God predes-
> tined (planned beforehand) for us [taking paths which He prepared ahead

of time], that we *should* walk in them [living the good life which He pre-arranged and made ready for us to live]. (Ephesians 2:10, AMP)

God planned your paths beforehand, but notice that Paul writes "that we *should* walk in them." The Holy Spirit didn't say through Paul "that we *would* walk in them." There is a huge difference. Free will comes into effect here because fulfilling these assignments isn't automatic. We have to cooperate in our labor. God has set the goals, but it's up to us to discover through prayer, reading His Word, and other spiritual means what's recorded for our lives. Then by His grace we fulfill them. For this reason Paul prays:

> We have always prayed for you, ever since we heard about you. We ask
> God to fill you with the knowledge of his will, with all the wisdom and
> understanding that his Spirit gives. Then you will be able to live as the
> Lord wants and will always do what pleases him. Your lives will produce
> all kinds of good deeds, and you will grow in your knowledge of God.
> (Colossians 1:9–10, TEV)

Knowing God's will for our life gives us the ability to always please Him. However, it is not inevitable. God has set extraordinary goals for us, and they will not be accomplished without prayer, faith, and fervent labor. For this reason we are called "fellow workers" with God (1 Corinthians 3:9). We must search out our personal assignments and move toward them, as Addison and his department did. If they hadn't prayed, believed, and labored diligently, the team would not have attained the mark.

Some people are not happy when I tell them about God's goals. Their perception of the Christian life is "take it as it comes and live the best you can," rather than seeking to fulfill God's specific plans for their life. They think, *You get born again, attend a church, treat people well, work a job, retire, die of some kind of sickness or disease, and go to heaven.* With that mentality, what do these dear saints miss? How sad to trade a divinely designed destiny for such a mundane existence!

Scripture states that every moment of our life is mapped out. What if my son had just taken it as it came? He and the team never would have experienced the joy of reaching a high goal. Our Father specifically states, "I know the thoughts and plans that I have for you, says the Lord, thoughts and plans for welfare and peace and not for evil, to give you hope in your final outcome" (Jeremiah 29:11, AMP). God expects us to seek and find His will for our lives. Paul writes, "Therefore do not be vague and thoughtless and foolish, but understanding and firmly grasping what the will of the Lord is" (Ephesians 5:17, AMP). Another version is more blunt: "Don't be stupid. Instead, find out what the Lord wants you to do" (CEV).

Isn't it great to know that God didn't plan out the lives of just Billy Graham, Oral Roberts, Abraham Lincoln, Corrie ten Boom, and other famous people? He planned out your life too—every day, every hour, every moment—and wrote it in a book. Your life is unique, special, and by no means an accident or lost among the myriad details of the lives of other "common" folks. No one is common or menial. We all were created for a unique path that is extraordinary.

Reflections for an Extraordinary Journey
In your life now, how are you pleasing God? How might you please Him more?

What do you believe are God's special plans for you?

4

Revealed as We Are

At the believer's judgment seat, Jesus will not only examine our labor, actions, and spoken words, but He will also conduct a thorough probe of the core of our being to include our innermost thoughts, motives, purposes, and intents. It's deep on the inside where we first and foremost please God, and as we'll discover in later chapters, our innermost being is where extraordinary living begins.

In regard to believers we read, "When the Lord comes, he will bring our *deepest secrets* to light and will reveal our *private motives*" (1 Corinthians 4:5, NLT). Ponder the words *deepest secrets* and *private motives*. It's clear—there's nothing hidden that will not be revealed. With this in mind let's again hear God's Word in regard to the believer's judgment, this time from the Amplified Bible:

> We are constantly ambitious and strive earnestly to be pleasing to Him. For we must all appear and be *revealed as we are* before the judgment seat of Christ, so that each one may receive [his pay] according to what he has done in the body, whether good or evil [considering what his *purpose* and *motive* have been, and what he has achieved, been busy with, and given himself and his attention to accomplishing]. (2 Corinthians 5:9–10, AMP)

Notice the words *revealed as we are*. All human beings have three images: their *projected* image, their *perceived* image, and of course, their *actual* image. Your *projected* image is the way you desire others to see you. Your *perceived* image is how others see you. Your *actual* image is who you really are.

Consider Jesus—He was rejected by many, slandered by the influential, lied about by the rulers, and viewed by the establishment as a heretic or even demon inspired. His *perceived* image was not favorable in the eyes of many, especially the notables. Yet His *actual* image was quite different, for Scripture states that He is the express image of the Father (see Hebrews 1:3). He pointedly said at the Last Supper, "He who has seen Me has seen the Father" (John 14:9).

Many who possessed reputation or had influence focused on their *perceived* image of Jesus, while God only saw His *actual* image. For this reason the Almighty spoke audibly more than once, "This is My beloved Son, in whom I am well pleased" (Matthew 3:17; 17:5; 2 Peter 1:17).

God's pleasure in the first occurrence here was not based on Jesus' accomplishments because He hadn't yet performed a single act of ministry (see Matthew 3:17). The Father's statement stemmed from the fact that Jesus had stayed true to who He was instead of giving in to the temptation of wanting to "be somebody." Think of it—His half brothers and sisters were probably well aware of who Jesus was long before He was revealed in power during baptism. His mother and step-father had both had angelic visitations and probably shared those stories with the rest of the family. I'm sure He was even harassed by his siblings—"Come on, Jesus. Do something amazing!" Even after Jesus was baptized, His brothers pressured Him to live a *projected* image: "'Go where your followers can see your miracles!' they scoffed. 'You can't become a public figure if you hide like this! If you can do such wonderful things, prove it to the world!'" (John 7:3–4, NLT). If as grown men they prodded Him this way, can you imagine the treatment they, his neighbors, and others gave Him prior to His launch into ministry at age thirty?

Jesus' *perceived* image is not what Scripture emphasizes, but rather who He really is. If you see Jesus, you see the Father. That is why Jesus said to Philip, "Have I been with you so long, and yet you have not known Me, Philip?" (John 14:9). Jesus was a person of integrity—He was the same with the people He met as He was with His Father. He did not try to boost His reputation and did not seek the accolades and approval of men. He only cared for what was important to His Father. We should be no different! We should be just like Jesus. That is our Father's goal for us, and it should be our goal as well.

However, for so many Christians, their *perceived* image is what matters. Simply put, their reputation is of greater importance to them than the true motives of their hearts. This causes them to project themselves in the way they desire to be perceived.

Their efforts are focused on appearances, status, titles, saving face, and so forth. But we must remember that our projected or perceived image is not what will be revealed before the entire assembly of heaven. Rather it will be our *actual* image, our true heart motives and intentions. To repeat Paul's words, "We must all appear and be *revealed as we are* before the judgment seat of Christ" (2 Corinthians 5:10, AMP).

You Will Serve Who You Fear

For this reason, directly after informing us of the judgment seat, Paul writes:

> It is because we know this solemn fear of the Lord that we work so hard."
> (2 Corinthians 5:11, NLT)

Notice Paul's words—"solemn fear of the Lord." The fear of the Lord keeps us in touch with our *actual* image. The opposite is true as well: the more we lack the fear of the Lord, the more we lean upon our *projected* image.

You will serve who you fear. If you fear God, you'll obey God. If you fear man, you'll ultimately obey man's desires. Many times it is harder for us to offend the person we are looking at, especially if we desire their love or friendship, rather than the One we don't see.

The apostle Paul feared God. Therefore he was more interested in his *actual* image, the one God sees, not his projected image. This kept him in obedience to Christ, even when he received the disappointment, disapproval, or rejection of others. Paul wrote, "Does this sound as if I am trying to win human approval? No indeed! What I want is God's approval! Am I trying to be popular with people? If I were still trying to do so, I would not be a servant of Christ" (Galatians 1:10, TEV).

I'm sure Paul's fire was fueled to write these words by what he'd recently dealt with, for in the second chapter of this letter he writes of a confrontation with Peter and some of the other apostles:

> When Peter came to Antioch, I had a face-to-face confrontation with him because he was clearly out of line. Here's the situation. Earlier, before cer-

tain persons had come from James, Peter regularly ate with the non-Jews. But when that conservative group came from Jerusalem, he cautiously pulled back and put as much distance as he could manage between himself and his non-Jewish friends. That's how fearful he was of the conservative Jewish clique that's been pushing the old system of circumcision. Unfortunately, the rest of the Jews in the Antioch church joined in that hypocrisy so that even Barnabas was swept along in the charade.

But when I saw that they were not maintaining a steady, straight course according to the Message, I spoke up to Peter in front of them all: "If you, a Jew, live like a non-Jew when you're not being observed by the watchdogs from Jerusalem, what right do you have to require non-Jews to conform to Jewish customs just to make a favorable impression on your old Jerusalem cronies?" (Galatians 2:11–14, MSG)

Remember, you will serve who you fear. Peter was afraid of his conservative friends from Jerusalem. He deeply desired the approval of James and the other leaders, which led him to hypocritical behavior. He was focused on his *projected* image because he so desperately desired their *perceived* image of him to be favorable. For this reason, Proverbs tells us, "It is dangerous to be concerned with what others think of you" (Proverbs 29:25, TEV).

Paul saw the problem and had the courage to rebuke Peter to his face, along with Barnabas and the others who'd caved into peer pressure. Paul told Peter that he lived in truth, his *actual* image, as long as the conservative Jewish leaders were absent. Therefore Peter was empowered to be a true representative of Jesus Christ by accepting, loving, and enjoying fellowship with these fresh Gentile believers. But as soon as the men Peter wanted to impress showed up, he switched to living a *projected* image. Such behavior was a bad example to the new Gentile believers, and God was not pleased.

We know what a saint Peter was, and he's now in heaven. However, this is the type of bad motive and behavior that will be examined at the judgment seat. Peter will have to answer for this incident, as will we for all the times when we've chosen to be controlled by how we want others to perceive us.

Now read carefully these words from the book of Hebrews:

> For the word of God is full of living power. It is sharper than the sharpest knife, cutting deep into our innermost thoughts and desires. *It exposes us for what we really are.* Nothing in all creation can hide from him. Everything is naked and exposed before his eyes. This is the God to whom we must explain all that we have done. (4:12–13, NLT)

What a punch those words pack! If you skimmed over these verses because you've read them before, go back now and slowly ponder each statement.

Notice that the Word of God pierces deep into our innermost thoughts and desires. It exposes us for who we really are, not who we project ourselves to be. If listened to and obeyed, the Word protects us from deception.

Heeding the Word of God keeps the fear of the Lord active in our hearts. It keeps us fully aware that: "Nothing in all creation can hide from him. Everything is naked and exposed before his eyes." In hearing and understanding this, you can now more perfectly comprehend why the Holy Spirit cries out, "My son, if you receive my words, and treasure my commands within you, so that you incline your ear to wisdom, and apply your heart to understanding; yes, if you cry out for discernment, and lift up your voice for understanding, if you seek her as silver, and search for her as for hidden treasures; then you will understand the fear of the LORD" (Proverbs 2:1–5).

When we are pursuing His Word in our inward parts as the greatest treasure to be found, and if we are seeking to know His ways as if there were no superior reward or pleasure, then we know the fear of the Lord. We will not deceive ourselves with a projected image but rather live in truth.

WHAT IS THE FEAR OF THE LORD?

So what is the fear of the Lord? First and foremost, it is not being scared of God. How can we have intimacy with someone we are scared of? Yet this is God's passion—to have close fellowship with us.

When Moses led the children of Israel out of Egypt, he brought them straight to Mount Sinai, the area where God had revealed Himself to Moses in a bush. Many think his destination was the Promised Land. That is not true. Moses said to Pharaoh several times that the word of the Lord was, "Let my people go, so they can worship me in the wilderness" (Exodus 7:16, NLT). Why would Moses want to lead them into the Promised Land before introducing them first to the Promiser Himself?

I see an amazing contrast in Moses and the people he led. The Israelites had been abused in Egypt—beaten, sons murdered, labored a lifetime to build the Egyptians' inheritance, slum dwellers, poor food, rags for clothing. Yet after getting out of Egypt, they constantly complained and desired to return!

Then I look at Moses: he had lived in the home of the wealthiest man in the world, dined on the best food, wore the finest up-to-date clothing, had personal attendants at his beck and call, and had the best education—yet he came out of Egypt and never once asked to return! Why the difference? Moses had had an intimate encounter with God at the bush; the Israelites were offered the same but refused. God offered to come down on the mountain and introduce Himself to the Hebrews, which He did three days later. But the people, instead of embracing His presence, fled from Him. Once Moses saw this he said to Israel,

> Do not fear; for God has come to test you, and that *His fear may be before*
> *you,* so that you may not sin. (Exodus 20:20)

In other words, "*Do not fear,* because God has come to see if *His fear is before you.*" This may sound like Moses was contradicting himself, but in reality he was differentiating between being *scared of God* and having a *reverential fear of the Lord.* The difference is that the person who is *scared of God* has something to hide—for example, the way Adam and Eve acted in the Garden of Eden after their disobedient act. They hid from the presence of the Lord because they had sinned and thought they could hoodwink God by hiding.

The person who *fears God* has nothing to hide. In fact, he or she is scared to be away from God. King David had a holy fear of God but still ran toward Him and said, "Search me, O God, and know my heart; test me and know my thoughts. Point out anything in me that offends you" (Psalm 139:23–24, NLT).

As you can already see, the "fear of the Lord" is a large topic and not the focus of this book, so I'll be brief. (I have written two other entire books on this topic— *The Fear of the Lord* and *A Heart Ablaze*—if you'd like to learn more.) To fear God includes, but is more than, respecting Him. It is to give Him the place of glory, honor, reverence, thanksgiving, praise, and preeminence He deserves. He holds this position with us when we esteem Him and His desires over and above our own or others'. We will hate what He hates and love what He loves. We passionately seek truth in our "inward parts." Holy fear is manifested by our unconditional obedience to Him, whether we understand what He's up to or not.

When we properly fear God, we know that we can't hide anything from our Creator and that we will stand before the Lord as we really are, not as our projected selves. The somewhat surprising result: *We feel very secure.*

The Danger of Deception

The danger of living out of our projected instead of our actual image is that we can be deceived! And there is one huge problem with deception: it's *deceiving.* People who are deceived believe with all their heart that they are right when in actuality they are wrong. That's scary! James tells us:

> Do not deceive yourselves by just listening to his word; instead, put it into
> practice. If you listen to the word, but do not put it into practice you are
> like people who look in a mirror and see themselves as they are. They take
> a good look at themselves and then go away and at once forget what they
> look like. But if you look closely into the perfect law that sets people free,
> and keep on paying attention to it and do not simply listen and then forget
> it, but put it into practice—you will be blessed by God in what you do.
> (1:22–25, TEV)

We deceive ourselves when we just listen to the Word of God instead of allowing it to penetrate deep into our heart to judge our thought processes, attitudes, perceptions, intentions, and so forth—thus changing the way we behave. If the

Word doesn't penetrate our inner being, then we will have the mental knowledge of God and His ways but only in the moment (when we are looking in the mirror). However, when we aren't consciously aware of our faith (once we've stepped away from the mirror), we'll act in a manner totally contrary to what we profess.

Let me give an example. My family has vacationed in Hawaii for a week in each of the past fifteen years. We've been able to do this at little cost because of all the frequent flyer and hotel points Lisa and I accumulate from our travel.

One of the benefits I enjoy in Hawaii is that my body clock is on mainland time, which means I wake up early and get more time for prayer before the day begins. I like walking on the beach and communing with the Holy Spirit in those early hours.

On one trip I recall walking along the beach and encountering a man who also was up early due to the time difference. He was outgoing and enthusiastically shared his excitement about Hawaii and how much he loved the island's benefits. He bragged about the girls he was meeting, how great the parties were, and so forth. His every sentence was full of profanity, and I learned, sadly, after asking him a few questions, that he was married and had two daughters.

Since my private time with the Lord had already been interrupted, I decided to share Jesus with him and was searching for the right opening. He asked what I did for a living, and I told him I worked for God as a minister of the gospel.

When I said that, his face lit up and he even more enthusiastically said, "That's amazing! I'm a born-again Christian and attend a great church in New York." He talked about his pastor and shared that he was part of one of the church's ministries. He was so happy to meet a minister of the gospel and could not stop talking about "his faith."

As he talked I was reeling at how deceived this man was. No longer was he using profanity while talking about the parties and girls, but he was now looking in the "mirror." He knew the Christian lingo, could quote scriptures, and talked enthusiastically about God. But if I had not held up the mirror by mentioning that I was a minister, I could have talked to him with equal ease of lewdness and revelry. I could have cursed with him, and it probably wouldn't have phased him in the least. In fact, it would have only fueled his fleshly passions. He felt no conviction: the Word of God was not judging his innermost intentions, desires, or thoughts.

As long as he looked in the "mirror of Christianity" by discussing his "faith" and his church, he knew what he looked like. But the moment he walked away from the mirror, his actual image appeared. Chances are good that he didn't truly know Jesus Christ, as was evident by his fruit (see Matthew 7:20–23). When around another Christian, he *projected* an image of who he thought he was rather than who he *actually* was.

This is an extreme case, but it illustrates perfectly what James is communicating. The same principle applies on other levels. How many people repetitively fight and quarrel, speak in a harsh manner to their family members, are unethical in areas of their lives, and live for pleasure and gain—then go to church and project the image of being loving, kind, patient, honest, and devout in their faith? A different person is seen at church (when they are before the mirror) than the rest of the week. They may truly be saints but are more concerned about their projected image than their actual image. They, too, are deceived and will be stunned before Christ's judgment seat.

A Firm Decision of the Heart

The sad fact is that if we choose to focus on our projected image, we will forsake the blessing of being changed into the image of Jesus Christ. We will be deceived and won't be capable of pleasing God or living an extraordinary life. We must ask, *will I live to bring pleasure to God or to be popular among people?* We must be sincere in our choice. We can't fool God by making a superficial acknowledgment of the importance of pleasing Him but departing from it when it isn't convenient. It must be a firm and never-changing decision, for upon it hinges whether we are capable of growing into the image of Jesus Christ or growing into an image that has the form of Christianity but is distant from the heart of God.

It's just that simple. You can read an abundance of Christian books, listen to numerous messages on CD or DVD, attend every church service in your area, gather frequently with believers, and even participate in evangelistic outreaches.

But if you don't truly fear God and are more focused on your reputation, you will grow distant from Him. For this reason we are told:

The fear of the LORD is the beginning of wisdom. (Psalm 111:10)

And again:

Friendship with the LORD is reserved for those who fear him.
    With them he shares the secrets of his covenant. (25:14, NLT)

The Lord will not reveal Himself or His true wisdom to those who lack holy fear. He must take preeminence in a person's life. Not just in word or form, but in a deep rooted heart decision: "My life is not my own; it belongs to my Lord, Jesus Christ."

One of the great tragedies in the Western church is that we offer people the blessings of resurrection power without the obedience associated with the Cross. Many leaders have labored diligently to present a Jesus who is Savior but isn't Lord in a person's life. Many messages are spoken Sunday after Sunday in churches that communicate "the good life" based on biblical principles, but they say nothing of the self-denial required for the advancement of the gospel.

Many pastors focus more on being life coaches rather than bona fide fivefold ministers. Their messages are formulated from secular leadership principles or psychology, with scriptures found to conform to these views. Instead of simply and emphatically believing what the Bible says, this other information is read into the Bible as the basis of belief. Hear again these powerful words:

For the word of God is full of living power. It is sharper than the sharpest knife, cutting deep into our innermost thoughts and desires. It exposes us for what we really are. (Hebrews 4:12, NLT)

Much like a skilled surgeon, the true Word of God cuts deep into our innermost thoughts and desires and reveals the state of the heart so that we can be truly healthy before God. Are we hearing messages according to this standard in our Western churches? If not, are we hearing the true Word of God? Is the true wisdom of God coming from our pulpits?

Have we honestly asked ourselves why we have so much selfishness and envy in our churches? Could this be a result of not fearing the Lord? James questions church members: "Who is wise and understanding among you?" (James 3:13). The heart of his question is, "Who among you truly fears God?" (Wisdom doesn't exist outside of the fear of the Lord.) He continues:

> Let him show by good conduct that his works are done in the meekness of wisdom. But if you have bitter envy and self-seeking in your hearts, do not boast and lie against the truth. This wisdom does not descend from above [the fear of the Lord], but is earthly, sensual, demonic. (verses 13–15)

The Word of God will protect us from the traps of deception—either messages that appeal to men or messages that tickle our ears. We are told, "Fearing people is a dangerous trap" (Proverbs 29:25, NLT). The scary thing about a trap is that you don't know you're in it until it is too late. No bird or animal would ever enter a trap if it knew beforehand what was waiting. Proverbs clearly shows that focusing on our *projected* image is a trap, and you won't know you're in it until it is too late.

Recently, while I was fasting, the Holy Spirit cried out in my heart, *Where are the people who are valiant for truth on the earth?* (see Jeremiah 9:3). I felt the sadness of the Lord at how many in our Western churches have slipped into the trap of the fear of man and have lost their passion for the Word of God.

I feel His sadness for Christian leaders who will not confront the lost so that they can be saved. Boxes are put in the back of multimillion-dollar buildings for seekers to place cards stating that they have an interest in becoming a Christian. This is done so no one will feel uncomfortable or singled out in making a decision for Christ. We want to "ease them into the faith." Yet have we forgotten our Lord's statement, "If any of you is embarrassed with me and the way I'm leading you, know that the Son of Man will be far more embarrassed with you when he arrives in all his splendor in company with the Father and the holy angels. This isn't, you realize, pie in the sky by and by" (Luke 9:26, MSG)?

Does this type of ministry line up with how Jesus did it? Look at the rich young ruler, for example. He came with great desire to be saved, passionate to make it to heaven (see Mark 10:17). Jesus told him to sell what he had, give to the poor, take up the cross, and follow Him. What strong words for this seeker! What was the outcome? This wealthy man, who was excited about finding salvation, left the presence of Jesus "sad." He walked away "sorrowful" (verse 22) after hearing the Word of God. It cut to his heart and discerned his thoughts and intentions. He couldn't bear its examination of his life.

Think this through carefully: the man came eager to hear and left feeling down after Jesus preached to him. How do our modern-day Western ministry methods compare? The young ruler wasn't offered a card to fill out and drop into a box Matthew carried. No, he was confronted with truth, and the truth was not backed down from when it was received unfavorably.

Jesus then told the others how hard it is to enter the kingdom of God: "It is easier for a camel to go through the eye of a needle than for a rich man to enter the kingdom of God" (Mark 10:25). It could also be said, "It's just as hard for men and women to enter the kingdom who trust in their *projected* and *perceived* images." The riches they trust in are not money, but rather how people view them.

How would Jesus fare as a guest speaker at some of these churches who have boxes in the back of the auditorium? How would He fare in churches that are bringing only encouraging and nice words to help people in their life journey? What would the leaders of these churches do when many people left their building sad and sorrowful after Jesus confronted them about their self-seeking lifestyle and called them to a surrendered life?

The good news is that it's not too late, and we can change. Rise up, leader! Rise up, Christian! Our God is calling us to make a huge difference in our generation. We've been called to confront the spirit of the age, the spirit that works in the sons of disobedience, the spirit of this world. We've been called to bring heaven to earth!

Reflections for an Extraordinary Journey

In what areas do you see particular tension between your projected image and your actual image?

How might a more accurate understanding of the "fear of the Lord" improve your relationship with God?

5

You Can Do It!

When it comes to pleasing God, the big question is, "Can we do it?" Do we have what it takes to make Him smile? Can we who live in an imperfect world, bring a perfect God delight?

My early years of ministry were focused on teenagers. As a youth pastor, I learned so much about parenting and family dynamics. One thing I repeatedly observed that broke my heart was how some young people just couldn't please their parents. No matter what they did or how hard they tried, these kids didn't measure up to their parents' (most often the father's) expectations.

I soon discovered a pattern. These frustrated young people would keep attempting to please, but eventually, after repeated failures, they gave up and spiraled downward to a careless and loose life. Disillusioned, they felt hopeless. If the parents had given their children more positive feedback, many train wrecks could have been avoided.

How about our heavenly Father? Can we actually please Someone who is flawless? Hear the apostle Peter:

> We have everything we need to live a life that pleases God. It was all given
> to us by God's own power. (2 Peter 1:3, CEV)

There's our answer—we have everything it takes to live a life that pleases our heavenly Father. So from the outset, settle this in your heart and don't ever let this knowledge slip away. God is the One who spoke these words through Peter. His Word is true and unchangeable. Never at any time accept the lie that you don't have what it takes to please God. The fact is you do!

Many believers look at certain Christians, especially great leaders, and think they could never measure up or be as delightful in the eyes of God as the apostle John, the apostle Paul, Billy Graham, Oral Roberts, Mother Teresa, or anyone else they admire. The truth is that no one has any more ability to please God than you!

With that said, I want you never to forget this statement either: indeed you have the ability to please God, but it is up to you to utilize the power and live it out.

Lisa and I have four sons. Our third son, Alexander, is challenged in conventional education. In fact, he was in special education for a few years. He is a brilliant young man who certainly has the potential to surpass the accomplishments of his parents. Alexander is extremely creative, thinks out of the box, has astounding ideas, and can carry on an intelligent conversation with the best of them. However, in school he struggled with reading because he is more visual in his thinking and learning process.

His oldest brother, Addison, is extremely gifted in conventional education. He can read a five-hundred-page book in a fourth of the time it would take me and afterward can recite and process the book's information accurately.

Both sons have what it takes to go far in life, and I'm very proud of each of them.

When both boys were in school, Lisa and I learned to have different expectations for each. I recall many semesters when Addison had straight As on his report card. Lisa and I rarely had to help him with his homework or studies. He normally worked hard until he figured things out and scored extremely well on his exams. We were pleased.

During one of those semesters, Alexander was in middle school, and we were having a difficult time with him. He frequently forgot to do homework, and the assignments he did complete were subpar. He scored Ds and Fs on his report card. We were displeased with his performance that semester.

A few semesters later, Alexander turned the tide and worked diligently. I'll never forget when I opened his report card and saw Bs and Cs and no Ds or Fs. We were so pleased! Even though he didn't match Addison's grades, Lisa and I knew he had worked diligently. We praised him over and over for the work he had accomplished. He knew beyond a shadow of doubt that his parents were delighted. And eventually, through hard work, Alexander became an A and B student too.

Another semester Addison came home with As and Bs. We were not pleased—not because he hadn't made straight As, but because we'd observed his study habits that semester and noticed he was focused more on friends and social events than on schoolwork. Even though at that time he had made better grades than Alexander's Bs and Cs, we knew Addison hadn't given it his all. (This happened only once, as Addison graduated with high honors and has consistently been a hard worker in all areas of life.)

The point is this: God expects us to be faithful in what He's given us, and He doesn't empower each child equally. Oh, how great it would be if believers firmly understood this truth. This is made clear in the parable of the talents. One servant was given five talents, another was given two, and still another was given one. Scripture specifically states that we are entrusted with gifts "to each in proportion to his own personal ability" (Matthew 25:15, AMP). As with our sons, each servant in the parable had different levels of abilities. In considering this we must also always keep in mind Paul's words:

Who made you superior to others? Didn't God give you everything you
have? Well, then, how can you boast, as if what you have were not a gift?
(1 Corinthians 4:7, TEV)

We must always pay attention to what has been given us by God. A person's ability to write, teach, preach, sing, compose music, design, manage, organize, lead, interact well with people, and so forth is a gift given by God. If I keep that in mind, it guards me from the deadly traps of pride or envy—pride in thinking I'm better than others, envy in coveting what another person has.

Returning to the parable of the talents, the man who was given five talents labored diligently and finished with ten. The man given two talents worked just as diligently but ended up with only four. Even though the first man ended up with six more talents than the other (far better results), both were rewarded equally. You can hear the pleasure in their master's voice:

"Wonderful!" his master replied. "You are a good and faithful servant. I left you in charge of only a little, but now I will put you in charge of much more. Come and share in my happiness!" (Matthew 25:21 or 23, CEV)

Notice the unusual Scripture reference here—*verse 21 or 23*. The two verses are identical. I don't believe this is an accident. God is emphasizing a very important point: verse 21 was for the man who gained ten; verse 23 was for the man who finished with four, less than half the first man's total. Yet the master's delight and pleasure for both servants was identical. Jesus says:

If God has been generous with you, he will expect you to serve him well. But if he has been more than generous, he will expect you to serve him even better. (Luke 12:48, CEV)

If you compare yourself with an admired leader, family member, or friend, then you may come up short. The fact is, God probably gave that person more gifts, more ability, more talents than you. Hear Paul's words:

I'm speaking to you out of deep gratitude for all that God has given me, and especially as I have responsibilities in relation to you. Living then, as every one of you does, in pure grace, it's important that you not misinterpret yourselves as people who are bringing this goodness to God. No, God brings it all to you. The only accurate way to understand ourselves is by what God is and by what he does for us, not by what we are and what we do for him.

In this way we are like the various parts of a human body. Each part gets its meaning from the body as a whole, not the other way around. The body we're talking about is Christ's body of chosen people. Each of us finds our meaning and function as a part of his body. But as a chopped-off finger or cut-off toe we wouldn't amount to much, would we? So since we find ourselves fashioned into all these excellently formed and marvelously functioning parts in Christ's body, let's just go ahead and be what we were made to be, without enviously or pridefully comparing ourselves with each other, or trying to be something we aren't. (Romans 12:3–6, MSG)

You were perfectly created by God to function in the kingdom and have the gifts and abilities to fulfill your specific assignment. So in regard to what we have, we cannot compare our measured results with others. However, in regard to what we *do* with what we have, we will be judged, and in this we bring pleasure, or a lack of it, to our heavenly Father.

Let me say it another way. If the two-talent servant had compared his two gifts with the one who had five talents, he would have fallen short. However, both servants doubled what they started with. They were equally faithful with what they had been given and equally delighted their master.

A SIMILAR PARABLE WITH A DIFFERENT EMPHASIS

After saying all of this, let's look at a similar parable with a much different emphasis. In the parable of the ten minas (see Luke 19:11–26), Jesus discusses ten servants rather than three. Each was given one mina. In this parable, the mina doesn't represent our different levels of calling or special gifts, as with the talents. Rather, the mina represents the grace, foundational faith, love of God, and other gifts He gives equally to all believers.

Let me make this clear with an example. If God has specifically called a person to lead multitudes into the presence of God through praise and worship, he or she has been given musical talents. However, these gifts will go beyond the natural realm, for the talent also ushers worshipers into the presence of God.

I can honestly say that this specific talent wasn't given to me. Every time I try to sing in front of my family, it's a disaster. They laugh, leave the room, or in jest throw something at me—and rightfully so. So it wouldn't be wise for me to try out for the worship leader position at my church. The talents God has entrusted to me to fulfill what I'm specifically called to do lie in other areas, such as preaching, writing, and leading. We each have talents that match our specific assignments.

However, in general areas of life, we all have received equally. Scripture tells us that each of us has the mind of Christ, the armor of God, the name of Jesus, foundational faith, the promises of God, the love of God—the list continues on and on. These are all represented in the story of the minas. In that parable, the first servant multiplied his one mina ten times. At the judgment he was rewarded handsomely and given authority over ten cities. The second multiplied his mina five times. He was not rewarded as greatly; he was given authority over five cities. His reward was less because he took what was given to him and multiplied it half as much as the first man. The third buried his mina, was sternly corrected for his laziness, and received no reward.

These two parables reveal how God equips each of us equally in general life situations (the parable of the ten minas), whereas we are equipped differently in areas of specific callings or assignments (the parable of the talents). For the remainder of this book, I will address what God has given equally to each of us. However, the material is also the very foundation required to operate successfully in our specific assignments.

Bottom line, you can never function to your full potential—the extraordinary—without the revelation of what I'm about to discuss.

Reflections for an Extraordinary Journey

What gifts and talents do you believe God has given you to accomplish His kingdom work?

What, if anything, is hampering you from fully using your gifts and talents to advance God's kingdom?

6

The Power to Please

At the risk of sounding redundant, let me reemphasize the main point of the previous chapter, because if you and I don't fully "get" this truth, our lives will consist of striving, doubt, and frustration.

You and I have what it takes to bring delight to our heavenly Father. The Message reads, "Everything that goes into a life of pleasing God has been miraculously given to us" (2 Peter 1:3). The Contemporary English Version says it this way:

> We have everything we need to live a life that pleases God. *It was all given to us by God's own power.*

I know the next question: "What is the *power* that has been miraculously given to us that enables us to please God?" The answer is, "His grace."

Grace. Much has been communicated about grace in recent times, yet it still isn't fully understood by so many. Grace is without a doubt one of the most, if not the most, important truths a New Testament believer should grasp because it's the very foundation of our *salvation* and *life* in Christ.

In regard to *salvation,* of course we are saved by grace. It's a gift, the greatest available to humankind. We are not brought into a relationship with God by keeping His laws, for then salvation could be earned and consequently deserved. Grace is indeed God's unmerited favor. We are told:

> For it is by free grace (God's unmerited favor) that you are saved (delivered from judgment *and* made partakers of Christ's salvation) through [your] faith. And this [salvation] is not of yourselves [of your own doing, it came not through your own striving], but it is the gift of God; not because of

works [not the fulfillment of the Law's demands], lest any man should boast. [It is not the result of what anyone can possibly do, so no one can pride himself in it or take glory to himself.] (Ephesians 2:8–9, AMP)

That sums up our salvation in a nutshell. It is by the grace of Jesus Christ that our sins have been eradicated and forever removed as far as the east is from the west. When we stand before the judgment seat, if God asks why we should enter into His kingdom, it will certainly *not* be because of our good behavior, weekly church attendance, faithful service, life of ministry, or any other goodness on our part. We will find acceptance from God because of what Jesus did on the cross two thousand years ago by shedding His own royal blood, dying a gruesome death, and being raised up three days later for our freedom. He's the divine ransom paid to free us from our slavery. Nothing else could have freed us! In believing in Jesus' sacrifice and committing our lives to His lordship, we can stand before God with confidence.

GRACE FOR LIVING

But what role does grace play from the time we receive salvation until we stand before our King? First, we must never forget that *grace for living* is still God's favor, which cannot be earned. It doesn't change after we come into a relationship with God.

Unfortunately, many view their life in Christ after conversion through the lens of the law. Instead of depending on God's grace to receive favor and blessings, they rely on their self-efforts. In frustration, Paul asks, "Have you lost your senses? After starting your Christian lives in the Spirit, why are you now trying to become perfect by your own human effort?" (Galatians 3:3, NLT).

Later Paul got more pointed and emphasized to this same church, "For if you are trying to make yourselves right with God by keeping the law, you have been cut off from Christ! You have fallen away from God's grace" (5:4, NLT). If we attempt to maintain our right standing with God by keeping the rules, regulations, and requirements of the Old Testament laws, we actually risk losing our fellowship with Christ and the benefits of grace! That is sobering. We must always remind ourselves that it is by grace we are saved, and by grace we continue to receive the benefits of salvation.

For this reason, Paul writes in almost all of his New Testament letters, "The grace of our Lord Jesus Christ be with you." Keep in mind that his letters were written to men and women who were already saved, not to people who were lost and in need of *saving* grace.

The apostle James wrote to believers, "He gives us more and more grace" (James 4:6, AMP). In other words, there is more grace available than what we already have!

Peter takes it to another level by writing: "Grace and peace be multiplied to you" (2 Peter 1:2). This is even better news: not only can grace be added to our lives, but it can be multiplied! If the apostles desired and prayed fervently for more grace, it must be crucial to our daily life in Christ as well.

Therefore, when it comes to our life in Christ, we are not only saved initially by grace but also kept saved. I know that many believers struggle with thoughts that they messed up so severely after making a commitment to Jesus Christ that God might have taken back their salvation. This is not true! We are told:

> If we confess our sins to him, he is *faithful* and *just* to forgive us and to
> cleanse us from *every* wrong. (1 John 1:9, NLT)

Notice the verse doesn't say *most* wrongs. The blood of Jesus cleanses *every* wrong. He forgives and cleanses us from all that would keep us from His presence.

He is *faithful* and *just* to forgive and cleanse us. *Faithful* means every time; *just* means that He will always be true to His covenant promise. He will never say, "I forgive others of a wrongdoing, but not you."

Are you still not convinced? Are you thinking, *I've sinned too many times to be forgiven. I've exhausted the mercy of God*?

No, Scripture says, "Oh, give thanks to the LORD, for He is good! For His mercy endures forever" (Psalm 136:1). His mercy continues eternally and is inexhaustible. In fact, the statement "His mercy endures forever" is repeated twenty-six times in that one psalm alone!

You are in good company if you struggle with the enormity of God's forgiveness. Even the apostle Peter had trouble wrapping his mind around this, so one day he asked Jesus, "Lord how often shall my brother sin against me, and I forgive him? Up to seven times?" (Matthew 18:21). Peter thought his "seven times" statement was magnanimous because the Old Testament law stipulated "an eye for an eye" (see Exodus 21:23–24). Peter was accustomed to people paying for their errors, sins, and transgressions.

Jesus' reply shocked him: "I do not say to you, up to seven times, but up to seventy times seven" (Matthew 18:22). That is 490 times! However, Jesus was not implying that forgiveness is limited to 490 times because in Luke's gospel He states, "Be alert. If you see your friend going wrong, correct him. If he responds, forgive him. Even if it's personal against you and repeated seven times through the day, and seven times he says, 'I'm sorry, I won't do it again,' forgive him" (17:3–4, MSG).

We're commanded to forgive every day up to seven times. However, if someone sins seven times a day for more than seventy days, he would exceed 490 times. So if it was only 490 times we could sin and be forgiven, then Jesus would have said "up to 490 times" in Luke's gospel. But He didn't. He said seven times a day and didn't put a cap on it. So if someone sins seven times a day in an average lifetime of eighty years, the total would be 204,400 times! This far exceeds the 490 times.

Jesus is communicating that our forgiveness is not to wear out! Why should it be inexhaustible? Because that describes God's forgiveness toward us, and we are commanded to "Forgive one another, as God has forgiven you through Christ" (Ephesians 4:32, TEV).

So if you somehow feel that you have exhausted God's forgiveness, you are listening to your feelings or to lies that do not line up with the Word of God. If you sin and are sorry and repent, then you are forgiven. Case closed.

Along with this good news it is important that I warn you to avoid presumptuous sinning. If you say within, "I'm saved by grace, so I'm covered no matter what my lifestyle. I'm going to forget self-control and live for pleasure," stop!

That's dangerous ground. You are deceived! Don't be offended, but you need to ask yourself, "Am I even saved?" Paul addresses this by stating, "Well then, should we keep on sinning so that God can show us more and more kindness and forgiveness? Of course not! Since we have died to sin, how can we continue to live in it?" (Romans 6:1–2, NLT). In fact, Paul warns Christians:

> It is obvious what kind of life develops out of trying to get your own way
> all the time: repetitive, loveless, cheap sex; a stinking accumulation of men-
> tal and emotional garbage; frenzied and joyless grabs for happiness;...
> cutthroat competition; all-consuming-yet-never-satisfied wants; a brutal
> temper; an impotence to love or be loved; divided homes and divided lives;
> small-minded and lopsided pursuits; the vicious habit of depersonalizing
> everyone into a rival; uncontrolled and uncontrollable addictions....
> I could go on.
>   This isn't the first time I have warned you, you know. If you use
> your freedom this way, you will not inherit God's kingdom. (Galatians
> 5:19–20, MSG)

It's clear we have freedom through God's grace. However, this freedom is not to be used to sin presumptuously. A person who is truly saved has God's heart and doesn't say within, "How much can I sin and get away with?" Rather, an authentically born-again believer says, "I don't desire to sin because it hurts the heart of Him who died for me as well as those He loves." But again, if anyone does sin, no matter if it is seven times in a day, and truly repents, God forgives.

FAR BEYOND FORGIVENESS

How wonderful—we are saved and kept saved by grace. However, there's much more! Grace goes far beyond forgiveness. Grace is God's *empowerment*. This is how we can live like Christ.

Read carefully these words: "Whoever claims to live in him *must* walk as Jesus did" (1 John 2:6, NIV). Notice the apostle doesn't say *should* but *must*. We *must* walk as Jesus did! This is not a suggestion or a goal; it's what God expects. The good news is that God never gives a command in the New Testament without supplying the power to keep it. So we can conduct ourselves as Jesus through the power of *grace*.

Listen to Paul's own testimony on this issue: "You are witnesses, and God also, how devoutly and justly and blamelessly we behaved ourselves among you who believe; as you know how we exhorted, and comforted, and charged every one of you, as a father does his own children, that you would walk *worthy of God*" (1 Thessalonians 2:10–12). Paul commanded believers to walk as he did, *"worthy of God"*! This is possible—for him and for us—and we can do it through the power of grace.

It's this aspect of grace that many overlook, largely because it's not taught with the same emphasis. For this reason, many believers struggle in their Christian walk and don't live an extraordinary life.

Let's first look at the meaning of the word *grace* in Greek, the original language. The Greek word for *grace* used most frequently in the New Testament is *charis,* which occurs roughly 150 times. The most common meaning for *charis* is "a favor done without expectation of a payback." This is the absolutely free expression of the loving-kindness of God toward us. It's completely unearned and unmerited favor.

If we take this initial definition of *grace* and couple it together with select scriptures Paul wrote in Ephesians, Galatians, Romans, and other epistles in regard to salvation from sin and eternal death, we come up with the definition of grace that the majority of Christians are familiar with. However, this understanding merely covers the *motive* and *end result* of the gift but doesn't define the present *nature* of grace. In other words, it shows grace as a free gift that saves us in regard to the life to come but doesn't define its power in this life.

SAVED BY THE GUN

Allow me to illustrate what grace really means through an allegory about a gun. Let's go back a few hundred years to 1717, the year prior to the invention of the first firearm. Due to a shipwreck, a fellow I will call *Island Man* is stranded alone on a deserted island in the middle of the ocean.

The interior of the island experiences normal tropical weather; however due to some unusual conditions, the coastline is always concealed by a dense fog. The island is off the normal shipping routes, but if a vessel does travel close by, no one aboard can see the island due to the fog.

The island has ample fresh water and some wildlife, including deer and wild boar. There's an abundance of coconuts, but they hang high in towering palm trees.

Island Man washed up several days ago and is very hungry because all of his attempts to track and catch an animal have failed. He tried making spears out of branches but couldn't throw them hard enough to wound a fleeing animal. Island Man thought about making a giant slingshot but found no elastic material. As a last resort, he chased after both a deer and a hog and hurled large stones at them—all to no avail.

Island Man also tried to harvest the coconuts by attempting to climb the high palms, but all that got him were bloody legs and bruised arms—no coconuts.

To make matters worse, this lonely survivor had to use extreme caution at all times due to some other island occupants—fierce and wily bears. Never fully aware of their whereabouts, he must constantly be on guard because it seems the bears are hunting him. In the hopes of staying sane, Island Man found a large boulder the size of a small house that the bears probably can't climb. He constructed a makeshift ladder and climbed to the top, pulling the ladder up behind him. Island Man felt relatively safe but also imprisoned—confined to the rock most of the day and night as protection from these hungry predators. Now not just hungry, Island Man is also very tired from a lack of restful sleep, as the rock has an uneven surface that makes lying down very uncomfortable.

At this point, this unfortunate man is extremely frustrated and exhausted, but even worse, he's hopeless. The reality of his desperate plight has set in: he's going to die either of starvation or by being mauled by a bear.

Suddenly a man appears from seemingly nowhere. He's a time traveler from the late twenty-first century. With technology he had the ability to look back to

Island Man's time and whereabouts. In doing so he discovered Island Man's dilemma, and out of love and concern gathered the knowledge and equipment needed to save Island Man and came to the rescue via a time machine. His name is Messenger.

Messenger tells an excited Island Man that a ship will come close to the island in exactly sixty-one days. He further informs him that this will be his only chance to get home because Messenger has looked back through time and discovered that it will be decades before another ship passes near the island. Messenger tells the exact hour of the day when the ship will pass and sets up a sundial to help Island Man tell time. "You'll hear a horn blow when the ship is closest to the island," he says.

Messenger then opens a strange-looking case he has brought with him that contains unfamiliar items. One of them is a gun, which of course Island Man's never seen before. He's completely unaware of what this seven-millimeter rifle can do.

Messenger enthusiastically shares, "This is called a gun and it will save your life!"

After pausing to get a reaction, he continues, "When the gun is loaded and you pull this trigger, it will make a very loud sound." To demonstrate Messenger reaches into the case and grabs another strange item, a bullet, loads it in the chamber, points the barrel to the sky, and squeezes the trigger. Island Man jumps at the loud *bang*.

"The sound of this gun will travel miles over the water," Messenger says. "When the ship's captain hears the *bang*, he will venture into the ring of fog and discover the eastern shore of the island. You should fire the gun a few more times once you see the ship. You'll be discovered, taken on board, and brought safely home!"

Island Man is ecstatic and thanks Messenger repeatedly.

"You are welcome," he answers, "but there's more you need to know. The gun not only makes a loud noise, but the bullet comes out of the barrel at a high speed that can kill any bear, deer, or wild hog on this island. So you'll no longer live in fear of being mauled to death by a bear. Best of all, you'll have plenty of food until the ship arrives. Not only will you have the deer and wild hog meat to eat, but for added nutrition you'll be able to shoot the coconuts down from the trees.

Messenger then shows Island Man how to use the rifle, which has a powerful scope. After firing a number of shells at random targets in the forest, the stranded man's aim improves. "You've got it!" Messenger says with a smile, then says enthusiastically, "And there's more!"

Back on the beach, he walks Island Man to a cave that has a sand floor. Not long after washing ashore, Island Man had discovered this cave and had longed to sleep there, but he feared the bears might attack during the night.

Messenger says, "You'll be able to cover the entrance to this cave with the skins of deer. Now you can sleep on the soft sand, and if you kill a couple bears, you could use their skins for a mattress and blanket. This way you'll be warm during the cold nights, and the cave will also shelter you during those pelting rains."

Messenger opens the gun case again to show the supply of bullets. There are hundreds. "Use the ammunition wisely," he warns, "but you should have more than enough for sixty-one days."

At this point, Island Man is overwhelmed with gratefulness. Suddenly an important thought comes to his mind, and he cautiously inquires, "Messenger, what do I need to give you for the gun?"

With a smile he replies, "I know you don't have any money, so you can't buy it, and even if you did, repayment is not why I've done this for you. I saw you through the time machine and wanted to help. The gun isn't for sale; just take it. Besides, my employer, a very wealthy man in my world who actually owns the time machine, provided me with this rifle to give you. I had the joy of delivering his gift."

"Oh, thank you, thank you!" Island Man is exceedingly grateful and shocked by the concern and generosity of Messenger and his employer. He accepts the gun, and the benevolent stranger disappears within seconds. Island Man is left with a weapon that will spare his life as well as comfortably sustain him during the two remaining months on the island. He is saved!

As you have probably figured out, Messenger in this allegory represents a servant of Jesus Christ who tells Island Man about the way of salvation. He could be an evangelist, pastor, family member, friend, or total stranger. Messenger's employer represents the Lord, who sent Messenger on the rescue mission. The gun represents the grace of God, His unmerited gift. Salvation from a horrible death on the island came not by Island Man's doing but by the gift from Messenger's employer. The sixty-one days left on the island represent Island Man's remaining life here on earth, and the ship picking him up represents his leaving this earth for heaven.

AN IMPORTANT FACT LEFT OUT

Now I want to retell the story and see the difference if one important element is changed.

In this second version, Messenger appears and declares that the gun will save Island Man's life. As before, he says that firing the rifle is the only way the ship's captain will know someone is within the fog. Messenger again points the rifle toward the sky and fires it, then lets Island Man load the weapon and shoot several bullets into the air. As in the previous version, this is the only avenue for getting off the island.

However, this time Messenger neglects to tell Island Man about the gun's other abilities. He doesn't explain that besides making a huge bang, a hard steel projectile comes out of the barrel at high velocity that can kill the animals to provide food, protection, and warmth. Erroneously, Messenger assumes that Island Man knows what the gun can do. He forgets the fact that the stranded man lives in a time before the invention of firearms. As before, Island Man thanks Messenger for the gift, and Messenger immediately vanishes back to his time period. Island Man is left with a way of escape but without the information he needs to live successfully on the island for the next sixty-one days.

In this scenario Island Man feels mixed emotions after Messenger's sudden disappearance. Our protagonist is happy to know there is a way off the island, but he also realizes he's in for quite a struggle. What will he eat for the next sixty-one days? Can he survive that long without food? Island Man has failed at every attempt to kill just one of the animals. Chances are zero that he can avoid starvation or a bear attack before the sixty-one days expire, and he still doesn't have a way to sleep well at night, nor does he have any protection from the pelting rains or cold nights.

Will Island Man make it? His mind fills with fear concerning the reality that he might not last until the ship arrives in two months.

Frustration again sets in. Island Man is ignorant about the potential of what's in his possession. How could this man who was so kind to provide a way off the island not give the information needed to live successfully during the remaining time on this island?

Now that we've looked at two presentations of this allegory, what's my point? Many of us have been taught that grace is an unmerited gift and by it we were given eternal life in heaven. However, what's been neglected in many evangelical circles is the understanding of how grace provides the power to live—*extraordinarily*—a successful life that pleases God *before eternity.* Bottom line: we've not communicated what "the gun" can do prior to the ship's arrival. Because of this lack of knowledge about grace, large numbers in the church are still living relatively the same as before salvation and are defeated in many areas of life.

GOD'S EMPOWERMENT FOR LIVING

Let's return for another look at the word *grace.* Strong's Greek dictionary brings to light the power of grace (*charis*) by defining it as "the divine influence upon the heart and its reflection in the life." Notice the words "reflection in the life." It's obvious that there is more to the meaning of grace than being heaven bound. It would seem from this definition that there is an outward differentiation between one who has grace and one who doesn't. In other words, grace is reflected, or *can be seen,* in the life of a believer. We see this in the book of Acts:

> Then news of these things came to the ears of the church in Jerusalem, and they sent out Barnabas to go as far as Antioch. When he came and *had seen the grace of God,* he was glad, and encouraged them all that with purpose of heart they should continue with the Lord. (11:22–23)

Barnabas perceived the outward evidence of God's grace in the lives of the believers he met in Antioch. The New Living Translation makes it even clearer:

"When he arrived and saw this proof…" The grace of Jesus Christ was bestowed on their hearts, and Barnabas was able to see the proof of it—the outward reflection.

The Zondervan *Encyclopedia of Bible Words* states, "This grace is a dynamic force that does more than affect our standing with God by crediting us with right-eousness. Grace affects our experience as well. Grace is marked always by God's enabling work within us to overcome our helplessness." This definition is cer-tainly backed by this New Testament scripture:

> Since we are receiving a kingdom which cannot be shaken, let us have
> grace, *by which we may serve God acceptably.* (Hebrews 12:28)

It's remarkably clear that grace gives us the power to serve God acceptably. The Amplified Bible goes beyond the word *acceptably* and states: "Let us therefore… offer to God pleasing service." What was impossible in our own strength, an acceptable and pleasing life to God, is now possible, and grace provides the ability. We are empowered to overcome our shortcomings.

The Greek word used in Hebrews 12:28, *charis,* is the same word found in Ephesians 2:8: "For by grace [*charis*] you have been saved through faith, and that not of yourselves; it is the gift of God." So the very Greek word used in the verse that most clearly identifies our free gift of salvation is also used to show that it empowers us to live a life that is not only acceptable but also pleasing to God.

Grace is not just God's favor that cannot be earned but also God's empower-ing presence that gives us the ability to do what thrills Him. Grace gives us the ability to exceed our own ability. It gives us the ability to live extraordinarily!

I find this thrilling! God didn't just rescue us; He empowered us so that we can live successfully here in this world. He didn't want children who would have the title of righteousness but not have the ability to overcome the sins and weaknesses that ensnared us in the first place. No, He designed salvation to be complete— triumphant living in this world as well as in the one to come.

Reflections for an Extraordinary Journey

Have you ever wondered if you have fallen out of the grace of God? Why is such an idea so potentially wrong and dangerous?

What part of the Messenger allegory helps most to expand your understanding of grace?

7

Grace and Truth

The apostle Peter made an intentional point in his final epistle that escaped my attention for a long time. I'd read this book time and again but had never noticed his deliberate strategy. Hear what he says:

> I plan to keep on *reminding* you of these things—even though you already
> know them and are standing firm in the truth. (2 Peter 1:12, NLT)

Notice the word *reminding*. Peter noted that his readers had already heard what he was writing about and were standing firm in the truth, but he intended to keep *reminding* them. Then he does it again: "Yes, I believe I should keep on *reminding* you of these things as long as I live" (verse 13, NLT). He states that he'll never stop bugging them!

And Peter wasn't done with this "reminding" idea yet:

> Moreover I will be careful to ensure that you always have a *reminder* of
> these things after my decease. (verse 15)

Again the word *reminder*! Here Peter declares he'll make sure they will always—yes, always—be *reminded* of what he'd just written, even after his departure from this world. The New Living Translation reads, "I will work hard to make these things clear to you."

On that day, I had a greater realization of the importance of the written Word of God. It seems that many sermons today lack the revelation and understanding of Scripture. I find numerous contemporary Christian books that contain little insight into the Bible. When I read the writings of the early fathers of the church, I see numerous references to the written Word of God—hundreds, sometimes even thousands of Scripture notations interwoven in their texts. One of the early fathers, Clement of Alexandria, lived from approximately AD 150–215. He was a leader in the church of Alexandria, Egypt, in charge of the school of instruction for new believers. Josh McDowell points out a stunning fact in his book *Evidence That Demands a Verdict:* in his writings, Clement took 2,400 quotes from all but three books in the New Testament. Why is there such a contrast in emphasis on Scripture between the first couple of centuries and now? The early fathers knew the importance of being reminded of the Word of God.

I attended a church denomination for nineteen years of my life that taught me to pray to dead people, to light candles for the purpose of getting people out of purgatory more quickly, to believe that Mary was the go-to person for a favorable prayer answer from Jesus, and to accept many other strange ideas not found in Scripture. While attending this church I felt sorry for others who attended different denominations because we had the truth and they were lacking.

Had I died during that time period, I wouldn't have gone to heaven because I didn't understand salvation. Shortly after receiving Jesus Christ as my Lord, I realized that I believed many falsehoods as truths. I had been misinformed and misguided. I had based my life on what men taught from their own perceptions rather than simply adhering to what God says in His Word. Do you think my former denomination had drifted from certain aspects of Scripture suddenly? Certainly not. All man-made doctrines usually begin with a gradual straying that eventually ends up far from the truth.

Shortly after receiving Jesus and being delivered from error, I was captivated by these words:

Every Scripture is God-breathed (given by His inspiration) and profitable for instruction, for reproof *and* conviction of sin, for correction of error *and* discipline in obedience, [and] for training in righteousness (in holy living, in conformity to God's will in thought, purpose, and action). (2 Timothy 3:16, AMP)

Every Scripture is God-inspired. Listen again to these words: "Every Scripture"—not some thoughts of Scripture, not some points in Scripture, but *every Scripture* is inspired by God.

I soon afterward discovered what Jesus said: "Heaven and earth will pass away, but my words will never pass away" (Mark 13:31, TEV). Why can heaven and earth pass away but not the "least point" or "smallest detail" of His Word (Matthew 5:18, TEV)? Because "By his own mighty word, he holds the universe together" (Hebrews 1:3, CEV).

God took great care in getting His Word to us, so why do we take it so lightly and not put more emphasis on it? Why do we try to make His infallible Word fit into or confirm our lifestyle or social culture instead of allowing it to shape our lives?

This is why Peter said, "I'll remind you again, will always remind you as long as I live, and keep reminding you long after I've left this world." If you ponder his statements, you'll realize the importance of scripture, particularly the prior points he'd just made.

Let's stay with the written Word of God. It's incorruptible, eternal, and can never be altered or changed. It is the rock where we're to stand firm and to base our lives on.

So once again, I'll remind you of what Peter wrote. I've quoted these words already, but interestingly enough, they are the specific words he would never stop reminding the early Christians of. So let's pay close attention:

> We have everything we need to live a life that pleases God. It was all given to us by God's own power.... I am still going to remind you.... In fact, I think I should keep on reminding you until I leave this body.... I am doing my best to make sure that each of you remembers all of this after I am gone. (2 Peter 1:3, 12–13, 15, CEV)

What he wrote is important for us to retain in our thoughts and firmly believe. For us to lose sight of this truth is detrimental to our life in Christ. This should be clear as we progress. Again, you already have all you need to live a life that pleases God. It was given to you by His power, and that power is none other than God's amazing grace!

THE MAIN DIFFERENCE

For many centuries before Jesus came to earth, died on the cross, and rose from the dead, the people who desired a relationship with God could have it only through the law. The primary purpose of the law God gave through Moses was to show men and women that they could never please Him by their own ability. The law revealed humankind's weaknesses and shortcomings.

However, what the law couldn't accomplish in enabling us to please God is now possible for us through His grace. Remember, we're specifically told, "He who says he abides in Him ought himself also to walk just as He walked" (1 John 2:6). This is a command, not a suggestion or even a strong recommendation! And it's only through grace that we can fulfill it. In his gospel, John writes:

> And of His fullness we have all received, and grace for grace. For the law
> was given through Moses, but grace and truth came through Jesus Christ.
> (1:16–17)

There is so much to these two verses that I need to carefully break them down. Please bear with me a few pages—the rich understanding we gain will be worth it. The first line reads:

> And of His fullness we have all received.

Take a moment and let the meaning of that sink in. Focus on the words "of His fullness." The *completeness* of Jesus has been imparted to us! Not the fullness of a prime minister, president, celebrity, rock star, great athlete, or scholar, but the comprehensiveness of Jesus Christ Himself. If you really hear this, you'll never envy another man or woman again. *You have the full nature of Jesus Christ in you!*

Let's look again at Peter's words:

We have everything we need to live a life that pleases God. It was all given
to us by God's own power [grace].... God made great and marvelous
promises, so that his *nature* would become part of us. (2 Peter 1:3–4, CEV)

His *nature*! The New King James Version is more descriptive: "You may be
partakers of the *divine nature.*"

What an amazing, almost incomprehensible gift—His *"divine nature."* The
word *nature* is defined as "the innate or essential qualities or character of a person."
With that in mind, hear what else Peter writes:

Having been born again, not of corruptible *seed* but incorruptible, through
the word of God which lives and abides forever. (1 Peter 1:23)

A *seed* has all the innate qualities of its parent plant—it is an actual plant
within a shell, made in the image of what formed it. According to Peter, the seed
that was planted within you is the Word of God.

It's important to keep in mind that Jesus Christ is the living Word of God. He
is called "the Word." John writes of Him, "In the beginning was the Word, and the
Word was with God, and the Word was God.... And the Word became flesh and
dwelt among us" (John 1:1, 14). He is called "the Word of life" in 1 John 1:1 (NLT).

Then again the writer of Hebrews states:

For *the word of God* is full of living power. It is sharper than the sharpest
knife, cutting deep into our innermost thoughts and desires. It exposes us
for what we really are. Nothing in all creation can hide from *him*. Everything is naked and exposed before *his* eyes. *This is the God* to whom we
must explain all that we have done. (4:12–13, NLT)

If you wrote these verses in an English class, your teacher would mark your
paper incorrect. The proper way of writing this would be, "For the word of
God...everything is naked and exposed before *its* (not *his*) eyes." However, this

definitely is not the way it's written. Scripture specifically states "His eyes." Jesus is the living Word of God.

The seed that was planted in you, which you were re-created through, is none other than Christ Himself. This seed is indeed incorruptible. We are in Christ, He is in us, and we have the fullness of His nature. The seed planted in us when we were born again is all that makes Christ who He is! How awesome. In this world we have the comprehensiveness of His nature! Has the reality of this hit you yet?

John says it like this: "As He is, so are we in this world" (1 John 4:17). So many believers think that someday, in heaven, we'll be as He is, but for now on earth we are struggling sinners who've merely been forgiven. This is a mammoth lie, and it keeps people in bondage and nullifies the power of grace in their lives.

As amazing as this reality is, it makes complete sense. The Bible tells us we are His offspring: "Beloved, *now* we are children of God" (1 John 3:2). Not in the future, but *now*. If we are *now* born of God, *now* His children or offspring, then it stands to reason that we *now* have His essential qualities. Just as a horse cannot give birth to a worm nor a lion give birth to a weasel, so we cannot possess inferior innate qualities if we are born of God Himself. His makeup is *now* part of us!

But it gets even better! If we'll allow it, He lives through us! As we're about to see, that's the power of His grace. A mother lioness cannot live through the life of her cub, yet Christ lives in us. Paul writes, "I myself no longer live, but Christ lives in me" (Galatians 2:20, NLT). And again, "For you died, and your life is hidden with Christ in God" (Colossians 3:3). What complete salvation God has given us!

Now let's continue our detailed study of what the apostle John writes:

And of His fullness we have all received, and grace for grace. (John 1:16)

Here is the point so many miss today due to incomplete teaching: John connects receiving the fullness of God's nature with grace. It is God's unmerited gift—a gift that not only saved us from eternal damnation but also gave us His characteristics. One aspect of grace is just as real as the other, and it was all provided the moment we were saved.

Notice that John uses the phrase "grace for grace." I have a Greek friend who lives in Athens. He's a minister who not only speaks Greek as his native tongue but has also studied ancient Greek. He shared with me that the apostle was actually writing that God has given us "the richest abundance of grace." That's for sure!

I've often thought, *It would have been just fine if God had made us like one of His angels or if He had left us as sinners—but forgiven sinners who would spend eternity with Him.* Either of those options would have been exceedingly better than where we came from. However, He's not only forgiven us but also made us His very sons and daughters, imparting to us His divine and comprehensive nature. Such unmerited favor is extraordinary!

This is why I believe John used the phrase "the richest abundance of grace." He had lived under the Law of Moses and knew its limitations. He knew it didn't have the power to change his nature; it only exposed his weaknesses and shortcomings. He knew the law could only constrain him, not change his inner man. For this reason he immediately followed his statement about receiving Jesus' nature through grace with the fact that the law was given through Moses but that grace and truth came through Jesus Christ. Look at his words again:

And of His fullness we have all received, and grace for grace. For the law was given through Moses, but grace and truth came through Jesus Christ. (John 1:16–17)

Let's take a closer look at the difference.

JESUS' COMPARISONS

To capture the magnitude of the full reality of grace, let's go to comparisons Jesus makes in Matthew 5, where He repeatedly says:

You have heard that it was said to those of old.... But I say to you... (verses 21–22)

You have heard that it was said to those of old.... But I say to you...
(verses 27–28)

Furthermore it has been said.... But I say to you... (verses 31–32)

Again you have heard that it was said to those of old.... But I say to you...
(verses 33–34)

You have heard that it was said.... But I tell you... (verses 38–39)

You have heard that it was said.... But I say to you... (verses 43–44)

Jesus contrasts life under the law (life prior to His nature being imparted to us) versus life under empowering grace. He quotes the requirement of the Law of Moses with statements such as, "You have heard that it was said...," and then introduces His way—*truth*—under empowering grace, by saying, "But I say to you...."

Jesus introduces here the dimension of grace that would deposit the ability of God within us and free us from the powerless formula of the law. One was an outer restraint, while the other was the reflection of an inward transformation.

I often hear ministers and other believers bemoan the harsh requirements of the law and then express their relief that they are under grace rather than such a rigid lifestyle. I also greatly rejoice that I am no longer under the law, but it is not because I find God's expectations of me more lenient now. In fact, just the opposite is true—His expectations are higher under empowering grace! Let's delve deeper:

You have heard that it was said to those of old, "You shall not murder, and whoever murders will be in danger of the judgment." But I say to you that whoever is angry with his brother without a cause shall be in danger of the judgment.... But whoever says, "You fool!" shall be in danger of hell fire. (Matthew 5:21–22)

If anger reached the point where one called a brother a fool, Jesus said he was in danger of hell. The word *fool* means "godless" ("The fool has said in his heart, 'There is no God'" [Psalm 14:1]). To call a brother a fool was a serious accusation. No one would say such a thing unless his or her anger had turned to hatred.

In the Old Testament, you were guilty of murder if you actually took a physical life. Under empowering grace, God now reveals His actual standard—*truth*—the way it's always been, not just a constraint because of the weakness of our hearts. God reveals that He equates hating your brother with murder! This same thought is found in 1 John 3:15: "Whoever hates his brother is a murderer, and you know that no murderer has eternal life abiding in him."

To put it bluntly, under the law you had to run a knife through someone to be classified a murderer. Now, in the time of the New Testament, when we have empowering grace, if you refuse to forgive or harbor raging prejudice or any other form of hatred, this is evidence that God's eternal life or grace does not abide in you. You are a murderer! That's *the truth*.

Many in the church today view grace as "The Big Cover-Up" because of the way it has been taught and misunderstood. What do I mean by "Big Cover-Up"? Have you ever heard someone say, "I know I'm not living the way I should, but thank God for His grace!" This is completely contrary to what the New Testament teaches about *grace*. Yes, grace does cover, but in addition to that it is the divine influence on our heart with the reflection of its power in our life. It gives us the ability to live in *truth*.

So I ask, is Jesus describing grace as "The Big Cover-Up," or does He reveal it as the power of His nature that enables us to live a life that pleases God the Father?

Let's examine another comparison:

> *You have heard that it was said to those of old,* "You shall not commit adultery." *But I say to you* that whoever looks at a woman to lust for [desire] her has already committed adultery with her in his heart. (Matthew 5:27–28)

A judgment of guilt was passed under the Old Covenant if an actual act of adultery was physically committed, but under the New Covenant teachings of

Jesus Christ, a man is identified as an adulterer if he merely looks at a woman and wants to have sex with her. Simply put, under the law you had to do it; under the New Covenant of grace, all you have to do is *want* to do it! Does this more strict meaning of adultery square with how we've both taught and lived out grace in America? Have we bought in to "The Big Cover-Up," or are we understanding grace as a God-given ability to live like Jesus?

GRACE AND TRUTH

Before examining another Old Covenant versus New Covenant comparison, let's look again at John 1:16–17:

> And of His fullness we have all received, and grace for grace. For the law
> was given through Moses, but *grace and truth* came through Jesus Christ.

The fact is that *truth* came with grace. Why does John point this out? Why isn't *truth* also sided with the law? In this lies another great key to these two verses we're exploring—the next comparison holds the key.

Jesus says, "*Furthermore it has been said,* 'Whoever divorces his wife, let him give her a certificate of divorce.' *But I say to you…*" (Matthew 5:31–32). For His answer I'll go a little further into the book of Matthew, where He expounds more comprehensively. The leaders came to Jesus and asked if it was lawful for a man to divorce his wife for just any reason. Jesus replied:

> Have you not read that He who made them at the beginning "made them
> male and female," and said, "For this reason a man shall leave his father
> and mother and be joined to his wife, and the two shall become one flesh"?
> So then, they are no longer two but one flesh. Therefore what God has
> joined together, let not man separate. (Matthew 19:4–6)

The leaders then replied, "Why then did Moses command to give a certificate of divorce, and to put her away?" (verse 7). Hear Jesus' reply:

Moses, because of the *hardness of your hearts,* permitted you to divorce your wives, but from the beginning it was not so. And *I say to you,* whoever divorces his wife, except for sexual immorality, and marries another, commits adultery; and whoever marries her who is divorced commits adultery. (verses 8–9)

Notice His words "but from the beginning it was not so." Jesus is stating the truth, for it never changes. It's the same yesterday, today, and forever. However, under the constraints of the law, when their hearts were not infused with the nature of God, they were not able to handle the truth in this area, as well as in other areas. So God permitted Moses to write certain things that were not really God's true "best."

However, once grace came, once God's divine nature was freely imparted to us, once hardened hearts were replaced by the seed of God's inherent characteristics, we now have the ability to live as He intended humankind to live from the beginning—extraordinarily. We now can live this life as sons and daughters of God, in His image, His likeness, possessing His ability through grace!

So under the law you could divorce your wife for reasons other than sexual immorality. However, under grace, the *truth* of God's desire from the beginning is once again a reality. *Grace and truth* meet together so that men and women are able to walk as light to a crooked and perverse generation. We have God's nature within; we can walk in a manner that is pleasing to Him.

Vows Replaced by Integrity

The next comparison further clarifies the joining of grace and truth. Jesus states:

Again, you have heard that the law of Moses says, "Do not break your vows; you must carry out the vows you have made to the Lord." But I say, don't make any vows!... Just say a simple, "Yes, I will," or "No, I won't." Your word is enough. To strengthen your promise with a vow shows that something is wrong. (Matthew 5:33–34, 37, NLT)

Under the law, someone showed that they intended to do what they said when they vowed a vow or swore an oath. God again had Moses write this because men and women didn't have the nature of Jesus Christ in them and their hearts were hard. So again constraints were legislated through the law, in this case in order to differentiate a serious commitment from a nonserious commitment.

However, under grace, now that we have the nature of Jesus Christ, we are now able to live in *truth* at all times. We now have integrity inbred in our very being. We are now capable of being men and women who are like God, able to say what we mean and mean what we say, and abide by the integrity of our word, for our hearts have been made new and clean by the incorruptible seed of His nature. This is why we are instructed, "Be imitators of God as dear children" (Ephesians 5:1).

One who doesn't live by integrity is living contrary to the nature of God within. Why would anyone who has been given such amazing grace want to live divergent to His character? In one who consistently exhibits a lack of integrity, it's questionable, in fact even doubtful, if that person has actually been saved by grace, for his fruit shows that he doesn't have His nature. Jesus makes this clear by saying, "The way to identify a tree or a person is by the kind of fruit that is produced" (Matthew 7:20, NLT). This is how we identify one who is truly saved by grace.

Let me now drop down to the final comparison Jesus gives in this chapter. This time I'll quote from The Message, for it beautifully brings forth the truth.

> You're familiar with the old written law, "Love your friend," and its unwritten companion, "Hate your enemy." I'm challenging that. I'm telling you to love your enemies. Let them bring out the best in you, not the worst. When someone gives you a hard time, respond with the energies of prayer, *for then you are working out of your true selves, your God-created selves.* This is what God does. He gives his best—the sun to warm and the rain to nourish—to everyone, regardless: the good and bad, the nice and nasty. (Matthew 5:43–45, MSG)

In this comparison, the key statement is "for then you are working out of your true selves, your God-created selves." Our true self after new birth, once we've received grace for grace, includes the nature and characteristics of God Himself. I must repeat: We are not sinners who've just been forgiven by grace. We are the sons and daughters of God who possess His nature and are exhorted to be imitators of Him.

In fact, Jesus completes His comparisons and instructions by putting a cap on all He's stated:

> But you are to be *perfect*, even as your Father in heaven is *perfect*. (Matthew 5:48, NLT)

We are to be *perfect*, even as God the Father is perfect! I used to glide over the word *perfect* by convincing myself that Jesus was only setting a goal for us that certainly couldn't be attained; we were merely to do the best we could.

Then I later thought, *Well, maybe He's saying that is the way we will be when we get to heaven.* This seemed better, for how could we even dream of having a goal to be perfect in character like God. It seemed too outlandish to comprehend.

However, if we truthfully examine what He's saying, it's amazing. The word *perfect* here is the Greek word *teleios*. Joseph H. Thayer defines this word as "brought to its end, finished; lacking nothing necessary to completeness; perfect." The Amplified Bible brings this definition out: "You, therefore, must be perfect [growing into complete maturity of godliness in mind and character, having reached the proper height of virtue and integrity], as your heavenly Father is perfect."

Notice the words "must be." It doesn't say "should be." There are "should be" statements in Scripture and there are the "must be" statements. We are wise to know and follow the "should be" statements; we are really foolish to take lightly the "must be" statements.

Examining other Bible translations reveals nothing different. We can't overlook His charge to us. Again it's not a suggestion, recommendation, or even an out-of-reach goal. It's a command.

This is why Paul writes, "For God has revealed his grace for the salvation of all people. That grace instructs us to give up ungodly living and worldly passions, and to live self-controlled, upright, and godly lives in this world" (Titus 2:11–12, TEV).

Grace not only instructs but also empowers us to live above our own human potential—extraordinarily. We've been born again; we're brand-new people; we're sons and daughters of God.

WHY ARE WE MISSING THE MARK?

I was getting ready to be a guest on an international television talk show. While praying in my hotel room before the program, I cried out to God, asking why there was so much moral failure in the church. "Why, God, are so many, even leaders, falling into gross patterns of sin?"

I heard the Holy Spirit say, *It's because of what you've taught.* (I sensed His referring to "you" wasn't limited to me, but to the collective leadership of the church.) He went on to show me that words are seeds, and seeds always produce after their own kind. It's an obvious law—if you plant an apple seed, a maple tree will not grow. If you plant a mango seed, you'll not get a cotton bush. The seed will produce after its own nature.

If we teach and preach messages contrary to the Word of God, such as telling people, "We are no different than sinners. We are just forgiven," then they won't have the ability to walk in the power of His nature—the power of grace. Recall that it's through the exceeding great and precious promises (seeds) that we become partakers of the divine nature. The free empowerment of grace is transferred through *words.* The converse is also true—disempowerment is released through words (seeds). The words coming from our pulpits, books, CDs, and personal conversations will produce after their own kind; they are seeds! Now, rather than people walking in the fullness of God's nature, we have many who are living in the weakness of their flesh. We essentially have stripped the incorruptible seed of its power.

You may be thinking, *Okay, John, now you've gone too far! How can you possibly believe that the teachings of man can nullify the power of God's work in a person's life?*

I find the answer in Jesus' words. He said to the leaders of His day something very similar to what He said to me in that hotel room:

Thus you are nullifying and making void and of no effect [*the authority of*]
the Word of God through your tradition, which you [in turn] hand on. And
many things of this kind you are doing. (Mark 7:13, AMP)

"The authority of the Word of God" of which Jesus speaks represents its
power to change a person's life. This power can be nullified! It's so amazing when
you think of it. The stars that sailors have set their course by for generations, the
sun that has given light and warmth to our atmosphere for thousands and thousands of years, and the constellations that have been shining for longer than
humans can remember can all fade out and die before the Word of God can fail.
The Word of God is so mighty that it holds all created things together! And it is
so powerful that God has exalted His Word even above His name (see Psalm
138:2). As mighty as His Word is, yet there is still only one thing that can nullify
its power, and that is teachings in the hearts of men that are contrary to truth!

The power of the Word of God has been nullified in people's lives by contrary
teachings and concepts sown in their minds. They've been held back from becoming mature, as their heavenly Father is perfect. Our traditions, our man-made
teachings that are contrary to Scripture, have hindered spiritual progress. Jesus
paid such a great and full price for our complete salvation, yet evangelical tradition can nullify its power.

Are you one of the many who has felt helpless, discouraged, and disheartened
in your walk with God? Have you felt a real disconnect in regard to an intimate
relationship with Him? Have you wondered deeply, "Oh, there must be more"?
There's a good chance you may have been told correctly that you're forgiven and
saved from eternal death, but you are reaping a harvest of corruptible man-
inspired seeds sown in your heart and mind. The authority of God's Word has
been nullified in your life!

If this is you, I've got great news. Your life can totally be turned around by the
power of His grace. Your harvest is about to change because you are being fed the
Word of God, not the tradition of men. Godly living according to Scripture starts
with correct believing. If your foundation has been wrong, you've had nothing to
build upon. His Word is about to change that. Get ready for the extraordinary!

Reflections for an Extraordinary Journey

Do you think that through incorrect teaching or other means you have received any corruptible seed? If yes, what is the incorruptible seed—the Word of God— that needs to replace the bad seed?

What can you do from now on to be sure your life is filled with more and more good seed?

8

Newness of Life

Once I discovered that grace includes not only God's amazing forgiveness and the promise of heaven but also His empowerment, my life changed dramatically. Prior to this I struggled with sin, found many of God's instructions too difficult to fulfill, battled inferiority and a poor self-image, and wondered why there was so little eternal fruit in my life. However, once the realization came that I now possessed His nature, my life stabilized, blessings flowed, and my impact on others for the kingdom increased.

One illustration of how I changed would be my experience with my first laptop computer. I remember booting the machine up and moving the cursor through several programs, but I could do very little.

Some time later, I sat down with a computer expert, and he started showing me what was possible. Overwhelmed by what I was seeing, I stopped him and asked, "Do you mean I can do that?"

"You could have done it all along," he answered.

Then he did another amazing feat on my computer in a different program, and I again questioned, "I can do that too?"

"You could have done that all along," he said with a smile.

What was transpiring? This man was only revealing the capabilities of my computer that had been there all along but had been hidden from me because of a lack of knowledge. God says, "My people have gone into captivity, because they have no knowledge" (Isaiah 5:13). Many are captive, suffering defeats in life as I was, because they don't possess the knowledge of grace's power in this life. This is no different than our stranded man on the deserted island. He had all he needed to live successfully for his remaining two months but lacked the knowledge of one of the gun's main functions.

Ignorance of God's Word can go beyond captivity to something worse: "My people are destroyed for lack of knowledge" (Hosea 4:6). How many believers have shipwrecked in their faith after trying to please God in their own strength and ability? The bottom line—Christians aren't flourishing and are even perishing in their walk because they've believed what men have taught out of tradition, wayward feelings, or intellectual Christianity rather than searching out what God declares in His written Word. The early believers at Berea were said to be "more fair-minded than those in Thessalonica, in that they received the word with all readiness, and searched the Scriptures daily to find out whether these things were so" (Acts 17:11). The New International Version states, "The Bereans were of *more noble character*." Paul brought his God-given revelation to these people, but they didn't just take it at face value. They diligently studied the Scriptures to validate what he taught, and God said they "were of *more noble character*."

I realize that God gives revelation to gifted teachers who diligently seek Him. However, no matter how exciting the teaching is, we should study it ourselves to see if the Scriptures back what's stated. I've been in services of large and popular churches and heard men make wacky statements like, "Don't be overly concerned with life's choices; many wrong roads taken will eventually lead to the will of God in our lives because He will always find us." Or, "We Christians are still sinners but have been forgiven by grace." Most in the congregation smile and nod assent: they take for granted what's said because it makes logical sense. But then they wonder why they struggle so much in their lives. Have they never read God's exhortation, "Lean not on your own understanding" (Proverbs 3:5)?

Seeds have been planted in their hearts that are corruptible, because the words are contrary to what God says in Scripture. Yet they receive these words as gospel. They don't search out the Word of God, especially the New Testament, to discover that believers are not struggling sinners who take wrong paths but, due to grace, end up in the right places in life. They've failed to remember that God says, "You will always reap what you sow!" (Galatians 6:7, NLT). They err in not searching out the truth that we are *now* children of God, and as He is, so are we in this world!

Let's be like the believers in Berea whether we preach or whether we are listening to preaching. Before I stand to preach, I make sure I've meditated thoroughly on my message in regard to the overall counsel of God's Word. I usually have many scriptures, but always at least two or three, to back up every statement I make. Why would I want to misrepresent God and then give an account before His judgment seat of how I misled or disempowered His people?

If you are reading a book or listening to someone teach, think about what you are learning. Does the content line up with Scripture (and not just a scattered verse or two but the overall counsel of God's Word)? Don't just accept everything because a pastor said it. Search it out! Once you see it's true, grab it and don't doubt it. Commit your life to it. God says those who do this are fair-minded and even of "more noble character."

SIN'S DOMINION IS BROKEN

Hear again what the writer of Hebrews states: "Let us have grace, by which we may serve God acceptably" (12:28). Grace is a free gift that empowers us to serve God in a manner that is acceptable, yes pleasing, to Him. It lifts us into extraordinary living.

This empowerment is first and foremost seen in our being given Jesus' innate characteristics. Scripture declares that God re-created us "to be molded into the image of His Son [and share inwardly His likeness]" (Romans 8:29, AMP). Another version reads "become *like his own Son,* so that his Son would be the first of many children" (CEV). We were reborn in the exact image and likeness of Jesus Christ in our inner person; for this reason He's called the firstborn of many brothers and sisters.

Recently, I was fasting and praying for a few days in the mountains of Colorado. Some friends let me stay in their cabin, which was in the middle of nowhere. All that surrounded me was wildlife and beauty.

On that fast I kept hearing in my spirit, *Look at Romans 6.* I'm sad to say, it took several repetitions of the same words in my heart before I finally sat down and read it. Once I did, this scripture jumped out at me:

> For sin shall not have dominion over you, for you are not under law but under grace. (Romans 6:14)

Why shouldn't sin have dominion over us? Because we no longer possess a sin nature that is living under mere constraints, but we have entered God's empowerment, possessing the nature of Jesus Himself.

We are free from the power of sin! Read the above scripture again, for it is amazing news! The Message says, "Sin can't tell you how to live." God's Word, *the truth,* is declaring that gossip, slander, and lying no longer have dominion over you. Adultery, sex outside of marriage, homosexuality, pornography, or any other impurity no longer dominates you. Hatred, bitterness, unforgiveness, prejudice, and envy no longer control you. Uncontrolled anger, rage, and outbursts of wrath have lost their authority in your life. Stealing, substance abuse, and alcohol addiction are no longer a master over you. Disobedience to authority, stubbornness, and insubordination have lost their dominion over you. And the list continues. You don't have to yield to such sins anymore because you are now under the empowerment of grace!

Look at it this way: You were once imprisoned by your own nature to some of these things, if not all of them, and unable to live a godly life. Jesus came and threw open the prison door. He took the keys to sin's powerful domination, and you can now walk out of the prison. You are no longer a slave to sin. You are free and a child of God!

WHY DO SOME STILL STRUGGLE?

So why do many believers still struggle with and are even controlled by these areas of sin? Why are they not free? I'll answer these important questions as we progress through the book, but to begin, let's examine what Romans 6 reveals:

> Well then, should we keep on sinning so that God can show us more and
> more kindness and forgiveness? Of course not! Since we have died to sin,
> how can we continue to live in it? Or have you forgotten that when we
> became Christians and were baptized to become one with Christ Jesus, we
> died with him? (verses 1–3, NLT)

When you read the words "were baptized," don't think of water baptism only. The word *baptize* comes from the Greek word *baptizo*. It's defined as "to immerse, submerge; to make whelmed [overwhelm]." Most often, *baptizo* is used in Scripture to denote water baptism. However, there are other incidents where it's used to represent an immersion into something else. This is clearly seen in Hebrews, where the writer discusses the "doctrine of baptisms" (6:2). Obviously there must be more than one baptism (or immersion). For example, there is the baptism of the Holy Spirit (see Luke 3:16), the baptism into Christ's body (see 1 Corinthians 12:13), and the baptism of suffering. Jesus said to James and John, "Are you able to…be baptized with the baptism that I am baptized with?" (Mark 10:38). He was not referring to water baptism, which He'd already accomplished, but to the baptism (immersion) of giving his life for the sake of the kingdom.

Knowing that baptism has several meanings, reread the scriptures above, replacing the word *baptized* with *immersed*. We've become one with Christ Jesus by being immersed into Him. Jesus describes this uniting by saying, "I in them and you in me, all being perfected into one" (John 17:23, NLT). You and Jesus are now no longer two but one. Just as you can't separate a vine from its branch, so you can't separate us from our oneness with Christ. We are now dead to sin because we are in Christ, possessing His nature. Keep reading:

> For we died and were buried with Christ by baptism. And just as Christ
> was raised from the dead by the glorious power of the Father, *now we also*
> *may live new lives.* (Romans 6:4, NLT)

We have the power to live new lives! The Amplified Bible states, "So we too might [habitually] live and behave in newness of life." Think of it this way. Once you gave your life to Jesus, you spiritually died with Him, and you were buried with Him, and just as He was raised from the dead by God's power, that same power has infused Jesus' resurrected nature in you.

This was all done by God's miraculous power! If you try to grasp this with your natural mind, it'll be as difficult as trying to grasp how a man and woman literally become one flesh once they are married. This is a mystery to our human understanding. But, nevertheless, it's real. You are literally immersed "in Christ." You no longer possess a sin nature, but His nature. This is why we can live in newness of life. Hear these happy words:

> Our old sinful selves were crucified with Christ so that sin might lose its
> power in our lives. We are no longer slaves to sin. For when we died with
> Christ we were set free from the power of sin. (Romans 6:6–7, NLT)

We are set free from the power of sin! It no longer has a grip on us. We no longer have a sin nature; we have the divine nature! (I'm repeating this statement frequently on purpose so that it becomes more than just a thought and becomes fixed in your conscience.) Sin has lost its control over our lives!

> So you should consider yourselves dead to sin and able to live for the glory
> of God through Christ Jesus. Do not let sin control the way you live; do
> not give in to its lustful desires. Do not let any part of your body become a
> tool of wickedness, to be used for sinning. Instead, give yourselves com-
> pletely to God since you have been given new life. And use your whole
> body as a tool to do what is right for the glory of God. Sin is no longer
> your master. (verses 11–14, NLT)

Sin is no longer our master, for we have been given a new life! Jesus has opened the prison doors. We are free now to live in His extraordinary life because grace has empowered us with His nature.

Are you seeing the potential of grace?

The Choice Is Still Ours

Before we were in Christ, we were slaves to sin and had no power over it. Now we do. We can choose to either submit to sin or we can walk in grace free from sin. For this reason, it is abnormal for a Christian to sin while not for a person who has never received Jesus Christ as Lord. Christians have power over sin because they possess Jesus' nature. The unsaved person is only operating out of his or her own sinful nature. For this reason God says to Christians through the apostle Paul:

> So, since we're out from under the old tyranny, does that mean we can live
> any old way we want? Since we're free in the freedom of God, can we do
> anything that comes to mind? Hardly. You know well enough from your
> own experience that *there are some acts of so-called freedom that destroy*
> *freedom.* Offer yourselves to sin, for instance, and it's your last free act.
> But offer yourselves to the ways of God and the freedom never quits.
> (Romans 6:15–16, MSG)

God did not set you free from sin so that you could continue to sin and be forgiven—without reaping its consequences. No, a thousand times no! God set you free from sin so that you could indeed be free from it, so you could walk in true holiness, as Jesus did.

The true believer's goal is *not* to sin. However, if we sin (notice I said "if," not "when"), forgiveness is still found in His provision of grace. John writes, "My dear children, I am writing this to you so *that you will not sin.* But *if* you do sin, there is someone to plead for you before the Father. He is Jesus Christ, the one who pleases God completely" (1 John 2:1, NLT). Did you see his words: "that you will not sin"? How much clearer can it be said?

Prior to being born again, you could have had a goal not to sin, but that would have been impossible because sinning defined your character. Now you're empowered with His character and nature to live free from sin. However, if you choose to practice sin, you will reap the consequences of losing your freedom. Hear again what Paul states to Christians:

> Don't you know that you are slaves of anyone you obey? You can be slaves
> of sin and die, or you can be obedient slaves of God and be acceptable to
> him. You used to be slaves of sin. But I thank God that with all your heart
> you obeyed the teaching you received from me. Now you are set free from
> sin and are slaves who please God. (Romans 6:16–18, CEV)

Grace empowers us to be pleasing to God, to live an extraordinary life! However, if we choose not to walk in our new nature and continually yield to sin, then we give up our freedom and again are captive. So in essence, we've received God's grace in *vain*. Paul pleaded, "We then, as workers together with Him also plead with you not to receive the grace of God in *vain*" (2 Corinthians 6:1). To receive something in vain is to not use its full potential. If grace were only a cover-up, then what Paul wrote here would make no sense at all. However, when we understand grace as it truly is—*God's unmerited empowerment, which gives us the ability to do what truth demands of us*—then we can understand how grace can produce no results or fruit from being received in *vain*.

Once again, this is what Paul says to the Romans: "Don't you know that you are slaves of anyone you obey? You can be slaves of sin and die" (6:16, CEV). These are very strong words to Christians. Could he have overstated this one sentence? The answer is absolutely not, for look at what he says a little later in the same letter:

Therefore, *brethren*...if you live according to the flesh you will die. (Romans 8:12–13)

Again, there is no question he is speaking to Christians (see the word "brethren"). So what does Paul mean by "you will die"? I will elaborate on this later, but for now let's be aware that, according to what we just read, we can fall back into the slavery of sin. Who would want that?

REPENTANCE

At this point you may be feeling fearful, saying to yourself, "Oh, oh, but I've done this! I've sinned repeatedly!" Think back to the good news shared in an earlier chapter: "But if we confess our sins to him, he is faithful and just to forgive us and to cleanse us from every wrong" (1 John 1:9, NLT). To confess our sins doesn't simply mean halfheartedly uttering, "I've sinned. I'm sorry. Please forgive me." No, if you study the Scriptures, you'll realize there's another key—*repentance*.

Repentance in the New Testament is different than in the Old Testament. People would wear sackcloth and ashes in the Old Testament to show their sincerity. Again, because of their hardness of heart, it was an outward form of abasing themselves. New Testament repentance is about *truth* and represents a complete change of mind or heart. It is when we are deeply sorry we've hurt the heart of God and are now committed to obeying His desire in this area.

Paul had to sharply correct the believers of Corinth, and in doing so he brought deep sorrow to them. Here's what he wrote about things said in a prior letter:

> I am glad I sent it, not because it hurt you, but because the pain caused
> you to *have remorse and change your ways.* (2 Corinthians 7:9, NLT)

Paul was very strong and didn't let them off the hook uncorrected from their error. However, notice that their deep remorse had caused them to change their ways. This was true repentance—a heart change and the determination to no longer follow the dictates of their flesh but rather their new nature of Jesus Christ. Now hear what Paul also says to these believers:

> It was the kind of sorrow God wants his people to have.... For God can
> use sorrow in our lives to help us turn away from sin and seek salvation.
> We will never regret that kind of sorrow. But sorrow without repentance is
> the kind that results in death. (verses 9–10, NLT)

Notice Paul says, "Sorrow without repentance is the kind that results in death." Again, he uses the word *death* in dealing with Christians who haven't followed their inner nature but have yielded to their flesh.

Paul points out that after truly confessing sins, the other key ingredient for a believer who wants freedom after going back into sin's slavery is repentance—a true heart change.

You may now be questioning why, if he is speaking to Christians, Paul says, "God can use sorrow in our lives to help us turn away from sin and *seek salvation.*"

The word *salvation* here doesn't mean to be "born again." The Greek word used is *soteria,* which is defined as "rescue, deliver, safety and health." Let's focus on the definition "deliver," which makes it clear that Paul wasn't writing to these Christians to tell them they'd obtained a new ticket to heaven. He told them their deep godly sorrow had led to genuine repentance (change of heart and mind), which *delivered* them out of sin's captivity.

It takes both confession and repentance to free a believer from sin's grip.

Mercy Versus Grace

The writer of Proverbs confirms this:

> He who covers his sins will not prosper,
>> but whoever confesses and forsakes them will have mercy. (Proverbs 28:13)

So again we see that it is not just confessing but confessing and forsaking (genuinely repenting) that brings prosperity and freedom.

Notice the word used is *mercy,* not *grace.* The difference in meaning between the two is easily explained:

> Grace is when we get what we don't deserve.
> Mercy is when we don't get what we do deserve.

Mercy manifests when we don't get justice for our sin. Grace, on the other hand, is imparted power we don't deserve that frees us from the tyranny of sin.

A good example of this in the gospels would be the woman caught in the act of adultery. The religious zealots dragged her before Jesus, out in the open temple square, in order to corner Him in public. The law said that she was to be stoned. They knew He'd been teaching forgiveness and hoped to reveal a flaw in His doctrine.

Jesus says, "All right, stone her. But let those who have never sinned throw the first stones!" (John 8:7, NLT). Oh, how I wish I'd been there to watch as these leaders began to slip away quietly, one by one, beginning with the eldest, until only Jesus was left with the woman.

"Where are your accusers? Didn't even one of them condemn you?" Jesus asked.

"No, Lord," she replied.

Why did she call him "Lord"? I personally believe that when He stood before her and she saw the eyes of her Creator God manifest in the flesh, her heart was affected mightily and she believed in Him.

"Neither do I condemn you," Jesus said (verses 10–11).

Because Jesus was without sin, He had the power to condemn her and could have executed justice by throwing the stones right there. But mercy triumphed: "Neither do I condemn you."

Jesus then said. "Go and sin no more" (verse 11, NLT). These final words conveyed His grace, so now she was empowered. For we read, "No word from God shall be without power or impossible of fulfillment" (Luke 1:37, AMP). His words "Go and sin no more" carried the power needed for fulfillment. His words gave her the ability to carry out their directive. Grace gave her what she didn't deserve.

So again, *grace* is getting what we don't deserve, whereas *mercy* involves not getting what we do deserve. Many Christians have lumped the two words together and assigned to both the same meaning. Am I splitting hairs here or is this just *semantics*? Not at all. Here's a way to think about it: Suppose you play both football and basketball with football rules. Football would go well; however, with basketball you'd lose the uniqueness of the sport in addition to incurring numerous injuries. We've lost the power of the identity of grace because so many have combined it with mercy. We've also incurred numerous injuries by playing grace with mercy's rules.

For this reason, writers frequently begin their New Testament epistles with: "Grace, mercy, and peace from God our Father and Christ Jesus our Lord…" (see 1 Timothy 1:2; 2 Timothy 1:2; Titus 1:4; 2 John 1:3).

These writers and others distinguish grace from mercy so that the amazing truth of neither will be lost. This is how we may live a powerful life, free from condemnation. Grace gives us the power to live, and mercy keeps us free from guilt, condemnation, and shame, all of which try to pull us back into sin's grip.

Let's confirm this scripturally. In regard to mercy, Jesus says, "But if you had known what this means, 'I desire *mercy* and not sacrifice,' you would not have *condemned* the guiltless" (Matthew 12:7). You can see that mercy frees us from condemnation and keeps our conscience clear of the judgment we deserve. We are told, "So now there is no condemnation for those who belong to Christ Jesus" (Romans 8:1, NLT). What amazing mercy God has shown us! On the other hand, see how grace is differentiated:

> Let us then fearlessly and confidently and boldly draw near to the throne of grace,…that we may receive *mercy* [for our failures] and find *grace to help* in good time for every need. (Hebrews 4:16, AMP)

Mercy is given for our failures, our sins we've repented of. However, grace is given to help, to empower us. What a great salvation our Father has given us— complete and lacking nothing!

Reflections for an Extraordinary Journey
In your own words, describe the difference between *mercy* and *grace*.

"It takes both confession and repentance to free a believer from sin's grip" (see page 81). Are there areas of struggle in your life that need both sincere *confession* as well as the deep godly sorrow and heart change of *repentance*?

9

Holiness

I t's God's grace that forgives us of all our sins, saves us from eternal death, gives us an inheritance in heaven, makes us one with Christ, imparts His divine nature, gives us His Spirit, and blesses us with every spiritual blessing:

> Let us give thanks to the God and Father of our Lord Jesus Christ! For in our union with Christ he has blessed us by giving us every spiritual blessing.... Let us praise God for his glorious grace, for the free gift he gave us in his dear Son! (Ephesians 1:3, 6, TEV)

Every blessing is a result of His unmerited favor—the glory of His grace. Our salvation is totally complete! He's left nothing undone.

It's quite clear that grace is God's unmerited gift, which stems from His abundant love and favor. Volumes could be written about this, but this book is focused on grace's empowerment. Let's continue to learn more.

HOLINESS IS IMPORTANT

One of the fruits of grace is holiness, which isn't discussed much in our churches these days. I believe there are two reasons for this. First, I blame meanspirited or legalistic preachers who have abused many who truly wanted to please God. These zealots have reduced holiness to a backward lifestyle and taken the joy out of living. This, of course, is far from God's heart. Thankfully a good number have found freedom from this tyranny, however not without consequences. One of the most damaging results is that they now recoil at the mention of holiness.

The proverb "A scalded cat fears cold water" illustrates that once people have been burned by something, they will fear anything that closely resembles what burned them. How tragic, but this is exactly what has happened with so many who were scalded by legalistic "holiness." They now fear true holiness, which is greatly beneficial.

Secondly, on a totally different note, true holiness takes effort on our part, which many are not willing to give. Because we must cooperate with God's grace to produce the fruit of holiness in our lives, many ministers will either unconsciously or purposefully avoid preaching it to avoid losing the appeal of the gospel. Many Westerners would rather have an easy gospel that requires no labor than the true gospel. Let's face it: you don't nonchalantly cruise into a Christlike life. Paul says, "We must through many tribulations enter the kingdom of God" (Acts 14:22).

True holiness is a very appealing and important topic. Jesus is not coming back for a contaminated, worldly church but a church "not having spot or wrinkle or any such thing." The church will be "holy and without blemish" (Ephesians 5:27). So if it's a holy church Jesus will be returning for, then I definitely want to know all about holiness.

Also, we are told that without holiness no one will see the Lord (see Hebrews 12:14). Why is this so important, not only in the life to come but in this life? One of my favorite promises in Scripture is that God says the overcomers will "see His face" (see Revelation 22:4–5). How marvelous! What even Moses was denied we will have the privilege of beholding before His throne.

In regard to this life, we are transformed into the image of Jesus Christ from glory to glory as we behold, or see, Him (see 2 Corinthians 3:18). If we're not seeing Him in our hearts now, we cannot be changed into His image and are, in essence, becoming more religious as our knowledge grows. Receiving knowledge void of transformation is a dangerous combination. I want no part of it.

SEXUAL PURITY

Hear Paul's strong exhortation:

Finally, dear brothers and sisters, we urge you in the name of the Lord Jesus to live in a way that *pleases God*, as we have taught you. You are doing this already, and we encourage you to do so *more and more*. For you remember what we taught you in the name of the Lord Jesus. *God wants you to be holy, so you should keep clear of all sexual sin*. (1 Thessalonians 4:1–3, NLT)

It *pleases God* when we live holy, especially in our sexuality. This is the area that usually goes haywire outwardly if there is a deeper problem inwardly. If you were able to look into the heart of a professing Christian who is enslaved to fornication, adultery, homosexuality, pornography, or any other sexual impurity, you would most likely find a deeper issue. It could be pride, rebellion, lust for power, bitterness, envy, or some other iniquity, but no matter what's there, the root is always a lack of true fear of the Lord.

Though sexual purity is not the full definition of holiness, sexual impurity certainly identifies the lack of it. For this reason Paul states that we are to abound *more and more* in sexual purity. We are to flee from all forms of sexual impurity and not even come close to associating with it. In fact, such impurity is so severe that Paul writes to the Romans, "being filled with all unrighteousness, sexual immorality…[and] knowing the righteous judgment of God, that those who practice such things are deserving of death, not only [those who] do the same but also *approve of those who practice them*" (1:29, 32). This strong warning is not just for those who participate in immoral behavior, but also for those who approve of it!

Leaders should remember this when making decisions, civil laws, or other guidelines for those they lead: to approve, condone, or look away from immoral behavior is a grievous offense to God (see 1 Samuel 3; 1 Corinthians 5). On the other hand, leaders should be quick to forgive and patient to restore those who genuinely repent of immorality.

For a believer to go against the Christ-given nature and become enslaved to sexual immorality is a serious offense. Paul says more about this in his letter to the Thessalonians by stating what God will do to Christians who practice sexual immorality:

God wants you to be holy and completely free from sexual immorality.... We have told you this before, and we *strongly warned* you that the Lord will punish those who do that. God did not call us to live in immorality, but in holiness. So then, whoever rejects this teaching is not rejecting a human being, but God. (1 Thessalonians 4:3, 6–8, TEV)

Why are we not stressing this solemn warning from our pulpits? I have a friend who pastors a great church that has birthed over 250 other churches world-wide. While I was writing this book, we had lunch together and were discussing how today's church has drifted from sexual purity. He was sharing numerous cases of impropriety that he and his leaders have dealt with, but one story stood out. The pastor's wife had recently held a women's conference in her church during which she taught about the husband-wife relationship. After the service a visitor came up and sincerely commented, "My boyfriend has not been having sex with me lately. After hearing you speak I now know what I've been doing wrong in our relationship. I'm going to make the necessary changes and am sure he'll want to start having sex with me again. I thank God for what you've shared!"

This "Christian" woman just assumed that this teaching applied to her illicit relationship with her boyfriend. She was not convicted of living in fornication because to her it was normal social behavior.

The same type of thing happened with another woman I know in ministry. She was visiting the home of a lady who faithfully attended one of the larger evangelical churches in her state. As they walked into the master bedroom, the woman showed my friend her closet and her boyfriend's closet. There was no embarrassment shown as details of her living arrangement became apparent. She even commented on how much she missed sleeping next to her boyfriend when he was on a business trip. To her it was acceptable for them to be unmarried and living together. They both had attended this huge evangelical church for years and yet felt no conviction about their sexual immorality. What is being taught in this popular church?

There have been numerous cases of ministers living a sexually immoral life. Their uncleanness often affects more than one family, and those they've fornicated with, committed adultery with, or had homosexual relations with have fallen away from God or gone cold spiritually as a result. For this reason Paul states in these same scriptures, "You must not cheat any of the Lord's followers in matters of sex. Remember, we warned you that he punishes everyone who does such things" (1 Thessalonians 4:6, CEV).

We are straying far from God's heart because we are so influenced by our society. In so many ways, the church has become a subculture rather than what we are called to be—a counterculture. The incomplete gospel of forgiveness and inheriting heaven is preached but not the complete gospel of also being set free from the dominion of sin. So we are easily conformed to this world, where it's common for a man and woman to live together, have sex outside of marriage or with the same gender, and divorce and remarry for reasons other than unfaithfulness. And these practices are becoming more common among Christians because the church has not proclaimed what Jesus has freed us from.

Paul wrote a stern warning to the Corinthian church, which in many ways was similar to our Western church today. Some of their members were engaged in sexual immorality, and Paul brought the hammer down. He first told of the similarities of the Israelites following Moses and New Testament Christians. Then warned:

> But just experiencing God's wonder and grace didn't seem to mean much—most of them were defeated by temptation during the hard times in the desert, and God was *not pleased.*
>
> The same thing could happen to us. We must be on guard so that we never get caught up in wanting our own way as they did. And we must not turn our religion into a circus as they did—"First the people partied, then they threw a dance." *We must not be sexually promiscuous*—they paid for that, remember, with 23,000 deaths in one day! We must never try to get Christ to serve us instead of us serving him; they tried it, and God launched an epidemic of poisonous snakes. We must be careful not to stir up discontent; discontent destroyed them.
>
> These are all warning markers—danger!—in our history books, written down so that we don't repeat their mistakes. Our positions in the story

are parallel—they at the beginning, we at the end—and we are just as capable of messing it up as they were. Don't be so naive and self-confident. You're not exempt. (1 Corinthians 10:5–12, MSG)

The point I want to highlight from these deeply inspired words is God's displeasure with their sexual immorality. Twenty-three thousand died in one day—that's a small city. This is a warning sign so that we don't repeat their downfall. Because of a cover-up grace, we are not exempt from failing as they did, and according to Jesus, we are actually expected to live by a higher standard (recall Matthew 5). Why have we nullified the power of true grace by drifting back to this sort of behavior? We've not owned the truth that grace has empowered us to *not* be impure in our heart, mind, or body. All we have to do is cooperate with our new nature.

The leading apostles wrote in unison to all believers about the four things we should pay close attention to concerning abstinence. Three of the four concerned diet issues forbidden in the Law of Moses; however, they added another that was not as unique in regard to the difference between a Jew and Gentile. In a letter, the apostles said, "For it seemed good to the Holy Spirit, and to us, to lay upon you no greater burden than these necessary things: that you abstain from things offered to idols, from blood, from things strangled, *and from sexual immorality.* If you keep yourselves from these, you will do well" (Acts 15:28–29). How amazing that they didn't mention stealing, lying, murdering, coveting, or any other such matters also found in the law. What they did highlight was sexual immorality.

Be Holy as God Is Holy

Now carefully read Peter's words, keeping in mind that he is speaking only to Christians, not all humanity:

So think clearly and exercise self-control. Look forward to the special blessings that will come to you at the return of Jesus Christ. Obey God because you are his children. Don't slip back into your old ways of doing evil; you didn't know any better then. But now *you must be holy in everything you do,*

just as God—who chose you to be his children—*is holy.* For he himself has said, "You must be holy because I am holy." And remember that the heavenly Father to whom you pray has no favorites when he judges. He will judge or reward you according to what you do. So you must live in reverent fear of him during your time as foreigners here on earth.
(1 Peter 1:13–17, NLT)

Hear his words—*you must be holy in everything you do, just as God…is holy.* Again, this is not a *should be* statement, rather it's a *must be* command. We are to be holy, *as God is holy.* There is no option with this, and according to Peter, we'll either be judged or rewarded in regard to this command. Again, as Jesus stated, we are told to be perfect as our Father is perfect.

Let's look at the word *holy.* It is from the Greek word *hagios.* Some words used to define it are *set apart, sanctified,* and *consecrated,* along with *pure* and *morally blameless.* The fundamental qualities of holiness are separation, consecration, and devotion to the service of God, sharing in His purity and abstaining from worldly defilement.

In the Old Testament, God's people were to be literally separated as a nation. Jews were not permitted to keep company with Gentiles in all areas of life. However, in the New Testament, we believers are to separate ourselves from evil while living among and interacting with people who are not in relationship with God. We are to go into the world as lights but not to be contaminated by the world. We are to not conform to this world's ways, but to the higher standard—otherwise we are no longer lights.

God says, "'For My thoughts are not your thoughts, nor are your ways My ways,' says the LORD. 'For as the heavens are higher than the earth, so are My ways higher than your ways, and My thoughts than your thoughts'" (Isaiah 55:8–9). When God says, "Be holy as I am holy," He is actually saying, "I don't think, talk, or live like you, so come up to My level of living." To put it in more blunt language, He's saying, "Why do you want to hang around the barnyard and live like turkeys when I've called you to soar like eagles? I've called you to an extraordinary life!"

His holiness, therefore, includes more than separation and purity. If holiness just dealt with purity, then the Pharisees would have been holy because they led an outwardly blameless life. Yet Jesus condemned their self-righteous ways. If holiness just had to do with separation, then the hippies of the sixties would have been very holy. It's not just purity, and it's not just separation. Nor is it purity and separation combined. It's a transcendent separation and purity. It's a call to the "high life." It's a call to the realm of extraordinary living! It is to live as He lives, to imitate God as His dear children.

When we think like God, talk like Jesus (speaking what the Father says), and imitate Jesus' lifestyle, we will not live like people of the world. Appetites and desires of the flesh will not drive us. We will be creative, innovative, pure in our morals, life-giving in our ways. We will be influencers and often envied by the world due to our success because we are thinking and acting at a higher level.

Those who live for drunkenness, perverted sexual pleasures, greed, lust, status, envy, revenge, pride, and so forth are living at a low, earthly, demonic level—anyone can do this. They're not living extraordinarily through the grace of God. Their sin may bring fleeting pleasure, but before long it becomes harmful and destructive. Its result or "sting" is pain and death.

To walk in true holiness is to experience liberation and freedom at the highest level. It's healthy and will positively affect every area of our lives.

CLEANSE OURSELVES

Paul writes to the Corinthian church:

> Beloved, let us *cleanse ourselves* from all filthiness of the flesh and spirit,
> perfecting holiness in the fear of God. (2 Corinthians 7:1)

Are we instructed to cleanse ourselves from some filthiness? How about 95 percent of filthiness? No, we are to cleanse ourselves from every bit of filthiness, and that's uncleanness according to *God's standard,* both inwardly and outwardly. Inward would be attitudes of bitterness, envy, jealousy, strife, unforgiveness, greed, lust, and the like. Outward would be acts of stealing, lying, gossiping, slandering,

sexual immorality, fraud, drunkenness, drug addiction, vandalism, physical vio-
lence, and the list continues.

One day while I was reading this verse the Holy Spirit caused the words
cleanse ourselves to jump up off the page. I was struck by the fact that it doesn't say,
"God will cleanse us"; nor does it say, "The blood of Jesus will cleanse us." It says
we are to *cleanse ourselves*.

Please don't misunderstand me: the blood of Jesus does cleanse us of all sin.
However, there is a huge difference between justification (salvation from eternal
death) and sanctification (holiness). We were justified the moment we received
Jesus Christ as our Lord and Savior. At that moment, our old self died, and we
became a brand-new created being, inwardly possessing the nature of Jesus. We
were immediately justified in the eyes of God, and all unrighteousness was eradicated from our spirit. We had nothing to do with this. We didn't earn it, nor did
our "goodness" deserve it. It was freely given by God's grace.

However, the moment we were born again, the work of sanctification (holiness) began. This was when what was done on the inside of us, in our spirit, started
working its way to the outside, into our behavior. Paul says it like this: "Work out
your own salvation with fear and trembling" (Philippians 2:12). What we must
not forget is that sanctification (holiness) is also a gift of God's grace. But this time
we have a part in the process and need to work in conjunction with it. God's gift
of grace supplies us with the power to cleanse ourselves, and we must do the scrub-
bing! Hear again the author's words:

> Let us have grace, by which we may serve God acceptably with *reverence
> and godly fear.* (Hebrews 12:28)

Grace not only justified us but also now empowers us to serve God acceptably
with holy fear. We cleanse ourselves from all filthiness inwardly and outwardly, per-
fecting holiness, in the *fear of God.* So even though grace is a free gift, we have to
cooperate with its empowerment to produce the fruit of holiness in our lives. For
this reason, let's again examine what Paul says to the Corinthians just prior to the
command to "cleanse ourselves":

We beg you who have received God's grace not to let it be *wasted.*

(2 Corinthians 6:1, TEV)

As I said earlier, if we look at grace as "The Big Cover-Up," we could never understand these words of the apostle. How can you *waste,* or not use the potential of, the kind of forgiveness-only grace that has been taught by so many? But when you understand grace as it truly is—*God's unmerited empowerment, which gives us the ability to do what truth demands of us, to produce the fruit of holiness*—then you can comprehend how grace can be wasted.

Consider again our story of Island Man, stranded on the deserted island. Messenger has explained fully how the gun works and will save him—how ultimately the gun will alert the ship's captain so Island Man can be rescued. He's also informed Island Man that the gun will kill any animal, whether for food or protection, and even knock coconuts off the palm trees. Island Man has also been shown the cave and told that he can shoot a deer and use the skin to make a door barrier for protection from a bear attack. And a bearskin would make a very comfortable mattress and warm blanket during those cold evenings.

Messenger departs back to his time in the late twenty-first century. The next day, he and his employer decide to watch Island Man through the time machine. To their surprise, nothing has changed in the way Island Man is living. He hasn't fired one shot at the deer or wild hogs. He's still trying to get food by trapping game or hunting with stones or spears made from sticks. Island Man is frustrated and miserable. Puzzled, Messenger asks his employer, "Why isn't he using the gun?"

The two fast-forward the time machine to see how Island Man is doing on the eleventh day after Messenger's visit. They observe sadly that he's still sleeping uncomfortably on the boulder, a few rocks piled close by for protection from the bears. Island Man is thin—he's lost so much weight from two weeks of not eating. A cold rain is falling, and Messenger and his employer grow concerned about hypothermia as Island Man shivers violently. They hear him curse his miserable situation and life.

The time machine is advanced to the thirteenth day. Messenger and his employer are encouraged to see Island Man, gun in hand, stalking a deer. The employer comments, "I think he's finally going to use it!" However, they recoil in horror when Island Man unknowingly wanders near a bear den. A mother and her cubs are inside, and when Island Man makes a noise, the enraged mama comes barreling at him. He's petrified, but instead of shooting the bear, he raises the rifle and fires several shots in the air in hopes of scaring the angry bear away. When the mother bear ignores the loud bang and keeps running at him, Island Man picks up a rock and hurls it at her face. She doesn't flinch and continues her charge. Island Man drops the rifle, turns, and runs away in terror. After a few huge bounds, the bear catches up and mauls him to death.

How do Messenger and his employer respond to what they have just witnessed? Much has been invested in this man, both in time and resources. Messenger had spent many days preparing to bring Island Man the right information and equipment—and it cost millions of dollars to use the time machine. How could Island Man *waste* it all? How could he throw away such a great gift? Their labor of love and sacrifice was in vain.

Their initial reaction to Island Man's choices is, first, great sadness for the loss of his life followed by significant disappointment and frustration. They look helplessly at each other and lament, "We gave so much, but it was all for nothing. He didn't use what could have saved his life; he *wasted* our gift."

The bottom line: Island Man failed to fully receive and cooperate with the wonderful gift that was freely given to him. He fell short of the goal.

What a sad epitaph that would be for anybody—He Fell Short of the Goal. By God's grace, such a grim statement never needs to describe the life of a saint. In the next chapter we'll find out why.

Reflections for an Extraordinary Journey

Until now, have you had a positive understanding of holiness? Why or why not?

How would you like your epitaph to read?

10

Never Fall Short

The fabulous news is that God has given us the resources we need to live a holy life that pleases Him! There's no need ever to fall short. Consider what the writer of Hebrews tells us:

Pursue...holiness, without which no one will see the Lord: looking carefully lest anyone fall short of the grace of God. (12:14–15)

The main point here is clear: we need the grace of God to walk in true holiness. Again we might ask, "If, as we've been taught, grace is only about forgiveness, then what does 'fall short' mean in this verse?" The Greek word here is *hustereo*. Strong's Concordance defines it as "to be inferior, to fall short (be deficient), come behind, be destitute, fail." Thayer's Lexicon goes into more depth by stating that this word's meaning is "to be left behind in the race and so fail to reach the goal, to fall short of the end."

Island Man was left behind, and he failed to reach the goal of freedom that was freely provided by Messenger's employer. He could have easily attained the goal, but he wasted what was given to him and fell short of the finish line. Holiness is crucial to finishing our race well. Hear the prophet Isaiah's words:

There will be a highway there,
    called "The Road of Holiness."
No sinner will ever travel that road;
    no fools will mislead those who follow it.
No lions will be there;
    no fierce animals will pass that way.

Those whom the LORD has rescued
    will travel home by that road.
They will reach Jerusalem [heaven] with gladness,
    singing and shouting for joy.
They will be happy forever,
    forever free from sorrow and grief. (35:8–10, TEV)

Before I go on, I do want to point out one flaw in the Island Man allegory. If the story actually happened in our world, there would still be a chance that even though Island Man actually used the gun, a bear might have killed him. There are many possible scenarios—a bear might have surprised Island Man so that he couldn't raise and fire the rifle in time. Or maybe he did fire the gun but missed. Or perhaps the bullet wounded but didn't kill the bear and in a blind rage it devoured Island Man.

However, God says that when we walk in the power of the grace of God, bearing true fruits of holiness, we are invincible because of Him. Isaiah says that no fierce animal, such as a bear or lion, will be able to take us out! (This includes our supreme enemy, Satan, who walks about as "a *roaring lion,* seeking whom he may devour" [1 Peter 5:8].) So unlike Island Man, we have no reason to fail when producing fruits of holiness through the power of God's grace—not because of us but because of Him. *However, this promise does not apply to believers who do not walk in true holiness.* Hear what Peter says about this:

But those who fail to develop these virtues [of holiness] are blind or, at
least, very shortsighted. They have already forgotten that God has cleansed
them from their old life of sin. So, dear brothers and sisters, work hard to
prove that you really are among those God has called and chosen. Doing
this, you will *never stumble or fall away.* And God will open wide the gates
of heaven for you to enter into the eternal Kingdom of our Lord and Savior
Jesus Christ. (2 Peter 1:9–11, NLT)

Peter says *we will never stumble or fall away.* We are invincible, not because of our own ability, but because of the ability grace provides. So, in essence, grace gives us the power to walk the *highway of holiness,* which secures for us the promise of finishing the race well. It keeps us from becoming shipwrecked in our faith and falling short.

Peter covers the opposite side as well. Those who do not walk in the power of grace fail to develop the virtues of holiness. The result is blindness and forgetting that God has cleansed them from their old life of sin. This blindness makes it very difficult, almost impossible, to stay on the narrow road of holiness. Quite easily they will venture back to a lifestyle captive to sin (and most often still believing they are covered and protected by God's grace). Later in his letter, Peter laments those choices:

> And when people escape from the wicked ways of the world by learning
> about our Lord and Savior Jesus Christ and then get tangled up with sin
> and *become its slave again,* they are worse off than before. It would be better
> if they had never known the right way to live than to know it and then
> reject the holy commandments that were given to them. They make these
> proverbs come true: "A dog returns to its vomit," and "A washed pig
> returns to the mud." (2:20–22, NLT)

How sobering. It reminds me again of the words the apostle Paul penned to Christians: "Don't you know that you are slaves of anyone you obey? *You can be slaves of sin and die*" (Romans 6:16, CEV). When we willfully and repetitively follow sin's desire, we become entangled in it and are once again its slave. Just as Island Man perished, so can a believer. For this reason Paul warns, "Therefore, brethren, we are debtors—not to the flesh, to live according to the flesh. For if you live according to the flesh you will die" (Romans 8:12–13).

Now you may wonder how the apostle Paul can write to Christians and say they will die. The apostle John, in similar fashion, instructs, "If you see a Christian brother or sister sinning in a way that does not lead to death, you should pray, and God will give that person life. But there is a sin that leads to *death*" (1 John 5:16, NLT). What kind of *death* is he speaking of that can affect a Christian brother or sister? Is it the same death the apostle Paul speaks of? Is it the same death Adam was warned of? Is he speaking only of physical death?

The apostle Jude writes of those who turn the grace of God into lewdness by using it as a cover-up in their practice of an immoral lifestyle. Although they regularly attend church services, Jude warns, "They are like trees without fruit at harvesttime. They are not only *dead* but *doubly dead,* for they have been pulled out by the roots" (1:12, NLT). Here are people who are physically living, attending church services, but are called not only "dead" but "doubly dead." What type of *dead* is he speaking of?

There are many theological debates over the meaning of this verse, but I would ask, "Why argue about this?" Bottom line—you don't want to find yourself dead in *any* way. The results of death are never good or promising. To put it bluntly, you don't want to find out the meaning of death firsthand. I propose that we get as far away from being dead as possible and abide in the grace of God in order to live extraordinary lives.

Again, the fabulous news is that God has indeed given us His grace. We've been given the nature of Jesus Christ and have been freed from the dominion of sin! Why would anyone who has been made free from the tyranny of sin want to venture back into its captivity and flirt with death?

So, my friend, don't fight for your right to habitually live in sin and still make it to heaven. That is the wrong way of viewing life. Rather, realize God has given you an amazing gift—*freedom*! You don't have to sin any longer; what you couldn't free yourself from before, you now can live free from through the power of His amazing grace!

GRACE REALLY WORKS

I received Jesus Christ as my Lord in 1979 and experienced the reality of the new nature of Jesus, and it changed my life. Immediately, I lost the desire for alcohol, and though I used to swear like a drunken sailor, my language was cleaned up.

Other sinful ways gradually disappeared the more I read, meditated on, and spoke the Word of God over my life.

However, there was one area of sin that didn't go away as easily. I struggled with lust and was addicted to pornography. If I saw pornographic pictures, I was overcome and drawn in. I had periods of freedom, but after time gravitated back to it. Lust definitely had a strong hold—a firm grip—on my soul.

In 1985, a man offered me his condominium so I could get away for extended prayer. At the end of that four-day fast, May 6, 1985, after an intense battle in prayer, I was set free from the stronghold of pornography and lust. Thank God, by His grace, I'm still free today.

However, once I was set free from pornography's grip, I still had to resist the desire to engage. Prior to May 6, it seemed I couldn't resist with any success. After May 6, I could resist, but I had to cooperate with grace to fight off the urge to look at pornography. Its power over me was broken after fasting and intense prayer, but I still had to steadfastly resist the attraction.

Over time, as I continued to pray and allow God's Word to saturate my mind, one day I noticed that my desires had changed. I no longer had to make myself turn away from pornography but rather I was repulsed by it. If a sexual image was somehow flashed before my eyes, I viewed the woman on display as someone's little girl. I grieved that this precious life was being reduced from a person created in the image and likeness of God to a piece of meat. God's grace had changed me thoroughly from the inside out. I had been renewed in the spirit of my mind and was truly free. My senses were changed by the power of His grace. The writer of Hebrews describes this blessedness:

> For everyone who continues to feed on milk is obviously inexperienced and
> unskilled in the doctrine of righteousness (of conformity to the divine will
> in purpose, thought, and action), for he is a mere infant [not able to talk
> yet]! But solid food is for full-grown men, for those whose *senses and men-*
> *tal faculties* are *trained by practice* to discriminate and distinguish between
> what is morally good and noble and what is evil and contrary either to
> divine or human law. (5:13–14, AMP)

I realized that God's Word, which I was constantly reading, quoting, pondering, and studying, had brought my senses and mental faculties into alignment with His desires and thoughts. Remember, holiness is to think, talk, and live as He does. It is to come up to His level of living.

It is for this very reason that a passion burns in my heart to write this book: so many of God's children are living on the milk. They are not being told that God's divine nature has been placed in them. Sunday after Sunday, they are told that they are forgiven sinners and that we all have weaknesses, but somehow we will get through to the finish line of life. This socially acceptable gospel will not empower their lives. Their senses and feelings, not their faith, are controlling their lives.

We must remember that the flesh can be trained, but it loves habitual patterns. This is why people often don't like change. The good news is that just as our flesh can be trained in unrighteousness, it also can be trained in righteousness. The writer of Hebrews supports this—"whose senses and mental faculties are trained by practice to discriminate and distinguish between what is morally good and noble and what is evil" (5:14, AMP). We can take dominion over our mind and flesh through the power of grace and retrain our mental faculties and senses with the Word of God. Our flesh responds to what it is fed.

Even though God's grace has freed me, I could revert back to looking at pornography. If I did it repeatedly over time, without any true heart repentance, I would once again be ensnared and become addicted. And my latter state would make me worse off than before. This I choose not to do because of my love for and fear of God.

His grace is more than enough! It's amazing!

AN EYE-OPENING INTERVIEW

Some years ago, while giving a radio interview with a station in a large southern city, I was talking about righteousness and training the flesh. I hadn't said anything about my deliverance from pornography but rather was stressing the importance of true holiness in a believer's life.

After thirty minutes or so the host opened the phone lines. The first caller was an irate man who tore into me: "How can you be serious about what you are saying? What about the man who's got bondages or addictions in his life? Are you telling me he's headed toward death?"

"I'm not saying this, sir," I responded. "The Word of God says it." Then I asked, "Can I get some clarification as to what you're stating?"

"Yes!" He was still very angry.

"So let me get this straight," I said. "Are you saying that there are some sins that the blood of Jesus and the grace of God can set us free from, but there are other 'special' sins that are just too strong, too powerful, for the grace of God? Is that correct?"

The man went completely silent. Suddenly he saw the foolishness of his argument.

I finally broke the silence. "Sir, I was bound to lust, and God's grace set me free in 1985. You can't tell me there are addictions or bondages too strong for the grace of God. I was completely bound, and now I'm free."

DIFFICULT TIMES

The apostle Paul wrote to Timothy and spoke about the time we are living in now: "In the last days it is going to be very difficult to be a Christian" (2 Timothy 3:1, TLB). We are living in the last days. There is no question about it, because all prophetic Scripture shows Jesus is soon to return. Paul foresaw that our day would be the most difficult time period to be a Christian. Why is this?

In Paul's era, he encountered great opposition. On five different occasions he received a brutal whipping with thirty-nine lashes on his back. Three separate times he was beaten with rods. Once he was stoned. And he spent years in prison. Everywhere Paul turned he faced terrible persecution. Yet he wrote that in our time it would be even more difficult to be a Christian! Here are his reasons:

People will be selfish, greedy, boastful, and conceited; they will be insulting, disobedient to their parents, ungrateful, and irreligious; they will be

unkind, merciless, slanderers, violent, and fierce; they will hate the good;
they will be treacherous, reckless, and swollen with pride; they will love
pleasure rather than God. (2 Timothy 3:2–4, TEV)

After reading this you may still wonder why Paul thought our day would be
that different from his. People in his society had all the same traits—they loved
themselves and money, were unholy, unforgiving, and so on. Peter had said on the
Day of Pentecost, "Be saved from this crooked (perverse, wicked, unjust) generation" (Acts 2:40, AMP). So why is Paul pointing to our generation as a more difficult time in history to be a Christian? In his next comments he gives the reason:

They will act as if they are religious, but they will reject the power that
could make them godly. (2 Timothy 3:5, NLT)

So that's it—we are living in a time (this is substantiated as well by many
other references in the New Testament) when there are many people who profess
being saved by grace and born again but who do not cooperate with the grace of
God in order to produce Christlike qualities in their lives. They *reject* the power
of grace that could make them holy while holding on to the belief that they are
saved by grace. They still own their life and live as they please, not surrendered to
His lordship. These "believers" are dangerous because through their lifestyle they
communicate a counterfeit gospel of Jesus Christ. It's for this reason that Paul says,
"You must stay away from people like that" (2 Timothy 3:5, NLT).

I believe the greatest battle the early church fathers fought was legalism. So
many were trying to get new believers back under the law rather than trusting in
God's grace for salvation. Today, after being in full-time ministry for over twenty-
five years, I've concluded that our greatest battle now is lawlessness—people in the
church who believe they can be saved yet live no differently than people in the
world. They are not submitted to the authority of God.

In speaking of the latter days, Jesus warns:

Sin will be rampant everywhere, and the love of many will grow cold. But those who endure to the end will be saved. (Matthew 24:12–13, NLT)

Since sin was rampant in Jesus' day as well, what makes our day so different? The shocking thing is that in talking about our time, Jesus is not speaking of society in general but about those who claim to follow Him. He is saying that in our day sin will be rampant among *professing Christians*. Otherwise why would He finish His statement with "but those who endure to the end will be saved"? You don't say to a nonbeliever, "If you finish the race, you'll be saved," for he hasn't started it. However, you would say that to one who is already in the faith, who has already started the race.

The bottom line is that walking in true holiness is more important now than ever before because of the deceptive nature of sin that Jesus said would run rampant in our time. The overwhelming great news, however, is that God has given us the power through grace to live a holy life in the midst of corruption.

We must be lights in these dark days for two reasons: first, for our own sake, and second, for the sake of the lost. Many in this world are crying out to see God. We are bone of His bone and flesh of His flesh, therefore let's imitate God as His dear children so the world may see His light.

We've got what it takes. It's called grace. Let's walk in its extraordinary power!

Reflections for an Extraordinary Journey

Are there any areas of your life that need cleansing? What are they?

Why is living a holy life impossible without God's grace?

11

The Kingdom Within

Grace enables us to serve God in the manner that pleases Him. First and foremost, we're empowered to live in holiness. True holiness includes sexual morality, yet is so much more. To be holy as God is holy is to live like Jesus, to walk as He did on this earth, bearing the same fruit. Jesus made this clear:

> You did not choose me; I chose you and appointed you to go and bear
> much fruit, the kind of fruit that endures. (John 15:16, TEV)

What enduring fruit is Jesus referring to? He revealed its nature during His Last Supper conversation:

> The truth is, *anyone* who believes in me will do the same works I have
> done, and even *greater works.* (14:12, NLT)

Greater works? Jesus didn't say, "You apostles who believe…" rather, He specifically states, "*Anyone* who believes…" I would have found these words difficult to believe if anyone other than Jesus had said them. However, this remarkable statement is straight from His lips, and His Word is infallible! We who have been brought into His family, made one with Him, and given His nature and Spirit are not only to do the miraculous works He did but to surpass them! How is this possible? By now you know the answer—*through His grace.*

Grace gives us the power to go beyond our own natural ability. It brings us into the extraordinary realm. Hear the words of the apostle Paul:

> And God is able to make *all grace abound toward you,* that you, *always*

having *all sufficiency* in all things, may have an abundance for every good *work*. (2 Corinthians 9:8)

In this scripture, Paul was specifically discussing finances and giving, but the principle applies to all areas of life. There are several keywords we need to highlight. First, Paul says *"all grace abound toward you"*—not a *little bit* of grace but *all*. Every spiritual blessing is ours in Christ Jesus (see Ephesians 1:3). This is why the Holy Spirit through Paul states, "No one, then, should boast about what human beings can do. Actually everything belongs to you…and you belong to Christ, and Christ belongs to God" (1 Corinthians 3:21, 23, TEV).

Paul continues by saying you will always—not just in some incidents, but *always*—have *all sufficiency* (total and complete) to abound in every good *work*. Jesus declares that each of us will accomplish greater *works*. So abounding, empowering grace gives us complete and total sufficiency to meet every need we may encounter, no matter what it is! There is nothing that cannot be accomplished in regard to bringing heaven's provision to earth, for grace has fully provided it all.

THE KINGDOM IS WITHIN

Jesus made a remarkable statement when teaching His disciples how to pray: "Your kingdom come. Your will be done on earth as it is in heaven" (Luke 11:2). This was a futuristic prayer for the disciples, but not for Jesus. And it's not futuristic for us either because this prayer applies right now. Allow me to explain. I urge you to carefully read these next few pages, for if you fully understand what I'm about to say, your life will change completely.

The Pharisees had problems with Jesus since He hadn't come on the scene the way they expected. Because of prophecies in the Old Testament, they were waiting for a messianic king. Isaiah had written:

A child is born to us!
    A son is given to us!
    And he will be our ruler.

He will be called, "Wonderful Counselor,"
  "Mighty God," "Eternal Father,"
  "Prince of Peace."
His royal power will continue to grow;
  his kingdom will *always* be at peace.
He will rule as King David's successor,
  basing his power on right and justice,
  from now until the end of time.
The LORD Almighty is
  determined to do all this. (9:6–7, TEV)

These leaders knew that theirs was the season of the coming Messiah. Recall when the wise men from the East came. The scribes were not taken back by Herod's request to learn where the King would be born.

Based on Isaiah's words, the Pharisees believed the Messiah could come only as a militant, conquering king who would deliver them from Roman rule and oppression. They anticipated that He would immediately set up the throne of David in Jerusalem and reign forever and ever.

But when Jesus showed up—a Nazarene, a common man, a carpenter from a poor family, and a friend of prostitutes and mafia (tax collectors were the mafia of the day), they didn't buy in to Him as Messiah. Even though many common people acclaimed Jesus "the One," the leaders rejected this because Jesus had different qualities than they'd anticipated.

So the Pharisees confronted Jesus: "Okay, if you're Messiah, where is the kingdom Isaiah said You would rule? Why are we still under Roman oppression?"

Jesus answered:

The kingdom of God does not come with observation; nor will they say, "See here!" or "See there!" For indeed, *the kingdom of God is within you.* (Luke 17:20–21)

"The kingdom...is within you"? We know "you" didn't refer to the Pharisees, for He had said to them, "You are of your father the devil" (John 8:44). Jesus was speaking of those who would be born again and filled with His Spirit. He had earlier promised to those who loved Him, "Do not fear, little flock, for it is your Father's good pleasure to give you the kingdom" (Luke 12:32).

When, though, was the kingdom to be given? His disciples asked Jesus this nagging question after He was raised from the dead. Put yourself in their shoes. It was finally clear: Jesus, alive and well, was standing before these faithful followers—He truly was the king Isaiah had prophesied would rule on the throne of David—but where was the kingdom? They were still confused about this even just before Jesus' ascension:

> When the apostles met together with Jesus, they asked him, "Lord, will you
> at this time give the Kingdom back to Israel?" (Acts 1:6, TEV)

They too were still looking for a physical kingdom to manifest itself, as it will one day when Jesus returns to earth on a white horse with "ten thousands of His saints" (see Jude 1:14–15; Revelation 19:11–16). While looking for this literal throne on earth, they forgot His words: "The kingdom…is within you." So He corrected the disciples' thinking, as He did the Pharisees:

> The times and occasions are set by my Father's own authority, and it is not
> for you to know when they will be [the establishment of His physical king-
> dom upon His return]. But when the Holy Spirit comes upon you, you
> will be filled with power [the kingdom within]. (Acts 1:7–8, TEV)

"Filled with power" from the Holy Spirit to do what? *Advance the kingdom!* This was not only for them but also for us, for Peter had proclaimed to the multitudes, "For God's promise [of the infilling of the Holy Spirit's power] was made to you and your children, and to all who are far away—all whom the Lord our God calls to himself" (Acts 2:39, TEV). You and I are certainly included in that number. So for this reason Paul writes to us all, "For the Kingdom of God is not just fancy talk; *it is living by God's power*" (1 Corinthians 4:20, NLT). Once the

Holy Spirit came to dwell within humankind, the kingdom and all its power would be within us! We now possess the *power* to advance the kingdom in the hearts and lives of others. This is why God's Word states, "For God's Kingdom is not a matter of eating and drinking, but of the righteousness, peace, and joy which the *Holy Spirit* gives" (Romans 14:17, TEV).

So in essence, Jesus answered the apostles' question—not about the outward establishment of the kingdom but about the inward establishment, which of course would affect people's lives outwardly. The amazing fact is that we can now do the works Jesus did in advancing the kingdom, and even *greater* works. Again recall His words: "Your kingdom come [which it now has]. Your will be done on earth as it is in heaven."

On Earth as It Is in Heaven

Let's discuss the manner in which Jesus brought heaven's ways to the earth. His mission of revealing the kingdom could be identified with one word: *righteousness*. We are told, "For the kingdom of God is...*righteousness*" (Romans 14:17). Jesus tells us to "seek first the kingdom of God and His *righteousness*" (Matthew 6:33). After His departure, He told His disciples that the Holy Spirit would come and "convict the world of...*righteousness,* because I go to My Father" (John 16:8, 10).

The Greek word most often used in the New Testament for *righteousness* is *dikaiosyne.* The *Expository Dictionary of Bible Words* reveals there is no gray area in the meaning of this word: it "indicates the state of being acceptable to God in every way." To put it simply, *righteousness* means "right in the eyes of God."

Scripture makes it crystal clear: "There is none righteous, no, not one" (Romans 3:10). Unless someone is born again by the incorruptible seed of the Word of God, it is impossible to be righteous or acceptable in the eyes of God. However, Paul states with equal clarity, "For as by one man's disobedience many were made sinners, so also by one Man's obedience many will be made righteous" (Romans 5:19). Do we become righteous now, or does it occur once we arrive in heaven? After the discussion in the previous chapters, we already know the answer. The Word of God declares:

Christ was without sin, but for our sake God made him share our sin in order that in union with him we might share the righteousness of God.
(2 Corinthians 5:21, TEV)

And again:

You are in Christ Jesus, who became for us...righteousness.
(1 Corinthians 1:30)

Because of what Jesus did for us, we are now acceptable to God in every way. Again, this refers to our justification, not to our walk of holiness. Right standing with God has nothing to do with our effort but is based on the amazing work of God through Christ. It's very sad to hear Christians refer to themselves as lowly worms or miserable sinners who have just been forgiven. It breaks my heart to hear someone speak in this manner when such a great price was paid for us to not only be forgiven and delivered but also to be re-created in the image and likeness of Jesus Christ.

First and foremost, the kingdom within speaks of the divine nature, which empowers us to live holy and fruitful in this present world. This power is most evident in the life of Jesus. He showed how humankind was created to live—not bound to the burning desires of fallen flesh, but motivated by righteousness, propelled by the power of the Holy Spirit in love, joy, and peace—abounding in forgiveness, healing, restoration, and lifting others to the higher life. This is the kingdom; it's not only to live holy but also to bring heaven's lifestyle to our lost and dying world.

This captures Jesus' life in a nutshell—it's easy to see His passion to give, heal, liberate, and reveal wisdom for successful and meaningful living. When reading the gospels, we can see how He is Light to those in darkness, Life to the dead, Comforter to the weary, the Door to freedom, the Way to the lost, Truth to the confused, the Shepherd of weary souls, the Savior of the helpless, the Redeemer of the captives—the list goes on and on. He brought heaven to earth, for He said, "To see me is to see the Father" (John 14:9, MSG). Now here is His charge to us:

As the Father has sent Me, I also send you. (20:21)

What a statement! We are to bring heaven to earth in the same manner Jesus did. This is why Jesus repeatedly says, "Make sure you get this right: Receiving someone I send is the same as receiving me, just as receiving me is the same as receiving the One who sent me" (John 13:20, MSG). In essence, this is how it should be: to see one of Christ's true followers is to see Jesus, just as seeing Jesus was to see the Father.

What a responsibility—and an opportunity—this is for each of us!

"HERE" AS OPPOSED TO "NEAR"

We see glimpses of this in the gospels in regard to the apostles, even though this was prior to the kingdom coming within. For example, consider the manner in which the disciples ministered: "And when He had called His twelve disciples to Him, He *gave them power* over unclean spirits, to cast them out, and to heal all kinds of sickness and all kinds of disease" (Matthew 10:1). Once Jesus gave this special ability (grace), He then directed them:

> Go and announce to them that the Kingdom of Heaven is *near.* Heal
> the sick, raise the dead, cure those with leprosy, and cast out demons.
> (verses 7–8, NLT)

They were to declare the kingdom. God's will was to be done on earth as it is in heaven. If there was a condition in a person's life that was not congruent with heaven's standard, it was to change. People in heaven are not tormented by demons. People in heaven do not have leprosy or any other diseases. People in heaven are not sick. People in heaven are not hungry. The power the apostles had received was to change what was contrary on earth to heaven! Are you seeing this? So they went forth and drove out demons, healed all manner of sickness and disease, fed and clothed the poor, and even raised the dead!

In regard to meeting physical needs, Jesus attempted to get His team to operate in this power as well, but they missed an amazing opportunity. They were without enough food in a deserted place away from any villages or towns. All that could be found were five loaves of bread and two fishes, and there were five thousand hungry men in their midst. The disciples pleaded with Jesus to send the vast crowd to get some food in the surrounding villages. But Jesus' reply was,

You give them something to eat. (Mark 6:37)

His desire was for the disciples to utilize the power of grace to meet the needs of these people. There was to be no lack, even as there is no lack in heaven. However, the disciples couldn't believe it was possible and responded accordingly: "It would take a small fortune to buy food for all this crowd!" (verse 37, NLT). They were still operating out of their own ability, not out of the extraordinary—the free gift of grace made available to them. So Jesus simply had to operate in this power Himself and feed the multitude.

In regard to sickness, disease, and freeing people from oppression, it was a slam dunk for the disciples. They returned from one ministry outing saying, "Lord, even the demons are subject to us in Your name" (Luke 10:17). The sick and diseased were healed; the captives liberated—it was just as Jesus said it would be.

However, it is important to note (see Matthew 10:7, NLT) that the disciples were to proclaim the kingdom only as *near*. Yet once the Day of Pentecost had come, it was no longer *near* but *here*!

The kingdom is now in the hearts of men and women who are born again and filled with His Spirit, just as the kingdom was in and manifested through Jesus as He walked this earth. This was made abundantly clear at the Last Supper. Jesus said of the Holy Spirit, "He lives with you now and later will be in you" (John 14:17, NLT). In the gospels, when the apostles went forth to bear fruit, the Holy Spirit was only *with* them and the kingdom was only *near*. However, Jesus shows that after the kingdom comes, the Holy Spirit will be in us—*within*. This is why

He instructed all of us just before His ascension to heaven, "As the Father has sent Me, I also send you" (20:21). We have the power *within* to advance the kingdom in the hearts and lives of people exactly as Jesus did; it's all because of His amazing grace!

GREAT GRACE

Let's briefly examine what transpires in the book of Acts once the kingdom comes within the hearts of God's people. On the Day of Pentecost, "they were all filled with the Holy Spirit" (Acts 2:4).

Those who were filled were 120 of Jesus' faithful followers—men, women, and most likely, children received the kingdom that day. Some were apostles, prophets, evangelists, pastors, and teachers. Most, however, were simply disciples of Jesus.

On that day, these 120 all spoke in foreign languages they'd never studied. They declared the wonderful works of God. This empowerment caused multitudes to stop and hear these simple people articulating God's Word in their native tongues. The onlookers finally exclaimed, "Whatever could this mean?" (verse 12). As a result of New Covenant grace, three thousand came into the kingdom.

We then read, "Through the hands of the apostles many signs and wonders were done among the people" (5:12). One miracle was particularly impressive. Peter and John were walking to the temple, and as they neared the entrance, they saw a crippled man who always laid in the same location to beg for alms. He asked them for financial help, but Peter said to him, "Silver and gold I do not have, but *what I do have I give you:* In the name of Jesus Christ of Nazareth, rise up and walk" (3:6). What did Peter have? The answer is simply the kingdom—Peter was enabled to bring forth heaven's normal living conditions to earth.

This man, who'd been crippled from his mother's womb, stood up and began to walk, leap, and praise God. When the people saw the kingdom's effect on this man, a mob gathered around Peter and John, and soon afterward the kingdom spread to five thousand more as they received Jesus Christ.

Peter and John were then arrested. Now Peter, the man who had been intimidated by a servant girl prior to Jesus' crucifixion and had denied Him three times, stood before the high priests and boldly declared the lordship of Jesus. The leaders were taken aback by Peter's boldness but couldn't say anything against what he spoke, for the man crippled for years was now standing—whole—before them. Peter and John were eventually released.

After this, the believers prayed and the building shook with God's power. We then read,

> With *great power* the apostles gave witness to the resurrection of the Lord
> Jesus. And *great grace* was upon them all. (Acts 4:33)

Did you notice how in this scripture *great power* is associated with *great grace*? Again we see grace being ascribed as God's empowerment to advance the kingdom!

Grace is not only the gift of forgiveness, His imparted nature, or empowerment to live a holy life; it is also God's empowerment to advance the kingdom! It's God's empowerment to do what Jesus did—and even greater works. It's the empowerment to live extraordinarily.

At first, many in the church believed that God's empowerment was available only to the apostles, not to every believer, as Jesus had clearly said at the Last Supper. However, this misunderstanding eventually changed, which we see glimpses of in Acts 5. Now instead of only Peter bringing the good news, all believers began to advance the kingdom through the empowerment of grace. "And daily in the temple, and in every house, they did not cease teaching and preaching Jesus as the Christ" (verse 42). There's no way that Peter in one day could preach in every house in Jerusalem. Television and radio didn't exist, so how was this possible?

The simple answer is that all believers were operating in this grace. The next verse says, "Now in those days, when the number of the disciples was *multiplying*" (6:1). This is the first occurrence of the word *multiplying*. Prior to this time period, when only the apostles were operating in the grace of God, we only hear the word *added.* Here are some examples: "And that day about three thousand souls were *added* to them" (2:41); and again, "And the Lord *added* to the church daily those who were being saved" (2:47); and again, "Believers were increasingly *added* to the Lord" (5:14).

However, once all the believers started operating in the grace of God, not only do we see the word *multiplying*, but we also see *great* multiplication: "Then the word of God spread, and the number of the disciples multiplied greatly in Jerusalem" (6:7).

There's a big difference between *addition* and *great multiplication*. If a minister in our day, such as the apostle Peter, was reaching ten thousand people a month and bringing them into the kingdom, it would take fifty thousand years to reach the world, provided that in those fifty thousand years nobody was born and nobody died. Of course, that's unrealistic.

How about if an evangelist reached half a million people a month? Reaching the world would take a thousand years. To give you a reference of how long this is, go back a thousand years when there is no United States. Christopher Columbus isn't known because he hasn't been born yet, nor is King Louis XIV of France or King Richard the Lionheart of England. A thousand years is a very long time, yet that is how long it would take to reach the world—provided that no one was born and no one died in that millennium. As you can see, it's an impossible feat for one person to evangelize the world, even reaching a half a million people a month.

In comparison, let's say one person operates under the empowerment of grace and reaches out to another person in a month's time and brings him into the kingdom. Then the next month these two reach two others each; then the next month these four reach two others each; then in the following month these eight reach two others each; and this pattern continues each month. With this multiplication process, everyone in the United States could be reached in one year and ten months! To go further, it would take only two years and nine months to bring the entire population of the world into the kingdom! Think of it—with no one reaching more than two people a month, the *entire earth* would hear the gospel in less than three years with no assistance from television, radio, or the Internet! This is easily attainable, and it's *great multiplication*!

And this is exactly what transpired in the early church. This is why we finally read:

Paul left and took the followers with him to the lecture hall of Tyrannus. He spoke there every day for two years, until every Jew and Gentile in Asia had heard the Lord's message. (Acts 19:9–10, CEV)

Every person who dwelt in Asia heard the Word of God in just two years! That's amazing when you think about it. *Every person!* Let's briefly ponder this claim. The Scriptures cannot *overstate* anything. An overstatement is when we declare something larger than reality. If I return from a fishing trip and say, "I caught every fish in that lake," what I'm attempting to communicate is what a great day I had fishing. However, in no way is it true that I actually caught every fish in the lake. This is an overstatement, an exaggeration. Honestly, it's a lie—but Scripture cannot lie or overstate. So if the report is that every person heard the Word of God in two years, then that means *every person!*

Paul taught in the same school each day, so there is no possible way *every person* in the *entire region of Asia* could have paraded through that small school in that time period. The population of Asia Minor at the time was estimated at over eleven million people! They weren't broadcasting Paul's teachings via satellite or cable television. They didn't cover him live on radio. So how could this actually have happened? The answer is obvious: Believers now understood that God had not only given them grace to be saved and to live holy but also grace to advance the kingdom. And they were doing it!

SIMPLY BELIEVERS

If you track the believers who were not apostles, prophets, evangelists, pastors, or teachers *after* the fifth chapter of Acts, you'll discover they too now walked in the extraordinary—manifesting the kingdom's ways on this earth. If there were situations in people's lives that were not congruent to heaven's ways, these believers had the grace to change them. Whether it was declaring freedom and delivering people through salvation, healing people who were sick, diseased, or demon oppressed, or simply releasing the higher wisdom of heaven to a fallen culture, these followers of Jesus just did it—they advanced the kingdom of God!

Stephen, a man who was a faithful member of his church in Jerusalem, worked in the restaurant connected to the ministry. He was an ordinary believer who waited on tables. Hear what Scripture says about him:

> Stephen, a man full of God's *grace* and power, performed amazing miracles and signs among the people. (Acts 6:8, NLT)

Great grace was upon not only the apostles to advance the kingdom but also on the ordinary church members as well. That was God's will then, it is God's will now, and it will always be God's will! Stephen was not an apostle, prophet, evangelist, pastor, or teacher in the church. He was an ordinary disciple of Jesus Christ, no different than you or me. Yet he was operating in great power—the grace of God—performing amazing miracles among the people.

Not only did Stephen operate in the miraculous; he was wise as well. Some zealots from the synagogue started a debate with him, and through God's grace he spoke the truth brilliantly: "None of them was able to stand against the wisdom and Spirit by which Stephen spoke" (verse 10, NLT). He could have easily backed down, confessing, "Guys, I'm not a theologian or an apostle. You need to talk to one of my pastors about this." But he didn't need to do that because he had grace—God's enabling power to meet the need of the moment.

Let me remind you again of Paul's words from earlier in this chapter: "God is able to make *all grace abound toward you,* that you, *always* having *all sufficiency* in all things, may have an abundance for every good *work*" (2 Corinthians 9:8). Paul is saying that we have not just barely enough grace (God's empowerment) but an abundance of it for any situation needed to bring heaven's ways to people's lives here on the earth! And this promise is valid for all believers.

Stephen never became a church leader and was not a full-time minister, as we know today. He was a simple believer who finished his race in an excellent manner by the grace of God. These were his final words before he departed this earth for heaven:

Then they put their hands over their ears, and drowning out his voice with
their shouts, they rushed at him. They dragged him out of the city and
began to stone him.... As they stoned him, Stephen prayed, "Lord Jesus,
receive my spirit." And he fell to his knees, shouting, "Lord, don't charge
them with this sin!" And with that, he died. (Acts 7:57–60, NLT)

Amazing. This restaurant worker was being stoned, yet he had the grace to forgive his murderers freely, even as Jesus forgave His murderers. He was able to do
this because there is no unforgiveness in heaven—the kingdom is *within*. Stephen
taught, did amazing miracles, walked in the character of Jesus Christ, and
advanced the kingdom of God—all by God's amazing grace! Yet he was simply a
follower of Jesus Christ.

The same was true for a common man named Ananias. Scripture says of him,
"Now there was a believer in Damascus named Ananias" (Acts 9:10, NLT). There
is no record of his being an apostle, prophet, evangelist, pastor, or teacher in the
church. He was most likely a businessman, a trade worker, schoolteacher, a store
clerk, a barber, or something similar. Yet hear what Scripture says of him:

So Ananias went and found Saul. He laid his hands on him and said,
"Brother Saul, the Lord Jesus, who appeared to you on the road, has sent
me so that you may get your sight back and be filled with the Holy Spirit."
Instantly something like scales fell from Saul's eyes, and he regained his
sight. (verses 17–18, NLT)

This common believer, who we never hear about again in the entire New Testament, obediently shows up and lays hands on Paul's eyes, and his sight is
restored. What an amazing work! Ananias didn't have a special gift, nor did he
have the reputation of being a miracle worker in the church. He simply needed to
access the necessary *grace* to do his part in advancing the kingdom. We all have
this grace; it's been freely given to us in Christ Jesus.

Jesus makes it crystal clear. Once the kingdom is within, we can advance it,
no matter if we are a businessperson, stay-at-home mom, doctor, schoolteacher,

mechanic, student, politician, investor, or real estate agent—our occupation does not matter. He commissions all of us to advance the kingdom:

> Go throughout the whole world and preach the gospel to all people. Whoever believes and is baptized will be saved; whoever does not believe will be condemned. *Believers* will be given the power to perform miracles: they will drive out demons in my name; they will speak in strange tongues; if they pick up snakes or drink any poison, they will not be harmed; they will place their hands on sick people, and these will get well. (Mark 16:15–18, TEV)

Notice that Jesus specifically states *believers* will be given the power, the same power, or "grace," Stephen operated in to do "amazing miracles" to advance the kingdom. Here is how another translation presents these words: "Everyone who believes in me will be able to do wonderful things" (verse 17, CEV). Jesus doesn't say "only apostles or full-time ministers." This power is for all believers—just as for Stephen, Ananias, Philip's four daughters (see Acts 21:9), the believers in Jerusalem, the believers in Asia—the list continues on to you and me and all who believe in Jesus Christ as Lord and Savior and are filled with His Holy Spirit.

I hope it's becoming crystal clear. Grace is God's empowering presence, which gives us the ability to live godly lives in the present and to do what is required to advance the kingdom. Grace gives us the power to go beyond our own ability. God said to Paul, "My grace is sufficient for you, for my power is made perfect in weakness." Once Paul realized this, he happily declared, "I will boast all the more gladly about my weaknesses, so that Christ's power [grace] may rest on me" (2 Corinthians 12:9, NIV).

Grace gives us the ability to go beyond our own ability in every area of life to please God, to live extraordinarily. The reason God set it up this way is simple: He gets all the glory, not us.

Look at the Macedonians. They didn't have enough money to give, but they didn't rely on their own ability. Hear Paul boast of their dependence on God's grace:

> And now, brothers, we want you to know about the *grace* that God has
> given the Macedonian churches. Out of the most severe trial, their overflow-
> ing joy and their extreme poverty welled up in rich generosity. For I testify
> that they gave as much as they were able, and *even beyond their ability.*
> (2 Corinthians 8:1–3, NIV)

The Macedonian believers gave as much as they were able. However, they didn't stop there, and by the power of God's grace gave a substantial gift *beyond their ability.* And God got all the glory!

Grace empowers us beyond our ability. This is why it is extraordinary! Oh, how I've seen this in my own life and in the lives of countless others. I've traveled for twenty years on a full-time basis, sometimes being away from home all but three days a month. Our children are now all in their teens and twenties, and all of them love God and serve Him wholeheartedly. My wife and I have never been so deeply in love, and our marriage so strong. People often look at me and ask, "How do you do it? How do you travel over two hundred thousand miles a year, continue to write books, stay fresh, and keep a healthy family life?" I just smile and reply, "The grace of God!"

I know my weaknesses and how utterly useless I am apart from His grace. Before I left my engineering career to enter the ministry, my own mother said, "John, I think this is a fad. You'll leave it in a few years like you've left everything else." Ouch! But she had a point—I had quit just about everything I'd tried before encountering God's amazing grace. This lack of staying power had even typified my relationships, so when I finally got married, I worried that I would get tired of my wife and want to leave her. Yet the opposite is true: I love my wife more today than I did almost three decades ago when we wed. I'm more fired up about the ministry today than over twenty-five years ago when I first began. How can this be? I've learned deep in my heart never to forget my weaknesses prior to His grace.

Grace has been freely given to me, so I can now do what would otherwise be impossible. I can go beyond my human ability to accomplish the extraordinary because of His grace—all to His glory!

It's very sad that God's grace has been reduced in so many Christian circles to mere "fire insurance." No! Grace is God's free gift that forgives us, saves us, re-creates us, and empowers us to live a holy life. It also enables us to advance the kingdom within by going beyond our own ability. Just as grace saves us from eternal death, it empowers us to live extraordinarily in all areas of life.

So now we come to the most important question in this book: Why aren't all of God's children living in the power of this amazing grace? Get ready for the answer. This is where the message really gets good!

Reflections for an Extraordinary Journey

Do you find it difficult to believe that you can do greater works as a believer than Jesus did? Give reasons for your answer.

In what areas of weakness do you need God's grace the most?

How do you think Christ is calling you to advance His kingdom?

12

The Access

Grace is God's gift to each of us. It cannot be earned or merited—rather it's freely given. Best of all, the very grace discussed in the previous chapters is available to everyone. Please don't ever buy into the fallacy that it's assigned only to certain individuals; no, it's available to all!

With this in mind, we must ask, "Where is the disconnect? Why are so many Christians living largely as they did before they were liberated by God's grace? Why is there so little evidence of empowering grace?" The apostle Paul has the clear answer:

> We have peace with God through our Lord Jesus Christ, through
> whom also *we have access by faith into this grace* in which we stand.
> (Romans 5:1–2)

The keyword in this scripture is *access*. The Greek word here is *prosagoge*, which according to several Greek dictionaries is defined as "access." *Webster's* defines it as "the ability, right, or permission to approach, enter, speak with, or use." A one-word synonym is *admittance*.

Think of the various ways we use this word. You're attempting to get important information from a computer; however, *access* is denied because you don't know the password. You desire to gain entrance to the White House to see the president, but *access* is denied because you don't have security clearance. You're the captain of the high school baseball team and you need equipment for practice. It's all in a locked storage room, but you don't have *access*. So what must you do? Find the coach who has the key that gives *access* to the equipment room.

Here's another way to illustrate the meaning of the word: say you are in great need of fresh water because your well has run dry. The city has a huge tower down the street that contains millions of gallons of fresh water. As a citizen, you are entitled to all the water you need from that tower, but you have no *access* to it. A main pipeline from the tower carrying an unlimited supply of water runs by your house. So what must you do? Simply go to the city and obtain a permit to tap into the main pipeline. After doing that you go to the local hardware store and buy some PVC pipe. You dig a trench in your yard and connect your home to the water main with the PVC pipe. The water flows into your house because you now have *access*.

Simply put, faith is the pipeline of grace. Hear Paul's words once again: "We have *access* by faith into this grace in which we stand." Let me insert the words from my water illustration to make it abundantly clear: "We have *access* by the pipeline of faith to all the water of grace we need."

Faith is the determining factor for whether we *do* or *do not* partake of grace. This means the grace we've carefully discussed in all the previous chapters cannot be accessed any other way than through faith! Keeping this in mind, let me reiterate this important fact: grace is the empowerment needed to please God. Therefore we are told:

Without faith it is impossible to please God. (Hebrews 11:6, NIV)

The Amplified Bible states, "Without faith it is impossible to please and be satisfactory to Him." Why? Without faith we have no pipeline and therefore do not have *access* to the grace that enables us to please God. Remember, we cannot please God in our own ability, but only through grace.

THE WORD OF HIS GRACE

Everything needed in this life is contained within God's Word. We know this from Peter's final epistle:

His divine power [grace] has given to us all things that pertain to life and godliness…by which have been given to us *exceedingly great and precious promises*, that through these you may be partakers of the divine nature. (2 Peter 1:3–4)

Two important truths are seen here. First, all things pertaining to life— extraordinary living—are found in the precious promises of His Word, and second, all that's needed for a godly life is summed up in one word: *grace.* So in essence, it could be said that God's grace is contained in His Word. We read of the believers, "Therefore they stayed there a long time, speaking boldly in the Lord, who was bearing witness to *the word of His grace*" (Acts 14:3). The writer specifically uses the phrase "the word of His grace." Later in Acts we see Paul's final exhortation to those he dearly loves:

So now, brethren, I commend you to God and to *the word of His grace,* which is able to build you up and give you an inheritance among all those who are sanctified. (20:32)

Notice again the phrase "the word of His grace." In other words, all grace— God's empowerment to receive every spiritual blessing—is all locked up in His Word. This is why we read that Jesus is "upholding all things by the *word of His power*" (Hebrews 1:3). It doesn't read "the power of His word" but specifically states "the word of His power." If it were said the first way, it would mean only that His word is powerful. However, the way the Holy Spirit has it written clearly communicates that all of His power, all of His grace, is contained within His word!

Grace is not given because we are nice, or because we love God, or because we are sincere, or because we work hard in ministry, or because we honestly want to please God, or because we hang around the right people, or because of any number of other things. All grace is contained within His Word, and His Word must be believed in order to activate, or access, the free gift of grace:

For indeed the gospel was preached to us as well as to them; but the word which they heard did not profit them, not being mixed with faith in those who heard it. (Hebrews 4:2)

This verse speaks of the children of Israel. Figuratively, the full load of heaven's blessings went right by their house, but they didn't hook in their PVC pipe of faith. Therefore they did not receive the wonderful blessings God had provided for them to live an extraordinary life because they simply didn't believe.

The biblical writer compares Israel to us. We too have the blessings of grace flowing by our house—even *greater* covenant promises than the Israelites did. However, if we don't hook up our pipe of faith, we too will not profit from grace because we'll have no access to it.

Salvation from Death

Let's look at some of the aspects of grace we've discussed in this light. Scripture states, "For God so loved the world that He gave His only begotten Son, that whoever believes in Him should not perish but have everlasting life" (John 3:16). God gave Jesus to be the ransom for every person in the entire world. Peter elaborates further: "God is patient, because he wants everyone to turn from sin and no one to be lost" (2 Peter 3:9, CEV). Not only has God's grace provided salvation through Jesus Christ, but it is also His desire that every person would receive it. It's His heart and will that all be saved from eternal death.

However, the reality is that not all will be saved. In fact, according to Jesus, the majority of humankind will be lost. Jesus says: "Go in through the narrow gate, because the gate to hell is wide and the road that leads to it is easy, and there are *many* who travel it. But the gate to life is narrow and the way that leads to it is hard, and there are *few* people who find it" (Matthew 7:13–14, TEV).

Why will only a minority of humankind enter heaven and the majority find themselves in hell forever? When such great pain, agony, and sacrifice was paid by Jesus Christ to bring all humanity into the kingdom, why will so few find it? The

Word will not benefit them because it won't be mixed with faith. Recall the words in John 3:16: "that whoever *believes* in Him should not perish." It takes *believing*, and that's *faith*. Hear Paul's words:

> For by grace you have been saved *through faith*, and that not of yourselves;
> it is the gift of God. (Ephesians 2:8)

Grace is God's eternal gift; it's the only means by which we can be forgiven, made new, and destined for heaven. However, it's clear that it can only be received through the pipeline of faith: "For we conclude that a person is put right with God only through faith" (Romans 3:28, TEV). Without the pipeline of faith, there's no grace, even though it's been abundantly provided.

Paul says, "How can people have faith in the Lord and ask him to save them, if they have never heard about him? And how can they hear, unless someone tells them?" (Romans 10:14, CEV). People must hear "the word of His grace" in order to have faith to be saved.

But hearing with our physical ears is only the beginning, for Paul continues, "Yet not everyone has believed the message" (verse 16, CEV). Why doesn't everyone who hears believe? There are various reasons; however, Paul states the primary one in the next verse:

> So then faith comes by hearing, and hearing by the word of God. (verse 17)

Notice that Paul points out two sets of hearing. The first is with our natural ears; the second is with our hearts. Jesus constantly repeats, "He who has ears to hear, let him hear" (Matthew 11:15; 13:9, 43; Mark 4:9, 23; 7:16; Luke 8:8; 14:35). Everyone He addressed could physically hear, but it was the hearing of the heart He referred to, for this is the seat of faith.

Our heart will hear when it's noble, hungry, and willing to respond (see Luke 8:15). Under these conditions, we'll receive when the word of grace is spoken, for only it can pierce our core being: "For the word of God is living and active. Sharper than any double-edged sword, it *penetrates*...the heart" (Hebrews 4:12,

NIV). To *penetrate* is to pass through and enter the desired destination. Only the Word of God can pass through our conscious mind, intellect, or emotions and reach into our core being, where true faith is spawned. Knowing this causes us to realize how important it is to speak the Word of God—not to speak tradition, leadership principles, philosophical ideas, concepts of God, and so forth. Only the *Word* can penetrate to produce true faith.

THE EVIDENCE OF FAITH

It's crucial to hear in our hearts, for we are not saved by mental awareness, warm emotions, or even intellectual assent. Rather, it's "with the heart one believes unto righteousness" (Romans 10:10). This is true faith that originates in our core being. Many have complicated this, but it's quite simple. Faith deeply believes God will do what He says, and it subsequently produces words of agreement *and* actions of obedience. The corresponding words and actions are simply *evidence* that our heart has laid hold of what God has spoken. That's it, plain and simple, yet so hard for so many to grasp.

Let's briefly discuss faith's corresponding words and actions, for together they represent *evidence* that someone has accessed grace.

First, faith has a language. Paul writes, "The righteousness of faith *speaks* in this way" (Romans 10:6). And again, "The scripture says, 'I spoke because I believed.' In the same spirit of faith we also speak because we believe" (2 Corinthians 4:13, TEV). So true faith speaks a certain way.

Jesus says,

Have faith in God. For assuredly I say to you, whoever *says* to this mountain, "Be removed and be cast into the sea," and does not doubt in his
heart, but *believes* that those things he *says* will be done, he will have whatever he *says*. (Mark 11:22–23)

Notice that Jesus emphasizes true faith in God will speak in agreement with what it believes; this is the language of faith. In fact, the word *says* is repeated three times in this one verse, and the word *believes* is mentioned only once by Jesus. He puts great emphasis on the language of faith. Genuine faith speaks in accordance with what it believes, for Jesus says, "Out of the abundance of the heart the mouth speaks" (Matthew 12:34). We don't prove we have faith by speaking what we know is correct. Rather, we spontaneously speak what we already believe. As the psalmist writes, "I believed, therefore I spoke" (116:10). Belief comes first; the evidence of speech follows. Paul affirmed, "We also speak because we believe." Under pressure, or when we are not consciously thinking, what comes out of our mouths is what we actually believe. This is evidence of our faith or the lack thereof.

This truth is vividly portrayed in an experience the disciples had with Jesus. He had taught all day on the principles of the Word of God and faith. He then questioned the disciples, "Have you understood all these things?"

"Yes, Lord," was their response (Matthew 13:51). Whether they did or didn't understand the day's instruction was about to be tested, for the Holy Spirit put it into Jesus' heart to cross the Sea of Galilee because God desired to liberate a demon-possessed man on the other side. "Let us cross over to the other side," Jesus said (Mark 4:35).

The disciples, several of whom were skilled fishermen and had been on this sea countless times, entered the boat and the voyage began. Jesus, exhausted from the busy day, fell asleep in the stern.

A great storm accompanied by fierce winds arose. The boat began to fill with water, and the shore was nowhere in sight. These experienced seamen concluded they were doomed.

Now observe their reaction: "Frantically they woke him up, shouting, 'Teacher, don't you even care that we are going to drown?'" (Mark 4:38, NLT). They cried out from the abundance of their hearts. They spoke the language of natural senses rather than the language of faith because they had no faith. The tragedy of it all was that Jesus had said to them, "Let us cross over to the other side." He hadn't said, "Hey, guys, let's get in the boat, go halfway, and then sink."

They had heard His word with their natural ears, not with the ears of their hearts. This is why He got up and commanded the windy storm, "Peace, be still!" (verse 39). Then He turned to them and said, "Why are you so fearful? How is it that you have *no faith*?" (verse 40). Jesus knew they had *no faith* because under pressure He had not heard any corresponding language of faith come out of their mouths. They spoke from the abundance of their hearts and with no faith they couldn't access the needed grace to get across the sea. They consequently had to operate out of human strength, subject to contrary and overwhelming circumstances, rather than rising above the ordinary to function through God's strength in the extraordinary.

The conclusion here is remarkable. They had said they understood and believed all Jesus had taught that day. Yet when pressure arose, what was really in their hearts came out. In the storm they spoke, and it wasn't the language of the extraordinary, rather what ordinary men would speak under these circumstances.

CORRESPONDING ACTIONS OF FAITH

In regard to corresponding actions of faith, the apostle James makes it clear, "You can no more show me your works apart from your faith than I can show you my faith apart from my works" (James 2:18, MSG). Let me further explain his words by returning to our water tower illustration. The proof we've installed and connected the pipeline is that water flows out of the faucet. You can stand at your kitchen sink and boldly declare that you've hooked your home up to the main pipeline; however, if you turn on the faucet and no water comes out, the reality is you're not connected to the source.

The same is true with grace and faith. You can repeatedly declare, "I'm saved by grace," boast of God's goodness, speak of love, and use other Christian clichés. But unless there are corresponding actions—such as a lifestyle that pleases God— your faith is empty chatter. It's for this very reason that Jesus states, "Thus, by their fruit [lifestyle] you will recognize them" (Matthew 7:20, NIV). The apostle James reinforces His words by writing:

My friends, what good is it for one of you to say that you have faith if your actions do not prove it? Can that faith save you?

But someone will say, "One person has faith, another has actions." My answer is, "Show me how anyone can have faith without actions. I will show you my faith by my actions." Do you believe that there is only one God? Good! The demons also believe—and tremble with fear. You fool! Do you want to be shown that faith without actions is useless? How was our ancestor Abraham put right with God? It was through his actions, when he offered his son Isaac on the altar. Can't you see? His faith and his actions worked together; his faith was made perfect through his actions.... You see, then, that it is by our actions that we are put right with God, and not by our faith alone....

So then, as the body without the spirit is dead, also faith without actions is dead. (James 2:14, 18–22, 24, 26, TEV)

Strong words, yet we must heed them. The book of James is an inspired book of the New Testament, just as are the books of Galatians, Romans, or any other epistle or gospel. James is protecting us from mere mental assent that leads to powerless Christian living and, worst of all, deceit. He's protecting us from intellectually agreeing with the Word of God and not tapping into the main power source—grace. Even as a human being's body is dead without the man or woman's spirit, so faith is dead, or not genuine, if there are no fruits of holiness and righteousness in a person's life. There is no true belief from the heart.

James speaks of Abraham, who is called the "father of us all" (Romans 4:16), the father of faith. Abraham was promised a son, but it took years for him to firmly believe this. His name originally was Abram. However, once he firmly believed God would make good on what He'd promised, under God's direction, Abram referred to himself as Abraham, which means "the father of a multitude."

Can you imagine what people thought about Abraham? At ninety-nine years of age he said, "Guys, my name is no longer Abram; it's now 'Father of a Multitude.'" They must have laughed and thought that age had taken its toll. "Old Abram has lost it or is in denial." It didn't matter what others thought or said though because Abraham believed in his heart. Therefore his words and actions were in line.

Before the promised child arrived, Abraham spoke what he believed and became what he spoke. It was his words of faith coupled with his actions of belief that solidified grace's power in his life. Read carefully what we are told about him.

We've always read in Scripture, God saying to Abraham, "I set you up as father of many peoples." *Abraham was first* named *"father" and then became a father because he dared to trust God to do what only God could do:* raise the dead to life, with a word make something out of nothing. When everything was hopeless, Abraham believed anyway, deciding to live not on the basis of what he saw he *couldn't* do but on what God said he *would* do. And so he was made father of a multitude of peoples. God Himself said to him: "You're going to have a big family, Abraham!"

Abraham didn't focus on his own impotence and say, "It's hopeless. This hundred-year-old body could never father a child." Nor did he survey Sarah's decades of infertility and give up. He didn't tiptoe around God's promise asking cautiously skeptical questions. He plunged into the promise and came up strong, ready for God, sure that God would make good on what he had said. (Romans 4:17–21, MSG)

We can see that Abraham's actions showed that he believed. He didn't act a certain way to convince himself and others that he had faith. No, first came faith, followed by the confident words and corresponding actions.

Years later, Abraham would again produce evidence of his faith. God asked him to go to the land of Moriah and sacrifice Isaac. Can you imagine how difficult this request must have been? Abraham had waited twenty-five years for the promised son he loved dearly, and now God was asking Abraham to put that son to death? Yet hear what is recorded: "*Early the next morning* Abraham cut some wood for the sacrifice, loaded his donkey, and took Isaac and…started out for the place that God had told him about" (Genesis 22:3, TEV). What amazing faith! Abraham didn't waver or hesitate; he left the next morning. How could he be so quick to put to death what was so dear to him? Why didn't he fight the emotions for weeks before finally giving in and making the trip? The answer is clearly found in his own words:

> On the third day Abraham saw the place in the distance. Then he said to the servants, "Stay here with the donkey. The boy and I will go over there and worship, and then *we will come back* to you." (Genesis 22:4–5, TEV)

Why does Abraham say, "We will come back to you"? If he were to put Isaac to death, how could "we" be returning? It was his faith speaking. He was holding on by faith to God's declaration that through Isaac the promise of a great nation would come forth. So Abraham concluded that somehow God would raise Isaac up from the ashes of the sacrifice. The writer of Hebrews tells us, "Abraham, who had received God's promises, was ready to sacrifice his only son, Isaac, though God had promised him, 'Isaac is the son through whom your descendants will be counted.' Abraham assumed that if Isaac died, God was able to bring him back to life again" (11:17–19, NLT).

Abraham built the altar, tied Isaac up, placed the boy on the altar, and lifted his knife—fully ready to put him to death. Then God called to him from heaven, "Do not hurt the boy in any way, for now I know that you truly fear God. You have not withheld even your beloved son from me" (Genesis 22:12, NLT). Abraham's corresponding actions of obedience were evidence that he truly feared God and *believed His Word* over anything else. His actions were mere evidence of his faith.

This is why James says of Abraham:

> You see, he was trusting God so much that he was willing to do whatever God told him to do. His faith was made complete by what he did—by his actions. And so it happened just as the Scriptures say: "Abraham believed God, so God declared him to be righteous." He was even called "the friend of God." So you see, we are made right with God by what we do, not by faith alone. (2:22–24, NLT)

God chose Abraham's story to teach us New Testament faith. For this reason, the apostle Paul writes, "But it's not just Abraham; *it's also us!*" (Romans 4:23–24, MSG).

These very same principles apply to us since true faith not only speaks its belief but also acts accordingly and ultimately reveals the empowerment of grace.

FOLLOWING ABRAHAM'S EXAMPLE

Let's return once more to the water pipe analogy. What we are to ultimately seek is not the pipeline of faith but rather the water of grace that flows out of the faucet. The pipeline is merely the passageway that brings what's greatly needed. So again, the end goal is not faith, but rather the result of faith, which is grace. By it we are forgiven, changed into His image, and empowered to live righteously and to bring heaven to earth. In summary—to experience an extraordinary life that pleases God.

Those who live by the law, whom Paul had to confront constantly, taught that righteousness was earned through our works. If we did good deeds, kept the commandments of Moses, and did not trespass God's statutes, we would be granted entrance into His kingdom. Since that's impossible for anyone except Jesus to do, this teaching robbed individuals of freedom and power.

This same type of thinking can filter over to the Christian life as well. People can believe they'll miss hell by God's grace, but on the other hand erroneously believe that they can only receive God's blessings if they keep all His commandments through their own strength. Of course, this approach again puts the individual in the driver's seat because it's as if by effort and goodness that God's blessings are merited.

This is legalistic thinking and will keep us from true faith and grace's empowerment. It's backward to what we've just observed with Abraham. He first believed; then empowered living followed. To those caught in the trap of legalism, Paul wrote, "Are you so foolish and so senseless and so silly? Having begun [your new life spiritually] with the [Holy] Spirit, are you now reaching perfection [by dependence] on the flesh?" (Galatians 3:3, AMP).

True faith knows that godliness is a product of grace, which can only be accessed by believing what God has said (His revealed Word). If we believe, we're consequently empowered, and as long as we choose not to live in our flesh but to stay in the Spirit, where grace is found, then our lives will please God and subsequent blessings will flow. So the sufficiency is of God, not of our own human efforts. We know we're empowered, and we depend on it. We know we have an ability that is not possessed by those who live without faith.

MY OWN STRUGGLES

When I was a young man, my father took me to see the movie *The Ten Commandments* starring Charlton Heston. During the movie I came under tremendous conviction. I was a rebellious teenager living an ungodly life, and the movie exposed my sin. When I saw the scene of the earth opening up to swallow alive Dathan and his rebel friends into hell, I was terrified.

I walked out of that theater repenting like crazy for my numerous sins. I made a firm decision to live a godly lifestyle from that day forth. As a result, my life was changed…for about a week. After that I went back to all my previous behavioral patterns. Why couldn't I live like I wanted to? The answer is simple—I'd not been empowered by grace. There was repentance but no grace because I hadn't given my life to Jesus Christ through *faith*. Therefore I still had the same sin nature.

A few years later I received Jesus Christ as my Lord. I genuinely believed and turned my life over to Him. I now saw some change in my life and my behavioral patterns. However, in many ways I still lived a powerless Christian life because I didn't know what I had inside me. I didn't know about my new nature, how I had been made the righteousness of God in Christ. I only knew I was forgiven and no longer going to hell or purgatory.

After a while I learned the importance of living a godly and holy life. So in my zeal to please God, I began to demand a holy lifestyle from myself and from others as well. This was chaotic and damaging. I made those closest to me uncomfortable, and some even avoided me. I was harsh, legalistic, and lacked compassion. I had begun in the Spirit but now was attempting to be made complete in my own strength.

As time progressed, God revealed through His Word what I've written in this chapter. I discovered that the strength and sufficiency was *of Him,* not of me. Just as I couldn't live a godly life after simply watching *The Ten Commandments,* even as a believer I still couldn't serve God acceptably without accessing grace through faith. The bottom line—I was trying to live a godly life without the power of grace, and it just can't be done.

In His Word, God says that His people perish or go into captivity because of a "lack of knowledge" (Hosea 4:6; Isaiah 5:13). I didn't have the knowledge of grace's empowerment because it wasn't a reality in my heart, so I certainly had no access to the very power I so desperately needed. Without faith I was not able to live a life pleasing to God, even though I believed the blood of Jesus had cleansed me from all sin and I would be admitted to heaven. Like so many today, I knew I was a Christian saved by grace, but I was living a very ordinary and, in some areas, even defeated life.

We have to face the facts: we cannot live godly lives in our own ability, nor can we please God in our own strength. We must remember Abraham's example: he decided to live not on the basis of what natural circumstances dictated he couldn't do but on what God said he would do. Abraham believed. That's all he could do, and that was more than enough. Even as it was impossible for Sarah and him to birth the promised child, so also we can't fulfill God's plan for our lives in our own ability. The only solution is simply to humble ourselves and believe. When we do that, we tap into Christ's great surpassing power by simply believing. This is what separates the person who overcomes the world's grip from the one still imprisoned by it: the first has faith; the second does not.

Without faith, it is impossible to please God. Without faith *and* grace, we live in the ordinary, not the extraordinary.

Reflections for an Extraordinary Journey

Have you experienced the power of God's Word in your life? List some examples.

How do you think you would have responded if you were in the boat during that terrible storm on the Sea of Galilee?

In what ways can you open up the pipeline of faith in your life so that God's grace will flow more freely?

13

Beyond Comprehension

Grace, though it's freely given, can be accessed only through faith, and we tap into its riches through believing. If you can settle this truth in your heart and mind, you'll avoid being misled by inaccurate feelings, contrary circumstances, or lies of the Enemy. Bottom line, it's not how nice, enthusiastic, sincere, or active we are; rather *it's all about* believing God's Word.

> This Good News tells us how God makes us right in his sight. This is accomplished *from start to finish by faith.* (Romans 1:17, NLT)

Our entire Christian walk, from the day we come into God's family until we behold Him face to face, *is all about* believing His Word over what we see, hear, or experience. Notice I keep repeating "it's all about." I'm not overstating; it indeed is *all about faith.* For this reason we are told, "The just shall live by faith" (Hebrews 10:38).

GOD GIVES GRACE TO THE HUMBLE

You may ask, "But what about humility? Doesn't the Bible say, 'God...gives grace to the humble' (James 4:6)?" It certainly does; however, who are the humble but those who believe and obey God's will over what they feel, think, or even desire? We are told:

> Behold the *proud,*
> his soul is not upright in him;
> but the just shall live by his faith. (Habakkuk 2:4)

Scripture portrays pride and faith as opposites. This verse could have been written, "Behold the one who's *not humble,* his soul is not upright in him; but the just shall live by his faith." It's clear that *humility* and *faith* go hand in hand; so do *pride* and *unbelief.* To not believe God is to say we know better than Him and are trusting in our judgment over His. Unbelief is nothing other than camouflaged pride.

Allow me to illustrate. When Israel was in the wilderness, spies were commissioned to go and search out the Promised Land for the children of Israel. The Lord spoke to Moses, "Send men to spy out the land of Canaan, which *I am giving to the children of Israel*" (Numbers 13:2).

Twelve leaders (one representing each tribe) were sent out; however, ten of them were very humble and two very proud (I speak facetiously). The group returned from the Promised Land after forty days of investigation. The ten humble men stood up first and said, "We've spied out the land, and it is indeed a land flowing with milk and honey. Just look at the fruit we brought back! However, there are strong armies with giants to contend with; they're skilled warriors with weapons much greater than ours. Let's face facts: We're just a bunch of recently freed slaves. We have to think of our wives and children. How could we subject our loved ones to cruelty, possible torture and rape, and certain death? We must be good fathers and husbands and report to you the reality of this situation: it's impossible to take the land" (see Numbers 13–14).

The crowd commended, even applauded, the humility and "wisdom" of these men. I'm sure the majority of fathers and mothers who heard their report were grateful for their meek demeanor. The people of Israel comforted themselves by saying, "We're so glad these men went before us. What great leaders; their ego hasn't gotten the best of them by putting us in harm's way. What would have become of us if it weren't for their common sense?"

Suddenly the "proud" leaders, Caleb and Joshua, interrupted and cried out, "Wait a minute! What are we doing here? We need to go and take the land—now. We can do it! We have the word of the Lord promising it to us. Let's move!"

Can you imagine how the other ten leaders must have reacted to Caleb and Joshua? "What are you talking about? Shut up, you egomaniacs. Are you out of your mind? We all saw those armies—they're skilled warriors. We're a bunch of slaves and no match for them. You're not considering our wives and children and the welfare of our nation. You're arrogant, foolhardy, and idealistic!"

The crowd sighed. "Whew, thank God the wiser ones are strong and aren't backing down. We are so fortunate that the majority of the twelve are humble and prudent. Can you just imagine what would become of us if they were all egotistical like Caleb and Joshua?"

Suddenly God steps in saying, "How long will these people treat me with contempt? How long will they refuse to *believe*?" (Numbers 14:11, NIV). It's clear He's not happy with them. What sounded like humility wasn't humility at all. In actuality their unbelief was pride. They were basing all their calculations on their own strength. God says elsewhere via the prophet Jeremiah, "Cursed are those who put their trust in mere humans.… But blessed are those who trust in the LORD and have made the LORD their hope and confidence" (Jeremiah 17:5, 7, NLT). Ten of the spies saw how big the giants were and based their prospects in battle on human strength. But Caleb and Joshua saw how big God was with respect to the enemy and based their estimates entirely on God's strength. These two ended up blessed; the other ten were cursed. So which of the leaders were the truly humble and proud? In God's eyes, the ten were proud and only two were humble.

It takes genuine humility to have faith in God because you must rely on His ability and not your own. Again, this is why God says, "Behold the *proud*, his soul is not upright in him; but the just shall live by his *faith*."

ESTABLISHED IN FAITH

It's important for each of us to be "established in the faith" (Colossians 2:7). If we're solid in our faith, we won't be moved easily from the heart and purposes of God. Paul's mission to those he was sent to, which certainly includes us, was to "supply what is lacking in your faith" (1 Thessalonians 3:10, NIV). Another version records Paul's words here as "mend and make good whatever may be imperfect and lacking in your faith" (AMP). This same purpose has compelled me to write this book: I'm carefully navigating New Testament revelations about who we are and what's available to us in Christ. As you systematically read this unveiling of grace, you're discovering your identity and, I trust, your faith is being solidified.

An illustration will help make this clear. Imagine being born the son of a king, heir to the throne of the kingdom you are destined to rule. But immediately following your birth, someone kidnaps you and takes you to a remote area in the countryside, far from the palace. As these scoundrels raise you, they repeatedly state that you were born in poverty and are a simpleton, a failure, and most importantly, a slave. What would be the outcome? Even though you're of royal descent, you'd grow up living, acting, talking, and thinking as a slave.

For years, your father, the king, has commissioned rescue parties to search continuously for you. One day, after almost two decades of combing the vast kingdom, one of the search parties locates and liberates you and delivers you home to the palace. There's a huge celebration because the heir to the throne has returned to his rightful place.

Though now in your rightful place in life, it would take extensive training and reprogramming to change your behavior patterns from a slave to an heir to the throne. Can you imagine your first day in the palace? You'd rise from bed and head out to the royal gardens and stalls to gather your food for breakfast. Upon your return to the palace with fruit, vegetables, and fresh milk, your attendants would question, "What are you doing, sir?"

"Just getting breakfast," you'd answer.

"But you have servants who do this," they would say, "including the royal chef, who makes the best dishes in the land." Soon afterward you'd go to your room to make your bed, straighten the room, and wash your clothes in the bathtub. Again your attendants would question, "Sir, what are you doing?"

"I'm fixing up my room and cleaning my clothes."

"But you have housekeepers to clean your room and clothes," they'd say.

When you had been held captive, there was no choice in these matters; it was the only way you were permitted to live. You were forced to fetch your cruel master's food, eat leftover scraps, and clean their clothes—not to mention your own. You were a lowlife slave in every respect.

Your behavior in the palace that first day would be extreme but easily altered. It wouldn't be difficult to convince you to allow attendants to do your cleaning and cooking. However, what had been instilled in the fiber of your being for years would be more difficult to address. Your overall thought processes would still have to be tackled on deeper levels. The way you think, interact with people, and make decisions would all have to be confronted and changed. Your slave mentality would have to be peeled away layer by layer and replaced with a prince's mentality. Even though you're heir to the throne, on many levels you'd continue to live the way you'd been trained. Your subconscious would have to be reprogrammed if you were to think as a prince. You'd have to be taught your new identity and what it means to have a prince's resources. This would take time and effort.

This is exactly what Paul is stating. Each of us was born enslaved to the "ordinary." Now we must be liberated to think and believe "extraordinarily." Paul desires to "mend and make good whatever may be imperfect and lacking in your faith" (1 Thessalonians 3:10, AMP). If we believe we are no different than those who haven't been liberated by the grace of God, we'll live as they do—in the ordinary. We'll live the way we were trained, captives of this world's system. However, if we allow the Word of God to change how we see ourselves, and we truly believe it in our heart, then we begin to live like heaven's royalty—the realm of the extraordinary!

God retrains the perceptions we have of ourselves, which exist deep in our core being. His Word says, "But you are the chosen race, the King's priests, the holy nation, God's own people, chosen to proclaim the wonderful acts of God, who called you out of darkness into his own marvelous light" (1 Peter 2:9, TEV). We are also told, "To Him who loved us and washed us from our sins in His own blood, and has made us kings" (Revelation 1:5–6). And again, "The Spirit Himself bears witness with our spirit that we are children of God, and if children, then heirs— heirs of God and joint heirs with Christ" (Romans 8:16–17).

You are an heir of the King of the universe! You are one of a royal company of people. You are set apart as God's ruling class of sons and daughters. We must know this and believe it in our hearts, for it's only then that we can access the power of the divine nature and bring glory to our Father in heaven.

It's all about believing the truth about ourselves, for if we do not believe, we do not have access to the amazing provisions of the grace of our God.

THE GREATNESS OF HIS POWER

Let's look closer at faith's role in our new nature's inherent power, as well as at how faith brings the kingdom's provisions to earth. Paul boldly states, "By the grace of God I am what I am" (1 Corinthians 15:10). What a statement! To say, "I am," means you know firmly who you are. That's the language of faith—no doubting, no floundering, no wondering. You speak confidently because you know in your inward being it's the truth. There is finality in saying, "I am." You are telling others, "You can call me what you'd like, you can accuse me of my despicable past or how insignificant my family is, or you can say I'm doomed to fail. None of this will phase me because I know who I am. My standing is not based on what I've done or what I deserve. I've received it by faith, and I am one with Jesus—all because of the grace of God!"

Not only did Paul himself live in the power of this knowledge, but he also earnestly prayed that the same reality would be in the heart of all Christians. He petitioned God that the eyes of our heart would be

> flooded with light, so that you can know and understand the hope to
> which He has called you, and how rich is His glorious inheritance in the
> saints (His set-apart ones), and [so that you can know and understand]
> what is the immeasurable and unlimited and surpassing greatness of His
> *power* in and for us who *believe,* as demonstrated in the working of His
> mighty strength, which He exerted in Christ when He raised Him from the
> dead. (Ephesians 1:18–20, AMP)

There is such depth in Paul's prayer. He states there is unlimited and immeasurable power in us who believe. The word *believe* is the key. In other words, this power is only available to those who have faith. Paul is basically praying, "I ask

God to grant you the ability to know who you are by the grace of God. Why? So
that you may have *faith that overcomes the world's influence and power.*"

John sheds further light on this:

> [God's] commands are not too hard for us, because every child of God is
> able to defeat the world. And we win the victory over the world by means
> of our *faith*. (1 John 5:3–4, TEV)

The reason God's commands are not burdensome or too difficult is because
we've been granted through grace the ability to keep them. God's laws no longer
restrain us, as with the people of the Old Testament, but rather we are empowered
to delightfully live in His ways. And this ability is accessed only through faith. For
this reason, John declares that "faith" is the victory that overcomes the world's grip
that keeps all unbelievers in slavery to sin. For this reason, we're told that "we walk
by faith, not by sight" (2 Corinthians 5:7). In other words, we live by what we
believe, not by what we see, hear, taste, touch, or smell. Everything that goes
against God's Word is subject to change. Only His Word is eternal, so our focus is
on what God says, not on always-changing circumstances.

However, it goes so much further than freedom from slavery. In Paul's prayer
he also passionately prays that we would "know and understand the hope to which
He has called you, and how rich is His glorious inheritance in the saints (His set-
apart ones)." He's praying that we would realize that we have not only been delivered out of sin's slavery, but have also become heaven's royal heirs. This is why he
further states that the same unlimited and immeasurable power that raised Jesus
from the dead has been imparted to us. Think of how amazing that is!

The Greek word for *power* is *dunamis*. It is defined as strength, ability, and
power. *Thayer's Greek-English Lexicon* defines this word as the "power residing in a
thing by virtue of its nature." This definition goes right along with what Paul
prayed. It is inherent power. Recall from John's gospel: "Of His fullness we have
all received, and grace for grace" (1:16). God's grace gave us a new nature, nothing short of His fullness, and it's inherent power is the very same power that raised
Jesus from the dead. It's almost too good to comprehend!

The same power that raised Jesus from the dead abides in us. This is why demons fear your discovery of what grace has imparted to you. This is why the Enemy has passionately strived to reduce grace down to "fire insurance" or "the big cover-up." If you find out who you are, you will rise up and be a great threat to his work. You'll live extraordinarily and bring great pleasure to your heavenly Father.

Now can you understand why Jesus says, "The works that I do [you] will do also; and greater works than these [you] will do" (John 14:12)? He tells us, "If you remain in me and my words remain in you [faith], then you will ask for anything you wish, and you shall have it. My father's glory is shown by your bearing much fruit" (15:7–8, TEV). God is glorified when we live as Jesus lived; He's not glorified by us suffering from inabilities that Jesus paid such a high price to free us from. We were made to reign in life—oh yes, *rule in life*. Hear Paul's words:

> All who receive God's *abundant grace* and are freely put right with him will
> *rule in life* through Christ. (Romans 5:17, TEV)

This means we are to rise above the norm. We're no longer living the status quo. We are influencers now, not followers. If you're a teacher, you should come up with the most creative and innovative ways of communicating knowledge and wisdom. Other teachers should be amazed by your ingenuity. If you're a designer, your creative ideas should be highly advanced, cutting edge, and fresh. You should be the leader in your field. As a businessman or woman, you should come up with inventive ideas and keen marketing strategies that are ahead of the curve. You should see what's profitable and what's not. You'll know when to buy and when to sell. Other businesspeople will scratch their heads trying to figure out why you're so successful.

If you're a stay-at-home mom, you should be the most imaginative, most compassionate, and wisest in your neighborhood. Others who haven't been saved by grace will approach you for advice. If they have sick children, you'll lay hands on them, as Jesus, and they'll recover. As rulers in life, we in essence meet people's needs by the exceedingly great power that's in us. This is the victory that overcomes the world, which causes us to rule in life—*our faith!*

Why don't we just believe? Why is our faith so complicated? Why are we not enjoying an overcoming godly life, advanced in all arenas of society, the most creative, innovative, winsome, and wisest people on earth? Why are we not compassionately healing the sick and freeing the captives? The reason Paul prayed this prayer is so we would get a revelation of the astonishing power available to us if we just have faith. This is why he further declares:

> Now to Him who is *able* to do *exceedingly abundantly* above all that we
> ask or think, *according to the power that works in us,* to Him be glory in
> the church by Christ Jesus to all generations, forever and ever. Amen.
> (Ephesians 3:20–21)

Did you grasp these words? He "is *able* to do *exceedingly abundantly* above all that we ask or think." Can you hear the adjectives Paul uses to describe the magnitude of what God can do through us and for us? And it gets better! Because it's not just His power, given periodically from the throne room or on rare occasions through angels. It's also not the special power that was upon the apostles when they were sent out by Jesus to heal the sick and raise the dead. No, it's *His power* that works *in us,* that resides in us. It's been imparted in our nature through His Spirit. When we get this revelation in our hearts, we'll then rule in life, overcoming the world's powers and influence. We will not be defeated, condemned, and fruitless. We will bear much fruit and indeed be imitators of God as His dear children.

Paul's words, as recorded in the Amplified Bible, are even stronger:

> Now to Him Who, by…the [action of His] power that is at work within
> us, is *able* to [carry out His purpose and] do superabundantly, far over *and*
> above all that we [dare] ask or think [infinitely beyond our highest prayers,
> desires, thoughts, hopes, or dreams]—to Him be glory.

How amazing are these words? It's not just *abundantly beyond* what we can ask or think, but *superabundantly, far over and above!* If that isn't enough, Paul goes on to say "infinitely beyond our highest prayers, desires, thoughts, hopes, or dreams"! Stop and ponder all this for just a moment. *Infinitely beyond* is past our human comprehension; it's extraordinary! So why are we not seeing this power readily operating through Christians?

GOD IS ABLE

The answer is found in one little word Paul emphasizes: *able*. Let's think this through by illustration. Say a hurricane just came through your city. There's widespread destruction with all electricity out. Worst of all, there is no fresh water.

The military quickly brings in massive tanker trucks filled with potable water. The announcement is made that they are *able* to give you as much water as you can carry away. All you have to do is bring empty containers, and they will fill them.

It would be interesting to see how people respond. One man comes to the tanker trucks with a large soft drink cup he'd gotten from a local convenience store before the storm. He walks away with 32 ounces of water. Another comes with an empty one-gallon milk jug and walks away with 128 ounces of water. Then another comes with a five-gallon bucket that holds 640 ounces. Finally, another man comes with a bathtub in the bed of his pickup truck; he leaves with 40 gallons, which is 5,120 ounces of fresh water.

The guy with the bathtub in his truck drives to his house, which as it turns out is next door to the man who got his water in the soft drink cup. When the guy with the cup realizes that his neighbor came home with 160 times more water, he becomes furious. He complains to other neighbors, to the city, and finally to the military: "Why didn't I get more water? Why did my neighbor get so much?"

The general in charge of the operation gives the simple answer: "We informed you that we were *able* to give you all the water you could carry away. Why didn't you bring a larger container?"

This is what Paul's communicating. God is *able* to do, through the power He has placed in us, *superabundantly, far over and above,* all that we can think or ask. So our "container" is how much we can think or ask, and of course this would be in accordance with what we actually believe in our heart. No matter how big you can think or how far-reaching your request may be, His power in us is *able* to do *more*. So in essence it's our thinking that limits the power of God residing in us.

Oh, how we've settled so far short of His ability! Why haven't we thought, imagined, prayed on a larger scale? The answer is simple: because our faith has not been developed. We've not searched out His covenant promises and simply believed. Influenced by the world, we've been more driven by our feelings, reasoning, and experiences rather than inspired by His Word.

Why does such common, even defeatist, preaching echo from our pulpits when God has made so much grace available to us through faith? The Enemy has fought tirelessly to hold back the truth of grace. He's done everything in his ability to convince preachers, ministers, authors, pastors, and other Christians to speak out of their own understanding, personal experiences, or examples of others who've lived far below their inheritance. These folks have declared and taught what makes sense to human reasoning and what has been witnessed in the past.

This is just plain wrong! We are to grow into God's image from glory to glory. If the Enemy can keep us bound to our former experiences rather than believing and exhibiting what the Word of God truly states, then Satan can keep us from growing into powerful and fruitful people. He can also keep the church from experiencing the glory God intends for it.

Too often today, instead of the church having greater power than the one described in the book of Acts, it looks more like a social club. In such a setting, even if we are people who truly desire to help others, we are reduced to doing it in our own strength. How is this any different than the ten spies? They desired the will of God but could only see obtaining it by their own ability. They deemed it impossible and influenced hundreds of thousands of people to see it through their perspective. Due to their lack of faith, they never entered into God's will for their lives. They died believing in God but falling far short of the destiny He had planned for them.

Many times the disciples wanted to get involved with what Jesus was doing— feeding thousands, helping the hurting, or healing the sick. They didn't want to die in the storm when the Master slept in the bow of the boat. But they continually failed because they could only envision offering assistance through their own strength. They fell short of what Jesus willed for them. However, after three and a half years with Jesus, this all changed.

Excuses for Our Lack of Power

The members of the early church didn't struggle with believing they had great power. We've already discussed ordinary believers like Stephen who moved unhindered in the grace of God. It was said of him, "Stephen, a man full of God's grace and power, performed amazing miracles and signs among the people" (Acts 6:8, NLT). Stephen wasn't an apostle or even a pastor. He was just a normal church member who had a day job as a full-time waiter in a restaurant.

If the early church lived this way, why do we struggle so much today? The answer isn't complex—they had Jesus as a role model. They had seen what He could do, so Satan couldn't convince God's people that the power had faded or passed away. They had no incorrect ideas or experiences of people that could fight against their faith. They simply believed.

Today we've allowed what people are thinking and saying to supersede truth. We hear this kind of thing all the time now:

"Grandpa Joe was a minister and prayed for someone to be healed, and the person died."

"Aunt Ruth asked God to save her baby, and she miscarried."

"My friend Sam asked God to heal his bad back, and he still suffers from it twenty years later."

We hear these stories and create conclusions not found in Scripture to explain why the power of grace is not for every believer or is no longer available. These explanations may actually comfort us, but they're false. So rather than act boldly in faith, we just don't ask God for much because we don't want to set ourselves up for a letdown. *Why even bother to ask when we really don't expect to receive?* However, if a situation arises where our back is against a wall, then we finally will ask, but more out of desperation than out of faith.

The early disciples were not allowed these excuses. If they failed in their faith, Jesus would make a statement like, "O you of little faith," or even, "You of no faith."

After Jesus ascended to heaven, a disciple like Peter had many fresh incidents to remember. Only a year or two before he'd seen Jesus walking on the water and had cried out, "Lord, if it is You, command me to come" (Matthew 14:28). Jesus had done so, and Peter had walked on the water. But when he noticed the boisterous wind and took his eyes off Jesus, he got scared and began to sink. Jesus then rescued him and said, "O you of *little faith,* why did you doubt?" (verse 31).

Many people say that Peter completely failed, but I disagree. It's the other disciples who missed a great opportunity because they had *no faith* and sat in the boat and watched. At least Peter had the guts to walk on the water for a short while with "little faith." Even so, he was still corrected by the Master for not having enough faith.

For Peter this lesson in faith was a recent memory, like us recalling what we did on vacation a year or two ago. What would happen today? How many are still in the boat, fearing to ask, "If this venture to help others is of You, Lord, command me to come."

There were other times Jesus strongly corrected His disciples for not having faith. Once He came down from the mountain and a father stopped him and asked why the disciples couldn't heal his son of epilepsy. Hear Jesus' response to His disciples: "How unbelieving and wrong you people are! How long must I stay with you? How long do I have to put up with you? Bring the boy here to me!" (Matthew 17:17, TEV). Jesus made these pointed statements to His own staff, the disciples. Can you imagine Jesus looking at you and saying, "How long do I have to put up with your unbelief?" Jesus then turned from correcting them, healed the young man, and gave him back to his father.

The disciples were confused, so they approached Jesus and asked why they couldn't heal the boy. Jesus simply said, "It was because you *do not have enough faith*" (verse 20, TEV). Since Jesus was physically in their midst, the disciples couldn't just come up with a nice-sounding spiritual explanation, like, "Well, the grace of God really doesn't apply to this situation because there are some diseases God wants us to live with so He can teach us something." How ridiculous! If we really believed that God wanted to teach us something from a hideous disease, then why would we continue going to the doctor or taking medicine? Why fight against God? If He is teaching us something, then let's not fight His lesson by trying to get a doctor to heal us. Do you see how absurd that thinking is?

God has made it clear: "Beloved, I pray that you may prosper in all things and *be in health,* just as your soul prospers" (3 John 1:2). Again we are clearly told, "Praise the LORD, I tell myself, and never forget the good things he does for me. He forgives all my sins and *heals all my diseases*" (Psalm 103:2–3, NLT). In the same sentence where we are told that God forgives our sins, we also are told that He heals all (not some) of our diseases. Why don't we say, "Well, God wants to teach me something by not forgiving me of this sin, so He's keeping me bound to it"? How absurd! If Jesus stood among us, as with the disciples, He'd let us know it's ludicrous to believe that God doesn't want us healthy.

The disciples were unable to heal the boy, and Jesus called them on it. They weren't able to say, "You know, I recall my Uncle Fred, who was a pastor; he told me that healing doesn't apply to us physically but only emotionally." *Are you kidding?* Jesus would have looked at them after a statement like that and bemoaned, "How long do I have to put up with you?"

Based on their experience, the disciples could not invalidate the power of grace. They just had Jesus to remind them:

- "Where is your faith?" (Luke 8:25, TEV)
- "Do you still have no faith?" (Mark 4:40, TEV)
- "What little faith you have!" (Matthew 6:30, TEV)
- "Why are you such cowards, such faint-hearts?" (Matthew 8:26, MSG)
- "You don't have much faith.... Why did you doubt me?" (Matthew 14:31, NLT)

After another situation that revealed their lack of faith, Jesus called them "runt believers!" (Matthew 16:8, MSG). Wow. He didn't put up with the kind of sloppy excuses we've dreamed up these days. He loved the disciples so much that He wanted to keep them from any false thoughts that would destroy their faith.

We must realize we've bought into so many teachings or theories that have robbed us of our faith. What would Jesus say if He were here in our American churches at this time? You might picture Jesus looking at your lack of faith with ten-der sympathy and kindness. Well, the truth of the matter is "Jesus Christ is the same yesterday, today, and forever" (Hebrews 13:8). He has not changed one iota, and He would speak as boldly now about a lack of faith as He did when on the earth.

The Holy Spirit is here today, but His voice can easily be drowned out. He's here to speak not from Himself but to point to what Jesus is saying. The difficult part is that because Jesus is not physically standing before us, we can ignore His bold statements of truth, spoken to us by the Holy Spirit. How terrifying. Let's be honest. Have we turned a deaf ear to Him? Are we really ministering with Jesus as the early church did? We can't avoid answering these difficult questions.

FAITH IN HIS NAME

The early church didn't have the convenience of making up excuses that would rob themselves or others of faith. I've mentioned this story earlier, but it's well worth another look. Do you recall the crippled man who begged for money at the entrance to the temple?

> When he saw Peter and John about to enter, he asked them for some money.
> Peter and John looked at him intently, and Peter said, "Look at us!" The
> lame man looked at them eagerly, expecting a gift. But Peter said, "I don't
> have any money for you. But I'll give you what I have." (Acts 3:3–6, NLT)

Peter didn't have a bagful of money, but he had something much better—the grace of God. Look at what Peter does next:

> "In the name of Jesus Christ of Nazareth, get up and walk!" Then Peter
> took the lame man by the right hand and helped him up. And as he did,
> the man's feet and anklebones were healed and strengthened. He jumped
> up, stood on his feet, and began to walk! Then, walking, leaping, and prais-
> ing God, he went into the Temple with them. (verses 6–8, NLT)

Jesus had said to Peter and the rest of His followers that when the kingdom of God came, His will would be done on earth as it is in heaven. Peter knew there are no lame people in heaven, so he looked inside for God's directive and sensed His desire to raise the man up. He listened to the Holy Spirit. How many times has the Holy Spirit attempted to lead us to minister to someone in need and we haven't listened?

Once the man was walking and leaping, a crowd gathered. Peter tells them how this man was made whole:

> And [Jesus'] name, through *faith in His name,* has made this man strong,
> whom you see and know. Yes, the faith which comes through Him has
> given him this perfect soundness in the presence of you all. (verse 16)

God's grace is available in the name of Jesus. Think of it in this light, it's through His name we are saved: "Nor is there salvation [grace] in any other, for there is no other name under heaven given among men by which we must be saved" (Acts 4:12). The grace of God is made available through the authority of His name, and the same is true for other areas of grace. However, it was not only the name of Jesus that healed this man but specifically faith in the name of Jesus. It took faith tapping into the power of grace. Look at Peter's words from The Message: "Yes, faith and *nothing but faith* put this man healed and whole right before your eyes" (3:16). Again, faith is the pipeline that connects us to the grace needed from God.

The fundamental problem is that we have cut ourselves off from the flow of grace. We may have faith to believe that God's grace has forgiven us from all sin and saved us from an eternal hell, but there are other areas of salvation, such as the power of our new nature, the power to walk in holiness, and the power to bring heaven's will to earth to meet the needs of humankind.

Here's an illustration to clarify what I'm saying. Let's say there's a river running through several fields managed by different farmers. The owner of all the lands is also the governor of the region, and he leases out the plots to these various farmers. The climate is very dry in this region, so water from the river is needed for any crops to thrive. Each of the farms grow different crops as illustrated below.

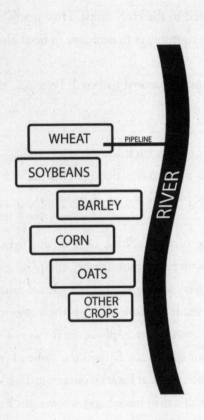

As you can see, one farmer grows wheat, another soybeans, another barley, and so on. However, only one farmer has been wise enough to connect a pipeline from the river to his field and install sprinklers to water his crops. The other farmers do not connect to the river. What's the result? Only the wheat farmer's field is watered, and over the course of time, his field flourishes and produces crops. However, the other fields do not flourish, their ground lies dormant, and they eventually become parched.

The governor of the entire region eventually comes to inspect the different fields. He compliments the farmer who'd connected his field to the river. However, he rebukes the other farmers for wasting the ground he'd entrusted to them, "Why didn't you connect your fields to the river? Why did you waste the ground?"

Now we will change our illustration slightly. Instead of fields of wheat, soybeans, barley, corn, and so forth, we now have fields called, "Forgiveness of Sin," "Living Holy," "Healing," "Resources to Meet the Needs of Humankind," and "Ruling in Life." There are other fields, too, but you get the idea. Instead of a region of several farmers, it is now the heart of a believer as illustrated on the next page.

In this scenario, again only one farm, "Forgiveness of Sin" is hooked up to the river of grace through the *pipeline of faith*. Therefore it is the only field of this believer's heart that is watered. Again, only this field flourishes and the others wither and produce no crop. As before, what is the determining factor of the different results? Why is it that one field flourishes and the rest go dormant—even though the river runs right next to each one? It's the pipeline of faith. All the fields could have flourished by the same water of grace from the same river, but only one field established access to it.

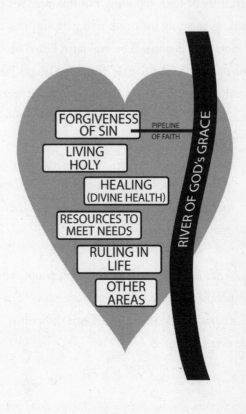

Each of these fields represents the different areas of life that grace affects and changes. This believer may have opened his heart to one area of grace— "Forgiveness of Sin"—but shut off grace from the other areas of life that needed empowerment because of unbelief. There's been no connection via faith to holiness, healing, resources to meet the needs of humankind, ruling in life, and more.

What will happen on judgment day when Jesus comes to examine the fields of our lives? How will we tell Him that we chose to not believe the Word of God in favor of excuses that nullified the power of His grace? How will we explain to Him that we didn't proclaim the full power of grace so that those who listen to us could be more fruitful? What will we say to the One who asks, "O you of little faith, why did you doubt?" (Matthew 14:31)?

Jesus clearly states, "And if anyone hears My words and does not believe, I do not judge him.... [T]he word that I have spoken will judge him in the last day" (John 12:47–48). Why do you think the Holy Spirit put so many examples in Scripture of Jesus rebuking His followers for not having enough faith in regard to healing, meeting the needs of the multitudes, calming storms, and many other scenarios? Our deeds will be evaluated based on His very words at the judgment seat. What Aunt Millie, Uncle Tom, our friend Jake, or our own experiences have dictated will not be heard at that judgment seat. Only God's eternal words of grace will be used to measure our faith and actions before the judgment seat. As it is written,

> For what if some did not believe? Will their unbelief make the faithfulness
> of God without effect? Certainly not! Indeed, let God be true but every
> man a liar. (Romans 3:3–4)

Let's not be people who doubt, people who don't believe what God says. Let's be people of faith. For Scripture says, "For whatever is not from faith is sin" (Romans 14:23). Besides, it's not difficult to believe God's Word, for how could He ever be wrong!

Reflections for an Extraordinary Journey
Why are faith and pride opposites?

Why do you think so many Christians live without power?

What challenges are you facing where you need to grab hold of the truth that "God is able"?

14

True Faith Is Relentless

I will never forget a life-changing encounter with the Lord. I'd been a Christian for only a few years, was still single and living in an apartment in North Carolina. One night, awakened from a deep sleep, I found myself jumping up from my bed and shouting, "I'm just looking for someone to believe!"

I shook myself fully awake, looked at my alarm clock, and discovered it was 4 a.m. It took a few moments to think through where I was and what had just happened. I turned on the light next to my bed and noticed that my sheets were soaked with sweat, yet I knew I had no fever or sickness. I was stunned as well as in awe: I realized God had just spoken out of my mouth. Once I concluded this, my next thought was, *Why wasn't the message more profound? I know He is looking for people to believe.* Still very sleepy, I turned the light off, laid down, and immediately fell back to sleep.

After I awoke that morning, the words kept reverberating through my being: *I'm just looking for someone to believe…I'm just looking for someone to believe…I'm just looking for someone to believe…* About midmorning, while walking though a vacant parking lot, the revelation suddenly hit me. I yelled out, "Wow, it is profound!"

From that moment I began to ponder two questions about Jesus' stay on earth: *What grieved Jesus the most?* and *What pleased Jesus the most?*

After thinking it through, I realized that He was most *pleased* when people simply believed and most *grieved* when people didn't believe that He would do what He said. Simply put, their lack of faith grieved Him deeply! Faith believes that God says what He means and He means what He says. God is not a man to lie; rather He backs His Word with the honor of His name. He swears by Himself since there is none higher. So when we doubt Him, we insult His integrity.

GOD RESPONDS TO OUR FAITH

Everything we receive from the Lord is through faith. There is a truth that I've discovered many Christians are ignorant of: *God does not respond to our need; He responds to our faith!* I could give many biblical examples to illustrate this, but allow me to give just a few. On a particular day, Jesus was leaving Jericho with His disciples and a huge crowd surrounded Him. As they traveled on the road, a blind man named Bartimaeus was sitting on the road. When he heard it was Jesus passing by, he began to cry out for the Master. Numerous bystanders scolded Bartimaeus, urging him to be quiet, not to trouble the Teacher. But Bartimaeus shouted even louder. Watch what happens due to his persistent faith:

> So Jesus stood still. (Mark 10:49)

How amazing! Jesus has set His face like flint to go to Jerusalem to fulfill what He had been sent to do, so He was focused on His assignment. Multitudes of people were surrounding Him, and I'm sure most of them had needs. Yet their needs didn't cause Him to stop and put a temporary hold on His mission. However, this one blind man cried out for Jesus and would not be quieted; no adversity could shut him up. It was his voice, not the silence of the others, that caused the Master to stand still.

Jesus then gave the directive:

> "Tell him to come here." So they called the blind man. "Cheer up," they said. "Come on, he's calling you!" (verse 49, NLT)

It's obvious the people surrounding Bartimaeus were not nurturing. In fact, they were contrary to his cause. This didn't faze him because Bartimaeus would not be stopped in his faith. He threw off his beggar's coat, jumped up, and hurried with some assistance to Jesus. Hear what Jesus asked:

> What do you want me to do for you? (verse 51, NLT)

Are you serious? What kind of question is this? A blind man, who has to be escorted to where Jesus stands because he can't see, is asked what he needs. It's obvious, so why does Jesus even need to ask? Is Jesus ignorant of his need? Is Jesus insulting or exposing him? Of course not. Jesus desires to see evidence of Bartimaeus's faith. Remember, faith speaks.

If Bartimaeus had said, "I know it's too much to ask for my sight, but could you please heal the arthritis in my hand?" then that is exactly what he would have gotten. I know this to be true by what Jesus states after Bartimaeus's eyes are opened:

Go your way. Your faith has healed you. (verse 52, NLT)

It's his faith that gets him in touch with the grace of God. There were other needs in the crowd, but his was the only one met. His faith spoke, and his faith received from God.

I recall praying for several young people in a particular service. It was a Friday night meeting, and many had come forward. I asked why each seeker had come for prayer and kept hearing the same answer: "I want more of God." For a short while I prayed for each, but there was very little power and presence of God. Sensing something was out of whack, I paused and then felt the Holy Spirit correcting my manner of ministry and leading me to confront the generality of these prayers.

The next person, a young man, approached and gave the same request: "I want more of God." He, like the others, had a look of desperation on his face—an appearance of "I'll pray all night if it's necessary." It wasn't hard to discern this young man's pure motives. However, *we can have a sincere heart yet not be in faith.*

I countered, "What specifically do you seek in asking for more of God? Until you identify exactly what you desire from Him, I will not pray with you."

There was an immediate change in his countenance. He now looked a bit puzzled and was speechless. The realization of his generality before God began to dawn on him.

Let's compare this to what we just saw in the story of Bartimaeus. All the people who surrounded Jesus on that day wanted more of God. That's why they had searched out and were following Him, but only this blind man got his sight.

I then said to the young man, "You stay here and think it through, and when you have something exact that you need from God, then I'll pray." I did the same with several others.

After a while, these men and women again approached me with specific requests. All of a sudden the presence and power of God was so very strong. Needs were now being met, and these seekers also got greater insight into God's ways. The reality of "more of God" was fulfilled.

Even though these seekers were so precious and hungry to please God, they'd slipped into a fruitless time of prayer because their faith was not directed toward a certain request. After the adjustment, they were now behaving more like Bartimaeus, who knew exactly what he needed and spoke what he believed. Both Bartimaeus and these young adults came away knowing more of God's ways than others in the crowd.

HEMORRHAGING FOR TWELVE YEARS

Let's examine another biblical example. A woman in a crowd following Jesus had been hemorrhaging for twelve years. Many doctors had treated her over the years, and instead of getting better, she only got worse.

> She had heard about Jesus, so she came in the crowd behind him, saying
> to herself, "If I just touch his clothes, I will get well."
> (Mark 5:27–28, TEV)

Notice she had heard about Jesus. I can assuredly attest that it could have been written, "She heard in her heart about Jesus," for the heart is the breeding ground of faith. After the doctors had failed to help her, she needed to hear in her core being. She did and had faith to be healed. So she speaks according to her belief: "If I just touch his clothes, I will get well." Unlike the young people in the service that night, her words were very exact. Watch what happens:

> She touched his cloak, and her bleeding stopped at once; and she had the
> feeling inside herself that she was healed of her trouble. (verse 29, TEV)

It happened exactly as her faith spoke. This is why the young people that Friday night all of a sudden started receiving. They believed, were specific, spoke their faith, and received. Now hear the rest of the woman's amazing story:

> At once Jesus knew that power had gone out of him, so he turned around
> in the crowd and asked, "Who touched my clothes?"
>   His disciples answered, "You see how the people are crowding you;
> why do you ask who touched you?"
>   But Jesus kept looking around to see who had done it.
> (verses 30–32, TEV)

Jesus didn't know this woman was coming for healing until after the power inside of Him already went out. It wasn't His faith, His initiation, or His will to find this woman and heal her. Every bit of this was initiated and carried out by this woman before He knew anything of it! This is why He turns, searches her out, and once finding her says:

> My daughter, your faith has made you well. Go in peace, and be healed of
> your trouble. (verse 34, TEV)

A MISSED OPPORTUNITY

Repeatedly throughout the gospels, you can see God responding to faith. On another occasion Jesus was teaching many leaders in a house:

> And the power of the Lord was present to heal them. (Luke 5:17)

I love how Scripture specifically tells us that God's power was present to heal these leaders. As a side note, we know that God never wastes anything. One example would be how Jesus collected all the leftover food at both mass feedings (the four thousand and five thousand), because God uses everything. So we can safely assume that if the power of the Lord was there to heal the leaders, at least one (and probably several) needed healing in his body, yet none received. Why? Because not one of them had faith to receive it.

However, all was not lost, for after a while a group of men brought a paralyzed man to the house on a stretcher, but they couldn't get in because of the huge crowd. So they brought the crippled man up on the roof, tore open the tile, and lowered him down on ropes before Jesus:

> When He *saw their faith*, He said to him…. "I say to you, arise, take up
> your bed, and go to your house." Immediately he rose up before them, took
> up what he had been lying on, and departed to his own house, glorifying
> God. And they were all amazed, and they glorified God and were filled with
> fear, saying, "We have seen strange things today!" (Luke 5:20, 24–26)

Jesus saw their faith. When ministering the Word of God, it's great to see faith in seekers and exhilarating to see them receive God's grace. However, sad to say, so often I've seen no faith. A person's countenance many times tells the story, for what is seen in his eyes is a reflection of what is going on in his heart. As Jesus states, the light of a human being is his or her eye.

The paralytic, along with those carrying him, knew that the Lord was good for His Word. They more than likely knew God's covenant states, "Forget not all His benefits: who forgives all your iniquities, who heals all your diseases" (Psalm 103:2–3). The faith of this crippled man and his friends was built upon God's Word.

The leaders, on the other hand, were amazed when they saw the paralytic healed and even glorified God, yet not a single one of them received healing because none of us can acquire even what God desires us to have unless we acquire it by faith! The Father's will was for those sick leaders to receive; yet they didn't! God responds when we believe, which is reflected by our actions and words of faith.

Receiving What Was Originally Denied

One of the most amazing miracles of grace in the gospels happens with a Greek woman. She came to Jesus pleading repeatedly with Him to heal her daughter, yet

Jesus gave her no reply—not even a word. (Matthew 15:23, NLT)

Wow, how many of us would have given up right there and become frustrated, hurt, or angry? She was begging for her daughter's life, yet it appeared she was being ignored. However, this woman was not to be denied, so in faith she continued to entreat Jesus. Finally, because she would not give up, He turned to her and said:

First I should help my own family, the Jews. It isn't right to take food from the children and throw it to the dogs. (Mark 7:27, NLT)

You can slice this pie however you'd like, but the truth is He called her a dog. She could have been insulted, accused Him of racial prejudice, and stormed away. However, she knew His character and immediately responded, "That's true, sir,…but even the dogs eat the leftovers that fall from their masters' table" (Matthew 15:27, TEV).

She knew she was in the presence of the Son of God and knew His goodness and believed He had no shortage of power. She was determined; she knew that all she had to do was stay with her request and she would not be denied. She stayed in faith, and for that Jesus says,

You are a woman of great faith! What you want will be done for you. (verse 28, TEV)

When she returned to her house, she found her daughter completely healed. We must not fail to grasp the ramifications of what happened here. What Jesus Christ—God revealed in the flesh, incarnate—originally denied her because she wasn't a covenant daughter was then granted because of her persistence. So again Jesus responded to faith not to need, for this woman's initial request was uttered out of need, but her reply to His initial denial was fueled by her faith.

Faith Is the Key to Receiving Everything

Is it clear why people don't receive what grace has already provided? Why they don't live in the extraordinary? James bluntly states, "The reason you don't have what you want is that you don't ask God for it" (James 4:2, NLT). It couldn't be put any plainer. He's not talking about halfheartedly asking but about asking with determined faith, as we've seen in the examples above.

This principle of God responding to our faith rather than to need applies to all areas of life, whether it's the ability to walk in holiness, live creatively, apprehend wisdom or inspired ideas, or receive healing or deliverance from habitual behavior—in short, to receive anything heaven has provided for our lives or, more importantly, for reaching our world with the gospel. We cannot minister effectively unless it is done in faith. In fact, James is bold enough to state that when we come to God for anything we must do it

> in faith, with no doubting, for he who doubts is like a wave of the sea driven and tossed by the wind. For let not that man suppose that he will receive anything from the Lord. (1:6–7)

This is really important, so let's look again at these words: "Let not that man suppose that he will receive *anything* from the Lord." Think of the words *not receive anything*. That's definitive with no gray areas and no exceptions! God is making sure we get this point-blank: He responds to faith and nothing else.

Speaking to a Mountain

In 2002, Colorado had the worst wildfire in its recorded history. Named the Hayman Fire, it was started by a woman who burned a letter from her former husband in a no-fire zone. In a month, more than 130,000 acres had gone up in flames. It was a catastrophe of enormous magnitude.

During the worst part of the fire, when putting it out looked hopeless, I was out of state ministering for a week and kept hearing news that the fire was moving closer to our office and house. Needless to say, I was anxious to get home because our township was already under a voluntary evacuation notice. Upon landing I headed straight to our office building. The sight on the road leading up to our ministry amazed me. Our building is located near the foot of the Front Range mountains, a line of smaller peaks running north to south that mark the beginning of the famous Rockies. Just beyond the Front Range, which is only a half mile west of our building, was a terrifying sight: massive billows of smoke and soot were rising to the sky, and ashes were falling on my windshield. It was like driving into a war zone.

As I pulled into the lot, I saw most of our employees carrying items from the ministry to a moving van backed up to the rear door. All our books and materials from the warehouse were stacked on pallets on our back parking lot along with filing cabinets, computers, furniture, and other items.

We had moved the ministry to Colorado only a year before, so many of our employees had been hired in Colorado. I'd learned that they all loved God passionately and lived good lives, but the majority lacked in the area of receiving from God. During our first year together I'd been teaching the staff weekly the foundational truths of Christianity because of the deficiencies in their faith.

After parking my car, I set out to find our director of staff, who we'd also hired in Colorado. He'd made the decision to evacuate, and once I located him, I said, "Stop loading the moving truck, and call all the employees into our staff meeting room so I can talk to them."

While the employees gathered, I got an update on the status of the fire and what evacuation policy was in effect. I learned we were still under voluntary evacuation. The leading edge of the fire, burning out of control in the mountains to the west of us, was now six miles from Rampart Range Road, only seven miles from our office. Once the fire crossed this road, the authorities had said they would issue a mandatory evacuation order for our township. The fire, pushed by a wind blowing west to east, was advancing toward our office at one mile per hour. Because of the direction of the wind, unless there was a miracle, our entire township of Palmer Lake would soon go up in flames, which according to expert calculations would happen later that day. Two ministries down the road had already evacuated the day before.

Once our employees had gathered in the meeting room, I opened my Bible to the gospel of Mark and wrote these three verses on the marker board:

Have faith in God. For assuredly, I say to you, whoever says to this mountain, "Be removed and be cast into the sea," and does not doubt in his heart, but believes that those things he says will be done, he will have whatever he says. Therefore I say to you, whatever things you ask when you pray, believe that you receive them, and you will have them. (11:22–24)

The first thing I said was, "Staff, these words in our Bible are in red letters. This means Jesus spoke them—not any teacher or preacher of our day or even of the past. So we need to keep in mind they are straight from the mouth of God."

After letting that sink in a moment I asked, "Did Jesus say we are to ask God to remove the mountain, or are we to speak directly to it?"

"We are to speak directly to it!" they responded. I quickly reminded them that other scriptures in the New Testament inform us to do this in Jesus' name, but it is still our responsibility to speak to the problem.

"What prompted Jesus to make this statement?" I went on. I took the staff back in the Bible story to the day before, when Jesus had sought fruit from a certain fig tree. None was found, only leaves, so Jesus "addressed the tree: 'No one is going to eat fruit from you again—ever!'" (verse 14, MSG). It was obvious: Jesus had spoken *directly* to the tree.

The following day, when Jesus and the others passed this same tree, it was shriveled into a dry trunk with bare sticks for branches. Peter remembered what had happened and commented, "Master, look! The fig tree which You doomed has withered away!" (verse 21, AMP). Jesus' response was the words I had written on the board.

The account of this event in the book of Matthew shows more specifically how Jesus responded to Peter's curiosity:

Assuredly, I say to you, if you have faith and do not doubt, you will not only do what was done to the fig tree, but also if you say to this mountain, "Be removed and be cast into the sea," it will be done. (Matthew 21:21)

I asked the staff, "Are you grasping this? Hear His words again 'You will not only do what was done to the fig tree, but also…' In essence, Jesus is saying, 'Guys, just as I got up and spoke to the storm and commanded it to be still, and it did; just as I spoke to the fig tree and commanded it to die, and it did; so My children are also to do the same!'"

Everyone was listening carefully, even as they could smell smoke from the fire and see ash collecting on the window of our conference room. I went on, "Not only are we to ask God, but also we need to speak directly to this adversity. We must speak from our authority of being one with Him, joint heirs with Him, ruling in this life through the abundance of grace. Let's look at Psalm 8:"

For you made us only a little lower than God, and you crowned us with glory and honor. You put us in charge of everything you made, giving us authority over all things. (5–6, NLT)

"As His ambassadors, we've been made only a little lower than God Himself and are to bring life as it is in heaven to earth! No buildings in heaven are burning to ashes! So it's not God's will for this building, which He gave us, to go up in flames. Jesus clearly states, 'The thief's purpose is to steal and kill and destroy. My purpose is to give life in all its fullness' (John 10:10, NLT). There is the dividing line of all matters. If it has to do with killing, stealing, or destroying, that's our enemy's purpose; however, if it correlates with heaven's lifestyle—fullness of life—then it's of God.

"This fire is not of God," I continued. "Its destruction is not of God. This fire was started by the thief, by darkness. We are not going to flee from it and just let our township and building burn to ashes. We are going to stand up and command it to stop!"

I saw expressions on the faces of my staff changing—fear was giving way to excitement. I could see their faith arising because it was becoming increasingly clear what Jesus had said about situations like this.

"All right," I said, "we are going to make a list of what will and will not happen, and this is what we shall pray and command." I started a list on the board. "First, we agree that our building will not burn, not one iota of it. Next, it would be wrong to believe that God wants to save our building and then watch all our neighbors suffer loss. Besides, we didn't pay a premium price for this beautiful lot with a view of the gorgeous mountains, quaint town, and beautiful vegetation to have it turn into a charred, burned-up landscape. So this fire will not burn one spot of what we can view all around our offices." This became the second item on our list.

I then said, "We are not going to lose all the time, energy, and money it would take to move out of our building, especially when we could use those precious commodities of time, energy, and money to minister to people. Can you just imagine how hard it will be to carry on effectively while operating out of a temporary location due to evacuation? So third on our list is that the fire will not cross Rampart Range Road. We will not have to evacuate."

Standing at the board, felt-tip marker in hand, I continued, "We also need the wind to change directions. We need it to blow from east to west." Item number four on the list.

The staff was really getting into it. Instead of seeing people weighed down by fear and defeat, I now saw new energy and determination among them. One suggested that we needed a rainstorm to come in and put the fire out. It had been burning for three weeks, and the firefighters couldn't get it under control because of little rain and high winds. We all agreed that a rainstorm should be fifth on the list.

The sixth and final point was that this fire would die. We would command it to cease, whether it was by a lack of oxygen or fuel or put out by water. *It would cease!*

During this meeting, I exhorted my staff much like a football coach would motivate his team before a big game. At this point they were so excited they couldn't wait to get out to that parking lot and speak to the fire. It was fun watching their eyes light up, to witness their rising faith removing the fear and worry from their faces.

"Okay," I said. "There's one more thing we need to discuss. When will we receive what we are asking for?"

No one said a word. It seemed the logical answer was "when the fire ceases." But our team is sharp, and they somehow knew that wasn't the right answer. A sudden quiet came over them, but in no way were they regressing in their surging faith. Even in the hush you could sense their newfound strength.

After a moment or two, I interrupted the silence and said enthusiastically, "Look at that verse on the board one more time: 'Therefore I say to you, whatever things you ask when you pray, believe that you receive them, and you will have them.'" I then read the same verse out of the King James Version:

When ye pray, believe that ye receive them.

"Staff, Jesus makes it clear: when we pray and command it to be done, that's when we believe and receive what we've asked for. As far as we are concerned, it will be done the moment we speak forth these six points. It doesn't matter what our eyes see or our senses tell us; we have a more sure report to believe—the Word of our God."

I then directed them to what Paul told the Corinthians: "'For we fix our attention, not on things that are seen, but on things that are unseen [the Word of God]. What can be seen lasts only for a time, but what cannot be seen lasts forever' (2 Corinthians 4:18, TEV). The fire we see is not what we will fix our attention on. Rather what we've determined in this room and will command out in that parking lot is where we will focus our attention. For that which is seen, the fire, is subject to change."

I turned to my director of staff and instructed him to tell the moving company we would not need their services. I then informed the staff that once we were done speaking to the fire, they were to gather all the items in the parking lot and put them back inside the building.

"So are you ready to go speak to the fire?" I shouted.

"Yes!" was their enthusiastic reply.

We all walked out to the parking lot. Then we prayed in this manner, "Father, thank You for giving us this beautiful building to minister to Your people. Thanks for the beautiful scenery You've blessed us with. We are petitioning You that not one thing would be lost, that the fire would not burn one part of our building or anything that lies in our view—other buildings or vegetation. We pray that we would not have to evacuate and that the wind would change direction and blow from east to west. And finally we ask that a rainstorm would come and put out the fire. We ask this in the name of Jesus."

The time had come to speak to the fire: "Now Holy Spirit, thank You for backing us up as we stand in the authority of Jesus' name and speak to this adversity." We all pointed our fingers at the direction of the large columns of smoke and soot rising above the mountain just to the west. I led and the staff all repeated in unison. We shouted, "Fire, we speak to you in the name of Jesus Christ. You will not burn our building, you will not burn our town, and you will not burn any vegetation we are looking at. We command you to stop in your progress, and you will not pass Rampart Range Road. You must die! We speak to you, wind, in the name of Jesus—you must change direction. We command you to blow from east to west. We also call in a rainstorm to dump water on you. We declare this all in the name of Jesus Christ!"

Everyone was praying passionately, for faith had arisen in our hearts. We were all in one accord, having one mind, united in purpose, and would not be stopped. We knew heaven was backing us.

All of a sudden the wind changed. God and my staff were witnesses to this! The wind had been blowing rapidly from west to east and had done so for many days. Now, just like that, the wind was blowing steadily from east to west. *Are we dreaming?* some of us thought. *We had faith for this to happen, but while we were in the process of speaking to the elements?*

Suddenly, just as we finished praying, our receptionist, who had stayed in the building to cover the phones, ran out to the parking lot and screamed, "The winds have changed!" She came straight to our director of staff and me and said, "The firemen are so excited; they are reporting the winds have suddenly changed and are blowing from east to west!" She had a radio by her switchboard that was tuned to the firefighters' frequency. She had been monitoring the radio traffic all day and had just heard the firemen shouting with excitement over the radio about the dramatic wind shift that had just occurred. They knew this would stop the fire's progress toward civilization.

We all spontaneously started shouting, "Thank You, Father! You are so wonderful! You are so faithful!"

That night I stood out on the back deck of my house and witnessed another phenomenon. Our house was a few miles east of the ministry office. The wind was still blowing from east to west, and as I looked out toward our offices I beheld a thunderstorm coming in from the west. I called my wife out onto the deck and said, "Lisa, how can the wind be blowing from east to west and yet the storm is coming in from west to east?" The rain fell heavily, and within a few more days, the fire was completely out. It truly was a miracle.

From that week forward our staff was never the same. They now are very bold and specific when they come to the throne room in prayer. They know deep down that "the earnest prayer of a righteous person has great power and wonderful results" (James 5:16, NLT). The Amplified Bible states that righteous prayer "makes tremendous power available [dynamic in its working]." We have a huge marker board in our conference room that has the specific requests of each department of our ministry. Numerous visitors have come to our offices during our morning staff prayer and are inspired by the faith and passion with which the team prays.

My question is, "How much are we not receiving for our own lives or, more importantly, to assist others in our arena of influence because we are not living by faith?"

How much is our Christianity driven by feelings, emotions, or intellectually processed information that kills our ability to believe? Are we like the Greek woman, who would not take no for an answer even when initially denied? Are we like Bartimaeus, who would not be deterred, even when fellow seekers close by were telling him to calm down, accept his condition, be reasonable, and act like the rest of them? Are we like the men who came with the crippled man and couldn't get close to Jesus, but because of their determination, climbed the roof and tore it open to receive from God? Are we like the woman who said, "Just let me touch Him," and pressed through the crowd, all the while crawling in the dust between the feet of the mob in order to grab the hem of His garment?

What kind of faith have we been operating in? Have we been determined to receive? Are we relentless in our pursuit? Or are we subdued, tolerating what Jesus paid such a great price to liberate us from? Are we the generation that Jesus questioned, "But how much of that kind of persistent faith will the Son of Man find on the earth when he returns?" (Luke 18:8, MSG)?

ARISING, NOT DESCENDING!

Isaiah got a glimpse of the glorious church Jesus is coming back for. He wrote,

> Arise, shine;
> for your light has come!
> And the glory of the LORD is risen upon you.
> For behold, the darkness shall cover the earth,
> and deep darkness the people;
> but the LORD will arise over you,
> and His glory will be seen upon you.
> The Gentiles [the lost] shall come to your light,
> and kings to the brightness of your rising.
>
> Lift up your eyes all around, and see:
> they all gather together, they come to you;
> your sons shall come from afar,
> and your daughters shall be nursed at *your* side.
> Then you shall see and become radiant,
> and your heart shall swell with joy;

because the abundance of the sea shall be turned to you,

the wealth of the Gentiles [the unbelievers] shall

come to you. (60:1–5)

Isaiah described the extraordinary life God has called the church to live. However, I've met too many people in my years of ministry who have the attitude or belief that God is going to one day soon fall upon the church with a great revival. It's almost as if we're looking for Him to all of a sudden awaken, arise, and bring a significant outpouring of His power on the church.

As the years have passed by and I've meditated more and more on this, I've come to the conclusion that He is waiting for us! *He is just looking for a generation to believe.* Isaiah declares the glory of God will be so strong upon us that the lost will come to our light. They will come in droves, and a great harvest of souls will be ushered into His eternal kingdom.

However, His glory and power will not descend. Instead, look at what Isaiah says: "The glory of the LORD is risen upon you." It's not coming down from heaven but rather it is rising up from within us. Could it be that we will take the lid off as a church and finally start believing God? Could it be that our faith will finally become like the early church, but even stronger? Will we really believe what Jesus says and go after it with relentless faith? I think God is waiting for us! He foresaw there would be a generation who would finally get it, that "the just shall live by faith" and finally receive and manifest the extraordinary glory that was available to all generations before but because of simply not believing, they missed out.

Are you seeing how important faith is? Can you now see why the Bible tells us it is impossible to please God without it (see Hebrews 11:6)? We're called to the extraordinary, but we can't attain it without relentless faith! Let's shake off our grave clothes. We are not people of this world; we are a royal priesthood, a holy generation, a different breed of people. We have the divine nature, sons and daughters of the light, with exceeding great power within us.

The devil is no match for the glorious church Isaiah prophesied. Why have we not gone after what belongs to Jesus with all-out persistence? He paid the price to free the nations, and they are His inheritance. He gave us His authority to go get the lost saved and to teach them how to live like Him. Jesus says to us:

> I have been given complete authority in heaven and on earth. Therefore, go and make disciples of all the nations, baptizing them in the name of the Father and the Son and the Holy Spirit. Teach these new disciples to obey all the commands I have given you. And be sure of this: I am with you always, even to the end of the age. (Matthew 28:18–20, NLT)

These are His words to you and me. All authority in heaven and earth is given to Him, but then He immediately says, "Therefore go…" He has transferred His authority to us and expects us to go and establish what He paid for. We are now to go in His name, in His stead, with His authority, because we're one with Him, and "as He is, so are we in this world" (1 John 4:17). Do you understand how much He has entrusted to us? We are to go forward relentlessly and bring heaven to earth—in our own life and in the world of our influence.

Is your faith arising? Please understand that it cannot be held back, overcome, or defeated by anything or anyone else. You are the only one who can give up. No force of darkness can stop your faith! Jesus says, "Listen! I have given you authority, so that you can…overcome all the power of the Enemy, and nothing will hurt you" (Luke 10:19, TEV). He's given us His authority, the authority that's superseded by nothing else. He's entrusted it to us and makes it clear—"nothing will hurt you."

It's time. Now is the time—not ten years from now, not even a year from now. Now is the time for the church to arise and walk extraordinarily in the power of grace through relentless faith. Quit looking at your ability, but focus in on His authority, His ability, His power that is residing inside you. He has given us so much! There is no limit to what we can do to help people come into fullness of life.

Reflections for an Extraordinary Journey
Will God respond to your need or your faith? Offer reasons for your answer.

Why do you think our faith is so important to God?

Are there "mountains" in your life you need to "speak to" in the name of Jesus? Do it now in His mighty Name!

15

What Are You Listening To?

Let's recap some of what we've discussed so far.

Our ultimate goal in life as believers is to please God: to thrill our heavenly Father is the passion of every true believer. On the contrary, you'll not find such a passionate motive in a "pretend" believer, for he or she views godliness through the lens of personal gain. This kind of twisted intent is not found in those who are extraordinary because they are not weighed down by self-preservation or self-love. Those living a grace-powered life are not driven by personal gain, an opulent lifestyle, or greed. They live to bring creativity, ingenuity, insight, resources, and other benefits of life and godly power to those they influence. In meeting the needs of a hurting humankind, they naturally flourish in all aspects of their personal life.

To please God in our own ability is an impossible task. However, "We have everything we need to live a life that pleases God. It was all given to us by God's own power" (2 Peter 1:3, CEV), and that power is none other than His magnificent grace. We've discovered grace to be more than forgiveness of sins; it's also God's empowering presence that gives us the ability to do what truth demands of us. Paul affirmed this by writing, "For God is working in you, giving you the desire to obey him and the power to do what pleases him" (Philippians 2:13, NLT), and extraordinary living on our part is what brings Him great pleasure.

God did this first by giving us a new nature. Not only are we forgiven, but we are also made brand-new creations, children of God made in the very image and likeness of Jesus Himself. Now, through the power of this new nature and in union with the Holy Spirit, we can live as Jesus—a holy, powerful, and extraordinary life, doing the works He did and bearing even greater fruit.

This amazing grace is all accessed through faith, and there is no other way to obtain it. Faith is the pipeline that transports grace into our lives. If we have faith only for being forgiven of our sins, then we will live a largely fruitless and defeated life. If we have faith only for being forgiven and achieving godliness, then we will live a pure life but find ourselves held back by obstacles and adversity that will prevent us from reaching those in need of the kingdom's power. However, if we have faith to be forgiven, live godly, and receive all the spiritual blessings God has provided for us in Christ, then we can accomplish what we've been charged to do: "Live just as Jesus Christ did" (1 John 2:6, TEV); bringing hope and solution to those in need.

We must remember Jesus lived with a focused mission; He came with a purpose and a cause. He didn't just come and float through life and haphazardly minister to people as the opportunity arose. Listen to His words and particularly note the words *purpose* and *cause:* "Let us go into the next towns, that I may preach there also, because for this *purpose* I have come forth" (Mark 1:38). And again, "For this *cause* I was born, and for this *cause* I have come into the world, that I should bear witness to the truth" (John 18:37). John says of Him, "For this *purpose* the Son of God was manifested, that He might destroy the works of the devil" (1 John 3:8).

Jesus then makes the most amazing statement to each of us just before ascending to heaven:

As the Father has sent Me, I also send you. (John 20:21)

He is saying to each of us, "As I came for a *cause* and a *purpose*—to bear witness of the truth, to bear eternal fruit, and to destroy the works of the devil—so I'm sending you." With that in mind, hear how Barnabas strongly exhorted each member of the church in Antioch: "When he came and had seen the grace of God, he was glad, and encouraged them all that with *purpose* of heart they should continue with the Lord" (Acts 11:23).

If we don't have faith to access God's grace to live extraordinarily, then we will not have the ability to bring forth eternal fruit and destroy the works of the devil. We will not be able to fully accomplish our purpose. How then can we please God?

Increase Our Faith

It is for this reason we are emphatically told, "No one can please God without faith" (Hebrews 11:6, TEV). Another translation reads, "But without faith it is *impossible* to please Him" (NKJV). Did you notice the word *impossible*? Here's the bottom line: no faith means no access to grace and no ability to please God; little faith grants little access to grace and little ability to please God; great faith equals great abundance of grace and great ability to please God. It all comes down to faith. It took the disciples quite some time to comprehend this fact. Once they did, it magnified their deficiency and brought clarity to why Jesus was so intolerant of their runt faith. They finally cried out:

We need more faith; tell us how to get it. (Luke 17:5, NLT)

Another version reads, "Increase our faith" (NKJV). Finally the apostles were aware of its importance, and I can only imagine the pleasure their realization brought to the Master's ears. These men He'd patiently worked with for years were finally requesting what was necessary to live successfully in the kingdom. This is His response to them:

If you have faith as a mustard seed, you can say to this mulberry tree, "Be pulled up by the roots and be planted in the sea," and it would obey you. (verse 6)

Notice Jesus talks about a mustard seed, which is so small it has a diameter of only two millimeters. That's roughly the size of a poppy seed or the dot of a Sharpie marker on a piece of paper. Jesus is conveying that faith originates from what seems insignificant. This is why so many miss out. They look for the extraordinary in logical places—in the substantial. They fail to realize the extraordinary starts out with His Word, which is a seed.

PLANTED IN OUR HEARTS

The key is getting His Word into our inner being: "For with the heart one believes" (Romans 10:10). The heart is the seat of our belief, so this is where the seed must be planted. Jesus discusses this pivotal truth in the parable of the sower. In fact, understanding this principle is so crucial that Jesus states,

> If you don't understand this story, you won't understand any others. (Mark 4:13, CEV)

Simply put, this parable illustrates the foundational principle of faith, and without understanding it, the principles of the kingdom will remain a mystery.

The Bible parable goes like this: A farmer went out into his field to plant his seed. As he scattered it, some fell on the road, where it was stomped down and the birds ate it. Other seed fell in the gravel and sprouted, but then the plants withered because they didn't have firm roots. Other seed fell in the weeds, where it sprouted and grew, but the weeds grew with it and eventually strangled it. Finally, the remainder of the seed fell in rich soil and produced a great crop and harvest.

Later when they were alone with Jesus, the disciples questioned what this parable meant. Jesus replied, "This is what the parable means: the seed is the word of God" (Luke 8:11, TEV). This is of critical importance. When Jesus says, "If you have faith as a mustard seed," He's referring to the word the Holy Spirit speaks to our heart, either from Scripture or from sources that line up with Scripture. As stated earlier, a seed contains everything needed to fulfill its destiny. All that's needed for life and growth is soil, and as we are about to see, the soil represents our hearts.

God desires to manifest His kingdom on this earth, to bring heaven's blessings to a dark world. Yet He's limited in what He can do through the body of Christ— ultimately by the heart condition of believers. When Jesus walked this earth, He perfectly believed the Father's words. There was no lack of faith, and this is why it is written of Him, "Behold, I have come—in the volume of the book it is written of Me—to do Your will, O God" (Hebrews 10:7). Jesus fulfilled God's desire perfectly. However, He returned to the Father and left the task of completing the work He began with us. Now the will of God—bearing witness of the truth and destroying the works of the devil—can be accomplished, not just through one Man, Jesus Christ, but through His entire body, which is a multitude of believers. The only condition is that we must cooperate, and it all begins in the heart.

Let's continue with Jesus' interpretation of this most crucial parable:

> The seeds that fell along the path stand for those who hear; but the Devil comes and takes the message away from their hearts in order to keep them from believing. (Luke 8:12, TEV)

The word is heard, but the devil comes and takes it out of their hearts for one purpose: he doesn't want them to believe it because faith will destroy his works. So the logical question we must ask is: "How does the devil take away God's Word?" His chief ways are through disappointing experiences, man-made "Christian" traditions, human reasoning, erroneous beliefs we cling to, and more—the list is long. We must remember that the devil doesn't come with a pitchfork, a pointed tail, and horns saying, "I'm the devil, and I've come to steal the Word of God." If he did, most would firmly resist and believe even more in what they heard. No, Scripture says Satan is subtle and crafty. His strategies appear extremely normal, which makes it difficult to discern it's him. His goal is to make God's Word appear abnormal and his wisdom normal. This is Satan's most effective strategy!

Listen to Jesus' statement once again: "The Devil comes and takes the message away from their *hearts* in order to keep them from believing." Again, it's the message planted in the heart, not the mind, that's a threat to darkness. When Jesus says, "If you have faith as a mustard seed," He is not talking about having the Word of God in our minds but in our hearts. Let me reiterate, "For with the heart one believes" (Romans 10:10). So the real focus of this parable is not the seed but the condition of the ground, or the heart. As we proceed this will become clearer.

Jesus continues,

The seeds that fell on rocky ground are the people who gladly hear the
message and accept it. But they don't have deep roots, and they believe only
for a little while. As soon as life gets hard, they give up. (Luke 8:13, CEV)

The key statement here is "they don't have deep roots" or, as Today's English
Version reads, "But it does not sink deep into them." They gladly hear the message and accept it mentally, and even in their hearts to a degree, but it doesn't get
deeply rooted and become more real than the natural world. Once adversity arises,
any conditions contrary to what God's Word states, they draw back, which simply reveals their shallow faith. Their belief is easily pulled up by the roots.

I've had numerous people approach me and say, "John, I believed God's
Word, but it didn't work out. My prayer was not answered." What happened to
them is really quite simple. Often there's a time period that begins when we originally believe God for something specific and continues until the work is com-
pleted or manifested. I call this time the "critical belief period." It's the period
when what you are "believing for" hangs in the balance; it can go either way, and
it's all according to your faith. I say to the people who are questioning why God
"did not come through" for them, "Somewhere in the critical belief period, you
believed more in the adversity than in God's Word."

I know this may seem like a hard saying that appears to place too much
responsibility on an individual's faith. But I think the overwhelming evidence of
Scripture supports my point here.

For example, recall how Peter originally believed Jesus' command, "Come and
walk on the water." For a time Peter believed, and he did walk on the water. Think
of it: if you get in a boat, go to the middle of a very calm lake, and step out, you
certainly will not walk on the water—you'll sink! Yet Peter walked. However, once
Peter began to focus on the adversity, he started sinking. Jesus later said that Peter
had "little faith." He didn't say His disciple had "no faith," but Peter's faith was not
deeply rooted.

Many are in that same place. Originally they do believe, but when adversity arises, their shallow faith is exposed. We must believe deeply. Just listen to Jesus' description of the final soil (I'm bypassing the third condition to focus on the point being made):

> The seeds that fell in good soil stand for those who hear the message and
> retain it in a good and obedient heart, and they *persist* until they bear fruit.
> (Luke 8:15, TEV)

Notice His words "*persist* until they bear fruit." When you believe deeply, you will endure, withstand hardship, and persevere through any adversity that opposes what God has revealed to you. This is why it is so important to hear His voice in our hearts from Scripture. Once we do, we should dwell on it, ponder it, focus on the image painted by it, then speak it.

WORDS PAINT PICTURES

It's important to understand that words paint pictures. Many have not stopped long enough to contemplate this. If I say "sunset," immediately in your mind a beautiful scene will appear. If you like the ocean and have fond memories of vacations near the sea, in your imagination you may see the sun in the midst of brilliant clouds just above the water. Or if you live in Arizona, you may picture a ball of red fire descending on a barren desert. If you live in Colorado, you may see the sun disappearing behind the jagged peaks of the Rockies with brilliant cloud formations reflecting an array of colors. God's Word paints pictures in our imagination in similar ways because He knows how we're wired.

Take what God did with Abraham [Abram], for example. He appeared and said, "Do not be afraid, Abram, for I will protect you, and your reward will be great" (Genesis 15:1, NLT). Can you imagine? God appears to you and makes a statement such as this? Amazing!

However, Abraham's response was skeptical: "What good are all your blessings when I don't even have a son?... You have given me no children, so one of my servants will have to be my heir" (verses 2–3, NLT). Abraham had no hope for a son since his wife was past childbearing age. The only image in his heart was what life had painted for him. Both experience and knowledge portrayed that once a woman passed a certain age she stopped having menstrual cycles and it was impossible for her to have children. Sarah had passed this marker years earlier, so Abraham's response made sense in the natural realm. However, God can supersede the natural realm, for all things are possible with Him. Abraham was not enlightened, so even though God appeared to him saying, "Your reward will be great," it didn't mean much in the old man's eyes since everything would one day go to his servant.

So watch what God does: "Then the LORD brought Abram outside beneath the night sky and told him, 'Look up into the heavens and count the stars if you can'" (verse 5, NLT).

I'm sure this interaction occurred early in the evening. Scientists say there are approximately eight thousand stars visible to the human eye under good conditions. However, in the ancient Middle East, where there was no pollution, humidity, or city lights to contend with, the number of visible stars would have been even higher. Can you imagine the task? I'm sure Abraham counted for hours and eventually, out of exhaustion, fell asleep. The next morning when Abraham woke up, I'm sure God was right there. I can almost hear Him ask, "Well, Abraham, did you count them all last night?"

"Are you kidding?" Abraham may have responded. "No way. That's impossible. They're innumerable!"

Then the Lord replied, "Your descendants will be like that—too many to count!" God painted a picture on the screen of Abraham's imagination. From then on, whenever he pondered God's promise about his descendants, he would see the night sky with innumerable stars. And in his imagination, suddenly these stars would transform into babies' faces all crying out, "Daddy Abraham!"

God also used the image of sand to speak this truth to Abraham: "I promise that I will give you as many descendants as there are stars in the sky or grains of sand along the seashore" (Genesis 22:17, TEV). Much of Abraham's pilgrimage had skirted the sea, so I would think Abraham was fond of it. He probably had great memories of feeling the warm sand under his feet. Isn't it possible that one day before

God spoke to him Abraham had thought to himself, *There is so much sand—I won-*
der how many grains there are? They must be innumerable! In Abraham's world, stars
and sand represented innumerability, so that's why God used them as examples.

If Abraham were alive today and were a biologist, God might have said, "Your
descendants will be as the number of cells in a human body."

Jesus did the exact same thing in communicating God's Word. He told stories
of fish to fishermen, stories of farming to farmers, stories relating to business and
finance to businessmen, and stories of weddings, family relationships, and other
general tales to the crowds. He did this so everyone could connect truth to something concrete in their daily experience. And God does the same thing today for
you and me—He uses words to paint pictures of what He desires on the screen
of our imagination. Since the Enemy and God are both contending for the screen
of your heart, this is the spiritual war zone, for whatever fills the screen and is
believed, that is what will come forth in our lives. The words we hear and heed on
a daily basis will paint pictures on our heart's screen. This is why Jesus says, "Be
careful what you are hearing" (Mark 4:24, AMP).

Satan speaks words into your mind of failure, defeat, poverty, sickness, hope-
lessness, inability to help others—the list is endless. He delights in you seeing yourself as ordinary and unable to experience godly change. Worry is his greatest tool
because it is the antithesis of faith. Worry paints a picture, even plays out the movie,
on the screen of your heart before it happens. What you fear dominates your screen.

God does just the opposite. He speaks words that produce images of hope.
This is why Scripture says of Abraham:

> Who against hope believed in hope, that he might become the father of
> many nations, according to that which was spoken, so shall thy seed be.
> (Romans 4:18, KJV)

God spoke these words right after Abraham failed in his attempt to count the
stars. Now a picture of hope was painted in his heart of a multitude of descendants. That picture replaced Abraham's former picture of his wife's barrenness and
his servant being his only heir.

Why did Paul write of Abraham "who against hope believed in hope"? The first hope is natural hope. Abraham's experience had left him thinking there was no chance of having a baby with Sarah. However, there is another hope—the God kind of hope, which is the second one Paul mentions. Unfortunately, we've reduced the word *hope* down to a "maybe so" word. When we say, "I hope so," we really mean, "It probably won't happen, but maybe it might." That is not a biblical perspective. The word *hope* in the Bible is defined as "a confident expectation." Abraham believed in the hope, the vision, God had painted on the screen of his heart. Because of faith, Abraham called himself the "father of a multitude" before he and Sarah had a son in the natural realm. He believed the deed was done because God could not lie. This explains why the writer of Hebrews communicates:

Now faith is the substance of things hoped for. (Hebrews 11:1)

Hope is the picture painted by God's Word on the screen of our hearts, and faith gives substance to it or brings it to reality. The reason so many struggle with faith is that they lack hope. If you have no hope, faith has nothing to give substance to.

Another way of looking at this is to describe hope as the blueprint and faith as the building materials. You can have tons of nails, wood, tile, windows, shingles, plumbing pipe, and so forth. However, if you don't have a blueprint, you can't build anything. Someone may counter, "Oh, I could still do it; I'd just build it out of my head." Yes, you possibly could, but you'd still have to have the image in your mind of what the house would look like; that would be the blueprint.

So let me repeat, if you don't have hope—the vision, picture, image, blueprint in your heart—your faith has nothing to give substance to. This is why Paul writes to the Roman Christians, who were suffering great persecution:

I pray that God, who gives hope, will bless you with complete happiness and peace because of your faith. And may the power of the Holy Spirit fill you with hope. (Romans 15:13, CEV)

This is a magnificent verse—one of my favorites—so let's look at other translations. The New International Version states, "May the God of hope…" Do you see? He's called "the God of hope"! Spending time with Him produces hope and vision. Today's English Version states, "May God, the *source of hope,* fill you with all joy and peace by means of your faith in him, so that your hope will continue to grow by the power of the Holy Spirit." Can you see how hope and faith work together to give joy, peace, and happiness? Do you also see where hope comes from? It comes from the power of the Holy Spirit. He is the person of the Godhead who desires to paint the pictures of truth in our hearts, and He does this through the words He speaks to us.

Again, this is the site of the great battlefield. The Holy Spirit and the Enemy both desire access to your heart's imagination screen. If the Enemy can get you to believe in failure, defeat, lust, pride, sickness, death, ineffectiveness, destruction, and more—all of which he paints pictures of with his lies—then he has you. Faith gives substance to things hoped for, but fear gives substance to our worries. Job said, "What I always feared has happened to me. What I dreaded has come to be" (3:25, NLT).

In my early twenties, just after I'd been saved, some of the battles I went through were enormous. In my mind I saw images of sexual perversion, and I also had dreams of the same things. These images were strengthened by hearing others speak, by watching movies or TV programs, and through advertisements. But most often these disgusting pictures hit me out of the blue. I was tormented by these thoughts, and fear had a grip on me. I wondered, *Will I ever have a healthy sexual relationship with the woman I eventually marry? Will it be impossible to look at a woman with right thoughts? How can I minister to others with this sin in my life? Am I abnormal?*

Then one day I discovered that God's Word states, "We are human, but we don't wage war with human plans and methods. We use God's mighty weapons, not mere worldly weapons, to knock down the Devil's strongholds" (2 Corinthians 10:3–4, NLT). What strongholds was Paul talking about? His answer—

Casting down imaginations, and every high thing that exalteth itself against

the knowledge of God, and bringing into captivity every thought to the
obedience of Christ. (2 Corinthians 10:5, KJV)

The first word mentioned is *imaginations,* or pictures painted on the screen of
our imagination. Next in line is incorrect knowledge and, finally, wrong thoughts
(I'll discuss these two later in the chapter). Paul makes it clear that strongholds are
part of a spiritual battle, not a natural battle. It takes the mighty weapon of the
sword of the Spirit—the Word of God—to knock down wrong imaginations and
replace them with God's hope.

Once I learned this, I gained the upper hand in the fight. I knew my future
was secure. I began to fight using the Word of God. I spoke *directly* to the images
and commanded them to come down in the name of Jesus, and I spoke what
God's Word declared over my sexual life. It was a tough battle, but I knew that
stronghold had to come down and be replaced with healthy images.

Once I overcame in that battle, I would face another. At first most of the battles dealt with my personal life. As I matured the battles came in areas of outreach.
These are the most important battlefields the Enemy wants to dominate, for they
concern how you affect others. Jesus looked at Peter and said:

Simon, Simon! Indeed, Satan has asked for you, that he may sift *you* as
wheat. But I have prayed for you, that your faith should not fail; and when
you have returned to Me, strengthen your brethren. (Luke 22:31–32)

Once while I was ministering in the Midwest, a pastor of farmers helped me
understand what Jesus was saying to Simon (Peter). I learned that if a wheat ker-
nel is sifted at the wrong time, it can be so damaged that it won't be able to reproduce. When I heard this explanation, I realized that Jesus was saying to Peter,
"Satan desires to take away your ability to reproduce—to bear fruit."

The Enemy really isn't so concerned about you living a comfortable Christian
life, making a lot of money, enjoying your earnings, and one day going to heaven.
What he fears most is that you will reproduce. Once you enter this arena, you are
in for a fiercer fight.

I could write an entire book on the spiritual fights Lisa and I have lived through in ministry, and so could anyone who's on the front lines of rescuing souls. I remember Lisa looking at me one night in 1988, three months after we had started preaching full time, and saying out of exasperation, "I didn't know there were devils this big!"

The battles we face are sometimes fierce and blatant, other times more subtle. Let me share a story of a subtle battle that illustrates beautifully what I'm discussing regarding the screen of our imagination.

A SUBTLE ATTEMPT TO SIFT

In 1992, God spoke to me one morning and told me to write a book. It was one of those divine encounters you never forget.

I hated English in school and flunked the national college entrance exam in the verbal category, which is why I had studied engineering. So when God told me to write, I really felt He had the wrong person. For ten months I was disobedient and didn't write. Then, within a two-week period, two women approached me with the exact same message: "John Bevere, if you don't write what God is giving you to write, He will give the message to someone else, and you will be judged for your disobedience." When the second woman said this, the fear of God hit me and I got out my paper and pen.

I wrote my first book, but I kept battling with the thought, *Who is going to publish this?* I wasn't well known, had only preached in churches of a hundred members or so, and was a former youth pastor who'd grown up in a little town of three thousand people in the Midwest. I couldn't figure out how my message would ever get published and out to the general population. But God had spoken; therefore I kept going.

I submitted the first manuscript to a Christian publishing house that happened to be in the city where I resided. For weeks I didn't hear anything. I finally called and was told by a man in upper management, "We don't want to publish your book because it's too preachy." If that wasn't hard enough to take, a few days later a friend of mine read it and said, "John, you use too many scriptures."

I fought discouragement. The words of both were painting a picture of failure in my imagination. I didn't fully understand then, but now I know it was a plot of the Enemy to keep me from reproducing. Satan desired to sift me. Yet God had spoken to me, and I sensed that the book would touch the masses. I had a choice: would I allow the words of those two influential people to paint a vision of failure in my heart, or would I hold fast to the hope found in the words God had spoken to me? I chose to believe God and warred against the "images of failure" by displacing them through speaking God's Word. Most of this was done in my prayer closet and with those who supported my God-given purpose, my wife being the greatest encourager.

I contacted another publisher and again was denied. Since I had already determined not to give up and no publisher wanted the manuscript, we chose to self-publish.

For the next year I sold my book in small churches where I spoke, but the message just wasn't getting out to the masses. Nevertheless, I wrote another book, we again self-published, and the same trend occurred the next year.

The following year, three years after God originally had spoken to me, I was again planning another book. This one would be on the subject of overcoming offenses. I was set to begin the long writing process, and plans were again to self-publish. I was determined to obey, not focusing on the fact that very few books had sold. God had told me to write and that the books would reach the masses. I refused to allow my hopes to be squashed.

Around that time I was invited to have lunch with a friend, and one of his friends—who happened to be the new leader of the publishing house in my city that had rejected my first book. We got through the introductions and small talk, and the publisher eventually asked about our ministry. I related how Lisa and I traveled and spoke at churches. I also shared that we had two self-published books.

His curiosity perked up, and he asked if I was planning to write another book. I told him I was working on the third, and he asked what the topic was. I shared some of it, and he asked more questions. Finally he said, "We only publish twenty-four books a year, and almost all of them are by established authors or nationally known ministers, so I really couldn't do your book. But I love this message!"

"That's fine," I said, and we kept discussing the subject.

Finally, he said enthusiastically, "I want to do this book, but I have to get the company owner's permission because this is out of our normal procedures."

In fact, that company did publish the book, which was titled *The Bait of Satan.*

During the first six months, the book sold very poorly and it looked as though it would be a flop. I fought against thoughts of why had I spent three hundred hours on each of my books when only a handful of people were reading them. I would comfort myself by saying, "If only one life is eternally changed, it was worth it." Yet I still battled discouragement and visions of failure. But I'd made a choice to believe God and to hope against hope. I refused to let the discouraging thoughts displace what God had spoken to me. I had an image of these books being read by people all over the world, and it was God who'd put that image on my screen.

During this time period a pastor came up to me and said, "John, God has shown me that you'll sell one hundred thousand books." You might think his words thrilled me because I had only sold a couple thousand, but they didn't. I was upset by his words because I'd had an image of *millions* of books selling. I just would not let go of the hope.

A little later I was invited to be a guest on a national Christian talk show. I was to engage in conversation for twenty-five minutes with the host and his wife about my life, ministry, and *The Bait of Satan.* But there was no conversation. I started speaking, and the host and his wife became speechless. It was as if God had invaded that studio. For forty minutes I spoke on the topic of "offenses" and was not interrupted once.

The next day, every bookstore in America was sold out of the book, and by week's end the publisher was completely out of books and had twenty thousand back ordered. They had to scramble. Now, at the time of this writing, the books I've sold number in the millions and have been translated into over sixty languages. I stand in awe, but I'm more aware than anyone else of who wrote these books—the Holy Spirit. My name is on them because I was the first to get to read them!

Looking back, I'm amazed at how consistently the Enemy tried to sift me like wheat, but in a very subtle manner. There were so many discouraging thoughts and words spoken that could have easily led to a very disheartening image that would have eventually caused me to let writing slide. God gave me an image of people all over the world reading en masse the messages He'd entrusted to me. He is the one who brought it to pass!

WHAT ARE YOU LISTENING TO?

Let me reiterate—the key is getting God's Word into our inner being: "For with the heart one believes" (Romans 10:10). This is why Paul emphatically charges us to be proactive in "casting down imaginations, and every high thing that exalteth itself against the knowledge of God, and bringing into captivity every thought to the obedience of Christ" (2 Corinthians 10:5, KJV). Notice he doesn't just state "imaginations," but knowledge and thoughts as well, because both can create wrong images in our hearts. And we must remember that the heart is the seat of our faith, where the seed must be planted. This is why we are told, "Above all else, guard your heart, for it is the wellspring of life" (Proverbs 4:23, NIV).

Paul tells us to cast down the knowledge that exalts itself above the Word of God. We guard our hearts by guarding what enters our minds, for our hearts cannot correctly believe unless we are feeding proper knowledge to our minds. For this reason, Jesus says to the wayward leaders of His day:

> You have taken away *the key of knowledge*. You did not enter in yourselves,
> and those who were entering in you hindered. (Luke 11:52)

Notice that knowledge is the key to believing. Feeding on improper knowledge breeds improper belief and, consequently, withholds the desired results.

I've met so many—and I mean vast numbers of—Christians who are very sincere but are way off the mark in what they believe. Countless numbers have based their walk with God on human logic, group reasoning, what's rational to the natural mind, past experience, or emotions rather than on the correct knowledge of the Word of God. It's scary to meet people who will not budge from, and even fight for, what is contrary to the overall counsel of God's Word. They do this because they genuinely believe a falsehood. They comfort themselves with this logic: *Since I'm sincere, I can't go wrong.* However, the fact is, you can be sincere in your heart but severely wrong in your head. The sobering truth is that *the error of your thoughts keeps you from the truth your heart desires.*

The Jewish people did the same thing. Paul lamented over his kinsmen by saying,

> I can assure you that they are deeply devoted to God; but their devotion is
> not based on true *knowledge.* (Romans 10:2, TEV)

Hear his words—"deeply devoted to God," not "deeply devoted to themselves," or "deeply devoted to humankind," or even "deeply devoted to their religion." No, they were deeply devoted to God, the God of our Lord Jesus, who created heaven and earth. In another version Paul says, "I know what enthusiasm they have for God" (NLT). No question about it, they loved God and were devoted in their service to Him, but their earnest and sincere desire was "not based on true knowledge."

The Jews Paul spoke of didn't have the key of knowledge in their minds, and because of this they could not apprehend the seeds in their hearts. Therefore, they did not have saving faith and, without it, could not access saving grace. Hear again the totality of his words with two translations put together: "I know what enthusiasm they have for God, but it is misdirected zeal [NLT], *their zeal is not based on knowledge* [NIV].... Instead, they are clinging to their own way" [NLT] (Romans 10:2–3).

In clinging to their own way, they missed out on true faith. Incorrect knowledge shut them out from the magnificent provision of Christ.

The same is true for us. We can be shut out of Christ's provisions because we don't have the seed of faith Jesus refers to—all due to incorrect knowledge. For this reason Paul passionately writes, "We have always prayed for.... God to fill you with the *knowledge* of his will, with all the wisdom and understanding that his Spirit gives. Then you will be able to live as the Lord wants and will always do what pleases him. Your lives will produce all kinds of good deeds" (Colossians 1:9–10, TEV).

Correct knowledge in our minds will mean the right information is fed to our hearts. This is why Jesus warns us, "Be careful what you are hearing.... For to him who has will more be given; and from him who has nothing, even what he has will be taken away" (Mark 4:24–25, AMP). How can the seed of faith be deposited in our hearts if we are hearing human logic, reasoning, or experiences contrary to the infallible Word of God?

INCORRECT INPUT LEADS TO UNDESIRED RESULTS

Let's use an illustration to help us understand how this mind-to-heart connection works. Say you own thousands of acres of land. One day you decide to build a large man-made lake on your property so you can stock it with smallmouth bass. Your dream is to let the fish mature and, once they do, open your lake annually for a major bass-fishing tournament.

When the lake is ready to stock, you research and select the best full-service aquaculture firm in your area. You drive to the company headquarters and spend a good amount of money purchasing your stock of smallmouth bass. However, there's a new employee at the company, and he makes a major mistake—instead of selecting the bass, he chooses and delivers catfish to your lake.

You wait out the four years it takes for the bass to fully mature. The time has now come; a lot of time, effort, and money have been spent for this dream. You set the tournament date and advertise. Your biggest claim, which will make your tournament most desirable, is that your lake is stocked with only smallmouth bass. There are no other fish in your lake because you've personally overseen the entire process. And since it is a man-made lake with no incoming rivers, there is no possible way any runt or undesirable fish live in your waters.

The day of the tournament arrives. Due to your exceptional conditions, people come from all over, some from hundreds of miles away, to fish in the tournament. You enthusiastically watch as all the participants launch and power their boats out into the lake. You're so excited to see just how large the bass have grown.

Less than an hour passes. You're a bit bewildered as you watch boats heading back early. You don't see smiles on the men's faces, rather disappointment, anger, and even rage. What could be wrong? The first competitors who come ashore hold up the catfish in disgust. "You falsely advertised!" they yell. "You claimed there were only smallmouth bass in this lake. Not only are there no bass to be found, but all we could catch were these ridiculous catfish!" They demand their money back. You've wasted several years, and all is lost. You meant well, you were sincere, but you didn't guard carefully the stocking of your pond.

The same is true in regard to our faith. We want to live a life pleasing to God, to have faith that will reach our lost and dying world. Yet all we've stocked our mind with is human logic, false reasoning from past experiences, inspiration from leadership manuals, or fickle emotional conclusions based on unbelief rather than on the correct knowledge of the Word of God. Our pond—our mind—is loaded with catfish. So what does our heart have to draw from?

So the questions we must ask are: What seeds are being stocked in our lives? What kind of knowledge is being input? What kind of teaching are we listening to? Is it the valuable smallmouth bass or the unwanted catfish? How does our Christianity make any sense when Jesus lived so fruitfully and extraordinarily, and the apostles did the same, yet we as a church have lived so normally, bearing little eternal fruit from what's been given to us? If we're honest, this question will make us uncomfortable. Even though we still attend church, we've drawn back, our heart has let go of the hope of living like Jesus and the early church. We have the form of godliness and are sincere, but we lack power. And it's all because we didn't listen to the truth in order to have seeds of faith deposited into our hearts.

The great news is we don't have to stay in this place. Jesus Christ is the same yesterday (in His ministry and in the early church), today (in our time), and forevermore (for all future generations). He is patiently waiting for the church to rise up and be the body of Christ on the earth. He hasn't given up. He never has and He never will. The divine nature has been imparted to us! We have extraordinary potential! But we have to feed correct knowledge into our minds, which will eventually be deposited in our hearts, and we must deeply believe. Then we will say to any adversity, "Be pulled up by the roots," and it will obey us. Even though it's not the end result, it begins with what we feed into our minds. For this reason Paul empathically states:

> Don't be like the people of this world, but let God change the way you
> think. Then you will know how to do everything that is good and pleasing
> to him. (Romans 12:2, CEV)

Hear the words "change the way you think." The people of this world operate with knowledge placed in them by the prince of the power of the air, the one who "works in the sons of disobedience" (Ephesians 2:2). Satan doesn't want you to know who you are in Christ Jesus because he desires that you settle for a fruitless Christian existence. He doesn't want you aware of the "power that works in us" (Ephesians 3:20).

We must remember, the same forces that influenced the Jews of Paul's day to keep the people from the knowledge of all Christ had provided for them are at work today to keep the church from accurately believing. These evil forces fear the seed of faith, so if they can keep sweet religious thoughts and powerless Christian teachings filling your mind, then they can keep you from destroying their territories. Hear Paul's words from the TEV: "Do not conform yourselves to the standards of this world, but let God transform you *inwardly* by a complete change of your mind."

When our mind lines up with God's Word, eventually our inward belief will line up as well. Paul boldly writes to another church, "Let the Spirit change your way of thinking and make you into a new person. You were created to be like God" (Ephesians 4:23–24, CEV). You and I were created to be like God. We are to imitate God (see Ephesians 5:1)! It all starts with correct thinking, though that is not where it culminates. The process is complete once we think in line with God's Word and that thought process gets planted like a seed in our hearts and firmly takes root.

Therefore you must "be renewed in the spirit of your mind" (Ephesians 4:23)!

Reflections for an Extraordinary Journey

What has the Enemy been attempting to paint on the screen of your imagination?

In what areas of your life do you need more hope?

How can you get more of God's good seed (the Word) into your heart?

16

The Flesh

U p to this point I've mentioned very little of the flesh. I've done this on purpose because many believers quickly resort to blaming their flesh's weakness for a lack of faith or absence of godliness. They attribute too much credence to the dominance of their flesh. In this chapter we'll see how damaging this incorrect mind-set is in regard to extraordinary living.

To set this up, let's first discuss a person's makeup. Human beings were made in God's likeness. In regard to the Godhead, first and foremost God is one. Jesus says, "The first of all the commandments is: 'Hear, O Israel, the LORD our God, the LORD is one'" (Mark 12:29). Paul confirms this by writing, "There is one God" (Romans 3:30).

Though God is one, there are three unique Persons in the Godhead. In creating man, "God said, 'Let *Us* make man in *Our* image'" (Genesis 1:26). Take notice of the words *Us* and *Our*. Peter testifies as to "how *God* anointed *Jesus* of Nazareth with the *Holy Spirit*" (Acts 10:38). The Father, Son, and Holy Spirit are each distinctly identified. This is again clarified during Jesus' baptism: "When He had been baptized, *Jesus* came up immediately from the water; and behold, the heavens were opened to Him, and He saw the *Spirit of God* descending like a dove and alighting upon Him. And suddenly a voice [of *God the Father*] came from heaven, saying, 'This is My beloved Son, in whom I am well pleased'" (Matthew 3:16–17). Again, the Father, Son, and Holy Spirit are each uniquely acknowledged.

In regard to the deity of each, there's no question that God the Father is God. He states, "I am the LORD, and there is no other; there is no God besides Me" (Isaiah 45:5).

We know that Jesus Christ is God, for Paul writes, "God was manifested in the flesh, justified in the Spirit, seen by angels, preached among the Gentiles, believed on in the world, received up in glory" (1 Timothy 3:16). John gives yet another confirmation of His deity: "In the beginning was the Word, and the Word was with God, and *the Word was God.*… And *the Word became flesh and dwelt among us*" (John 1:1, 14).

Finally, we know the Holy Spirit is God for He is "the Spirit of God" (1 Corinthians 2:14 and numerous other references). Scripture states, "The Spirit of God has made me, and the breath of the Almighty gives me life" (Job 33:4).

In a similar but not exact manner, humans are triune. Though we are not three distinct persons in one, we are a spirit, possess a soul, and live in a physical body. This is clearly seen in Paul's words:

> May the God who gives us peace make you holy in every way and keep your whole being—spirit, soul, and body—free from every fault at the coming of our Lord Jesus Christ. (1 Thessalonians 5:23, TEV)

Paul identifies our entire makeup as spirit, soul, and body. To simplify and assist in understanding this, we could view a human being as three circles within each other creating one—an outer, middle, and core. The outer layer would represent our body, the middle our soul, and the inner circle our spirit (see illustration 1).

The outer, our flesh, is the part of our being that has contact with the nat-

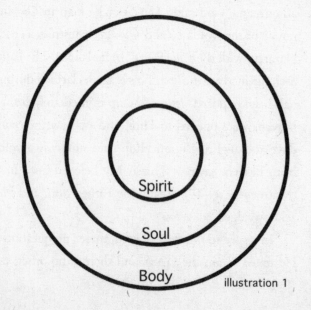

illustration 1

ural world through our five senses. The middle layer represents our soul. Some have attempted to oversimplify the soul by stating that it is merely our mind, will, and emotions. Though the soul does consist of these attributes, it is much more complex. The soul of a human being is what makes him or her unique; it's his or her distinguishing essence.

The inner circle represents our spirit. Our spirit is the life source of our being. If the spirit of a person is taken out of his or her body, the body collapses. When God created man, He took the elements of the earth, which He'd already created, and formed a body. Once this was accomplished, God "breathed into his nostrils the breath or *spirit of life,* and man became a living being" (Genesis 2:7, AMP). Our spirit, illustrated by the inner circle, is our seat of life.

The crucial point illustrated by the three circles is that either our flesh (outer) or our spirit (inner) can influence our soul (middle). Understanding this reality is vital to extraordinary living, for our soul determines the direction we'll follow. I'll discuss this in depth shortly.

In regard to an unsaved person, his or her spirit is dead. This doesn't mean it doesn't exist, but rather the lights are off and there's no contact with God, for it's in a fallen state. Therefore, the unsaved are completely influenced by their flesh and fully controlled by a mind that's alienated from God. The ways of God are foreign to them; they're truly in darkness.

However, once a person is born again, his or her spirit becomes brand new and alive unto God. Divine communication now flows through the spirit. Scripture states, "The spirit of man is the candle of the LORD" (Proverbs 20:27, KJV). Again we're told, "Spirit can be known only by spirit—God's Spirit and our spirits in open communion" (1 Corinthians 2:14, MSG). Christians have direct contact with God in their spirit, but it's their soul that determines which input they'll heed—either their flesh or spirit.

In reflecting back on our previous chapter, the logical question that now arises is: *What about the heart? Where does it appear on our illustration of the three circles?* Answering this will also make our illustration more realistic, for the circles oversimplify the border of our spirit and soul. Read carefully the following words:

For the word of God *is* living and powerful, and sharper than any two-edged sword, piercing even to the *division* of soul and spirit,…and is a discerner of the thoughts and intents of the *heart.* (Hebrews 4:12)

The writer refers to the area where soul and spirit meet as the *heart.* The spirit and soul are so closely intertwined that it takes the Word of God to penetrate this dividing line. The Amplified Bible states it exactly this way, "penetrating to the dividing line…[of the deepest parts of our nature], exposing and sifting and analyzing and judging the very thoughts and purposes of the heart."

After hours of study and pondering the Scriptures, I personally believe the region where the spirit and soul integrate is the heart; therefore both are included. In regard to the soul, it's our deepest *thoughts, beliefs, purposes,* and *motives;* in regard to our spirit, in some aspects it's what many refer to as *intuition* and *subconscious.* So if we were to illustrate the heart's location in our circle diagram, I believe it would appear as follows.

As illustrated here, the spirit and soul are both included in the region I've labeled *heart.* It's here they intertwine, and only the Word of God can separate them. The Weymouth translation states, "It pierces even to the severance of soul from spirit." Another supporting thought regarding their closeness

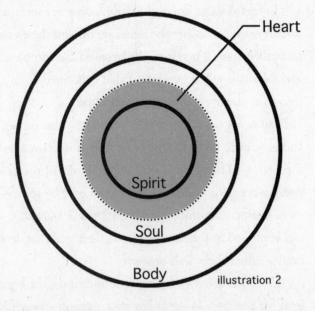

illustration 2

is the reality of death. Once the body dies, the spirit, along with the soul, leaves and goes to his or her eternal home. In like manner, when Paul visited heaven, his spirit and soul took the journey. But in regard to his body, Paul wasn't clear.

In his own words: "I really don't know if this took place in the body or out of it" (2 Corinthians 12:2, MSG). His soul was entwined with his spirit in this experience, but not his body.

SALVATION OF THE THREE

Before discussing how the flesh, soul, and spirit interact, it would be good first to show God's plan of salvation for each. Let's begin with the spirit, move on to the soul, and finally discuss the body.

As I've discussed extensively earlier in this book, a person's spirit becomes a brand-new creation the moment Jesus is received as Lord. The person's spirit is instantaneously made in the likeness of Him. This is affirmed by John's statement: "As He is, so are we *in this world*" (1 John 4:17). He distinctly addresses those believers who are here on this earth rather than those who have already gone on to their reward. A person who is truly born again by the Spirit of God is made perfect in spirit, here and now.

The moment we become a child of God, the process of our soul's salvation begins. Our soul is saved, or transformed, by the Word of God and our obedience to it. The apostle James writes:

> So then, *my beloved brethren*.... Lay aside all filthiness and overflow of
> wickedness, and receive with meekness the *implanted word*, which is able to
> *save your souls*. But be *doers* of the word, and not hearers only, deceiving
> yourselves. (James 1:19, 21–22)

It is important to note that James is speaking to *brethren* in regard to their souls' salvation, not to unbelievers. His words show the soul of believers is not made perfect at conversion, as is their spirit. It doesn't take a rocket scientist to figure this out; for if our soul was made perfect, we'd have no difficulties in the church. We're still working on that one!

James emphasizes both the planting of and obedience to the Word of God for the process of the soul's salvation. Our soul is the only part of our being in which we determine the rate of salvation. We cooperate by hearing, believing, and obeying, which in turn speeds up the process or, conversely, slows it down. The transformation of our soul is crucial to extraordinary living on earth, along with finishing well as believers. As with the spirit, we've extensively discussed this facet of salvation earlier, so we'll move on.

The final aspect of salvation is our body. Read carefully Paul's description of this:

> For we know that when this earthly tent we live in is taken down—when
> we die and leave these bodies—we will have a home in heaven, an eternal
> body made for us by God himself and not by human hands. We grow weary
> in our present bodies, and we long for the day when we will put on our
> heavenly bodies like new clothing. For we will not be spirits without bodies,
> but we will put on new heavenly bodies. (2 Corinthians 5:1–3, NLT)

These words lend strength and tremendous hope. Notice he doesn't just mention but *dwells on* the fact that we will have eternal bodies. In another place Paul states, "For the perishable must clothe itself with the imperishable, and the mortal with immortality" (1 Corinthians 15:53, NIV). Our body will be no different than Jesus' body, for Scripture states, "We also shall be in the likeness of His resurrection" (Romans 6:5). And again, "Beloved, now we are children of God; and it has not yet been revealed what we shall be, but we know that when He is revealed, we shall be like Him" (1 John 3:2).

A glimpse of what this body will be like is gained by observing Jesus' body after His resurrection: any physical trait He possesses, we'll also enjoy in our new bodies. So let's take a quick peek. Once risen from the grave, He appeared to the disciples and said:

> Why are you troubled? And why do doubts arise in your hearts? Behold
> My hands and My feet, that it is I Myself. Handle Me and see, for a spirit
> does not have *flesh* and *bones* as you see I have. (Luke 24:38–39)

He has flesh and bones! However, notice He says nothing about blood. That's because His blood was sprinkled on the mercy seat of God. Now what flows through His veins is the glory of God. We, too, will have flesh and bone, but as Jesus, I believe the life of our flesh will not be its blood but in the glory of God!

Jesus' appearance wasn't different from a normal man. He didn't look like an alien from a sci-fi movie. Mary thought he was the gardener (see John 20:14–15), and the disciples on the road to Emmaus mistook Him for a normal traveler (see Luke 24:13–35). He had a body very similar to what we possess, yet it was incorruptible and perfect.

Jesus also was able to eat physical food, for He asked his disciples, "'Have you any food here?' So they gave Him a piece of a broiled fish and some honeycomb. And He took it and ate in their presence" (Luke 24:41–43). He didn't eat with them just once but on two other occasions: once in the home of the men He met on the road to Emmaus and the other time when He cooked breakfast for the eleven by the sea (see John 21:1–14). I'm happy to report that in our eternal bodies we'll be able to eat!

Jesus could speak, sing, walk, hold objects, and so on as a normal man in His glorified body, but He could also walk through walls and disappear in a flash!

> That evening, on the first day of the week, the disciples were meeting
> behind locked doors because they were afraid of the Jewish leaders.
> Suddenly, Jesus was standing there among them! (John 20:19, NLT)

In this encounter Jesus asked Thomas to put his fingers in His hands and his hand in His side. So again, it's confirmed He had flesh and bone. And as quickly as Jesus could appear, He also could disappear. After breaking bread with the men He met on the road to Emmaus, we read:

> Then their eyes were opened and they knew Him; and He vanished from
> their sight. (Luke 24:31)

In our resurrected body we, too, will have the capability of vanishing in one place and suddenly reappearing in a different location. This explains how we'll be able to travel great distances in the new heavens and earth. Think of it—the New Jerusalem, our eternal home city, will be fourteen hundred miles long and wide. How will we get around? Not by monorail or plane. Will we engage in inter-galactic travel by spaceships? Hardly. Our body will not be limited by time and distance. How fun!

Once we leave our mortal body, our entire being—spirit, soul, and body—will be completely redeemed and perfect. Then when worshiping God at the throne, our body will not tire, need a break, or have to eat, rest, or sleep unless we desire. We will have unlimited energy and amazing physical abilities.

Best of all, we'll be able to behold God. Oh yes, what Moses was denied because of the frailty of the fallen human body will easily be experienced in our new body. It is written that we "shall see His face" (Revelation 22:4)! His glory will not knock us over, as it did John on the island of Patmos or Paul on the road to Damascus. How exciting!

THE DECISION MAKER

But what about our body in the here and now? It's obvious that our present body is not redeemed but is still corruptible. However, we're no longer slaves to appetites, lusts, pride, selfishness, and other traits of fallen flesh unless we choose to be. We can now draw upon the strength of our new nature and live by it rather than by the flesh. The determining factor is our soul, for it's the decision maker. This is the piece of the puzzle many don't understand.

Look at it this way: Imagine you're a POW, and for years you've been bound in a prison cell, held captive by the Enemy. The name of your cell is "Ungodly Desires of the Flesh." Time passes, and one day your king wins the battle to free you. One of his servants arrives and opens your cell door. You now have a choice: will you walk out into the freedom your great leader provided, or will you stay in the place you're familiar with after all these years? Your king is a gentleman and won't force you to leave the cell. The decision is yours.

Prior to the opening of your cell door, you had no choice and couldn't get free. Now you can walk away from the cell of "Ungodly Desires of the Flesh." Should you choose to stay in the cell, even though the war for your freedom has been won, you're still in that same place of captivity. The soul is the part of us that makes this decision: will we walk out of the prison or stay bound? This illustration helps us to comprehend the sadness of a redeemed man or woman still living for the appetites of the flesh.

In the light of this, let's return to our circle illustration. As previously stated, the outer (flesh) is the part of us that has contact with the natural world; the inner (spirit) is influenced by the Holy Spirit. Paul writes, "But he who is joined to the Lord is one spirit with Him" (1 Corinthians 6:17). Pause and ponder these words—we are literally one with the Spirit of God. This is why we are told, "No one can say that Jesus is Lord except by the Holy Spirit" (1 Corinthians 12:3). We can't live extraordinarily apart from the Holy Spirit. But that's not a problem because we're not separate from Him, rather made one together. This is where our imparted divine nature comes from, our union with Him! I hope you're capturing the magnitude of this reality. Jesus said, "I do not pray for these alone, but also for those who will believe in Me through their word;…that they also may be *one in Us*" (John 17:20–21). The "Us" includes you and me!

Jesus was no different. Listen to the statements He makes in regard to His oneness with the Holy Spirit: "The Son can do nothing of Himself" (John 5:19). Again He testifies, "That you may know and believe that the Father is in Me, and I in Him" (10:38). And again,

The Father who dwells in Me does the works. (14:10)

Let's now ask: Who is the Father dwelling in Jesus? It's not God the Father, for Jesus Himself prayed, "Our Father in heaven, hallowed be Your name" (Matthew 6:9). Clearly God the Father is in heaven, so Jesus is referring to the One who conceived Him, the Holy Spirit. He's the Person of the Godhead who implanted the divine sperm into Mary's womb. Recall the angel's words to Joseph: "For the child within her has been conceived by the Holy Spirit" (1:20, NLT). God the Father "sent" Jesus, and the Spirit of God is the Father who "dwelt" in Him. Jesus declares, "I and My Father are one" (John 10:30). As Jesus is one with the Holy Spirit, so are we, for "he who is joined to the Lord is one spirit with Him" (1 Corinthians 6:17).

THE LAW OF OUR NEW BEING

It's time for a quick review. In regard to the circles, our soul is located in the middle because it can choose to follow either the flesh or the spirit. Keep in mind the flesh's input comes from the natural world, but the Holy Spirit influences our spirit. With this truth established, we now turn our attention to Paul's pivotal chapter to the Romans. He writes:

> Therefore, [there is] now no condemnation (no adjudging guilty of wrong)
> for those who are in Christ Jesus.... For the law of the Spirit of life [which
> is] in Christ Jesus [the law of our new being] has freed me from the law of
> sin and of death. (Romans 8:1–2, AMP)

The "law of our new being" (our new nature) has made us free from the law of the sin nature that came on humankind as a result of Adam's transgression. Notice Paul speaks of two different laws. Allow me to illustrate.

We have a natural law referred to as earth's gravity. In layman's terms, it's the attractive force that earth exerts on any object on or near its surface. To make it even simpler, if you go to the top of a sixty-story skyscraper and unwisely step off the roof, you'll come plummeting down at a very rapid velocity to the concrete sidewalk below. This is true of any physical object. All human beings are under the constriction of this law.

However, there is another law, discovered by Daniel Bernoulli in the 1700s, referred to as the law of lift. Simply put, this law gives an airplane the ability to fly. So if you board a jet plane and apply thrust through the engines, upon exceeding take-off speed, you'll break free from the law of gravity and fly high into the air. Thus the law of lift will free you from the law of gravity!

This illustrates what the law of the Spirit of life (the law of our new being) did for us in regard to the law of sin and death. Prior to receiving our new nature, we had no airplane to fly into the friendly skies and free us from the law of sin and death. However, once we came into the knowledge of God, we entered our airplane of grace and, through the thrust of faith, flew to freedom. Now we're no longer bound to live as we once did, ensnared by unbridled and ungodly desires of the flesh. We're now free to stay in the plane of our newborn nature and live extraordinarily. Let me say it again—we don't have to live according to the flesh anymore. We are free!

However, let's suppose I decide to turn off the airplane's engines at thirty-nine thousand feet and somehow stop the plane's forward momentum. Guess what? Gravity still exists. I'm once again under its control and falling to earth at a very rapid rate. Gravity didn't cease while I was free from it. Bernoulli's principle didn't do away with gravity; it only removed its influence.

It's not much different in regard to our flesh. If the soul of a believer decides to repeatedly listen to the flesh rather than to the new nature influenced by the Holy Spirit, before long the flesh will be in control and the believer can no longer please God. Hear Paul's words to the Roman Christians:

For those who live according to the flesh *set their minds* on the things of the flesh, but those who live according to the Spirit, [*set their minds on*] the things of the Spirit. For to be carnally [*fleshly*] *minded* is death, but to be spiritually *minded* is life and peace. (Romans 8:5–6)

In light of this scripture, think again about our circle illustration. Those who set their minds—their souls—on the things of the flesh will live accordingly. They'll be subject to the appetites, lusts, and passions of this fallen world because their soul is drawing from the wrong source. However, those who set their minds to receive input from their spirit will live in life and peace.

The mind of the flesh [with its carnal thoughts and purposes] is hostile to God, for it does not submit itself to God's Law; indeed it cannot. So then

those who are living the life of the flesh [catering to the appetites and
impulses of their carnal nature] *cannot please or satisfy God, or be acceptable
to Him.* (verses 7–8, AMP)

If our minds are feeding off our flesh rather than our spirit, then we cannot
live in the realm of the law of the Spirit of life because we are still bound to the
law of sin and death. Even though we *may* one day die and make it to heaven, we
are still under the law that bound us when we were unbelievers; we've stayed in,
or returned to, our prison cell.

This explains why many in the church live no differently than those in the
world: our divorce rate is high; we quarrel, bicker, and live in strife and bitter
unforgiveness; we gravitate toward certain factions; we are addicted to pornography or substances; we turn a deaf ear to the cries of the poor, the widows, and the
fatherless. The list is endless. Isn't it interesting that Paul says that those who
receive their input from the flesh cannot please God and are still under the "law
of sin"? For this reason Paul goes on to say:

Therefore, *brethren,* we are debtors—not to the flesh, to live according
to the flesh. For if you live according to the flesh you will *die.* (verses
12–13)

It's crystal clear that Paul is not speaking to unbelievers, but to Christians,
because he uses the word *brethren.* So my question is how can believers say so flip-
pantly, "Oh, I just got in the flesh!" It's not insignificant, for Paul says if we dwell
in the flesh, we will die! As I said earlier, I'll leave the research to you to determine
what the word *die* means. However, nowhere in all of Scripture was it a happy or
desirable end when God said someone would die. He said these words to Adam:
"For in *the day* that you eat of it you shall surely die" (Genesis 2:17). Adam died
physically, but it was many years after his rebellion. Yet God said Adam would die
the day he ate the fruit. What happened? What manner of death came to him the
day he rebelled?

RESTORED LIFE TO OUR MORTAL BODIES

The question now arises: How do we keep from gravitating toward a carnal mind? How do we overcome the urge to follow the influence of the flesh? Paul gives us the answer, and it's twofold. First and foremost, we resist carnality through the power imparted by the Holy Spirit into our spirit; second, we take advantage of the Holy Spirit's amazing effect on our physical body. Paul says:

> But if Christ lives in you, [then although] your [natural] body is dead by reason of sin *and* guilt, the spirit is alive because of [the] righteousness [that He imputes to you]. And if the Spirit of Him Who raised up Jesus from the dead dwells in you, [then] He Who raised up Christ *Jesus* from the dead will also *restore to life* your mortal (short-lived, perishable) bodies through His Spirit Who dwells in you. (Romans 8:10–11, AMP)

This has to be one of the most liberating statements Paul makes in this epistle. Listen to his words from The Message: "With his Spirit living in you, your body will be as alive as Christ's!" Again, from the New Living Translation, "He will give life to your mortal body by this same Spirit living within you." The Holy Spirit not only re-creates and empowers our human spirit, but also infuses life into our mortal physical body! Why have we not proclaimed this more?

Once I became saved, I discovered the ungodly desires of my flesh waned due to the imparted nature of Christ in my spirit, but also because of the effect the Holy Spirit had on my physical body. Sin lost its appeal. I formerly used a lot of bad language. However, soon after my conversion, I realized I wasn't cursing any longer. Before knowing Christ I loved parties and drunkenness. I lived for the pre-weekend and weekend parties at my fraternity or on campus. Afterward, the desire for revelry and drunkenness was gone. I'd walk down to my fraternity's social room on any given party night and observe the guys moving in on the girls, drinking to inebriation, and making fools of themselves. The thought came to me: *How did I ever enjoy this, let alone love and live for it?*

It became a reality after I had become one with God's Spirit that if I did sin I didn't like it, whereas prior to salvation I had enjoyed sin. This was the effect of the Holy Spirit's empowerment in my new spirit, along with His infusion of life into my mortal body. My inner man was now alive. Before salvation, the carnal appetites of my flesh were strengthened by the sin nature of my spirit. Now my new nature was not at all in favor of sin. I now detested what I used to crave. My spirit desired to follow the Holy Spirit's leading. I yearned for His fellowship, ways, and wisdom. For this reason Paul continues,

> God's Spirit beckons. There are things to do and places to go!
> This resurrection life you received from God is not a timid, grave-tending life. It's adventurously expectant, greeting God with a childlike "What's next, Papa?" (Romans 8:14–15, MSG)

Life in Christ is adventurous, exciting, and expectant. In a word—extraordinary! We are now free from the law of sin and death that once enslaved us. We no longer have to follow our fallen flesh's desires. Our spirit, along with our body, has been affected by our new life in Christ. What an amazing salvation!

CALLED TO A FREE LIFE

Paul also addresses this awesome freedom from the flesh in his letter to the Galatians. He writes, "Christ has set us free to live a free life. So take your stand!" (5:1, MSG). We're liberated from the law of sin and death because our spirit is new and our flesh is energized by the power of God's Spirit. Let's hold fast to what's been provided, living the high life in our airplane of grace, powered by our faith, free from the bondages that ensnare the children of darkness. Paul warns:

> It is absolutely clear that God has called you to a free life. Just make sure that you don't use this freedom as an excuse to do whatever you want to do and destroy your freedom. (verse 13, MSG)

This information needs to be passionately proclaimed in our churches. Paul's warning could be compared to a man who is a repeat criminal. He's lived in poverty and has had to resort to stealing in order to live. Due to his persistent thievery, he's spent years in jail—incarcerated five times in a twenty-year time period, each time for armed robbery of a convenience store. Once released from prison, he always found himself back in jail within weeks due to his addiction to stealing. Now, because of his repeated offenses, he's been sentenced to life imprisonment.

Then one day a doctor comes up with a revolutionary drug that frees this prisoner from the habitual desire to steal. At the same time a high-ranking government official pardons this guy and obtains asylum for him in another country so he can get a new start. In this new country, a retailer gives the man a good job where he'll earn enough to pay his rent and buy food, clothes, and other necessities. This ex-prisoner will even have enough money to buy some luxury items. Now he's completely free, not only from his life sentence, but also from the compulsive need to steal.

Things go well for a couple years. However, some of his old ex-con friends learn his whereabouts, travel to the new country, and entice him. The leader of the gang says, "My mates and I have discovered a way to break into a major bank in your new city and get the mother lode. We'll be set, living in luxury and pleasure till we die! Are you in?"

He loves the thought of luxurious living and not working for it. He thinks, *What an amazing way to spend the rest of my life.* So he joins these hoodlums.

A few weeks later they pull off the job, but the next day they're all arrested and given life sentences. Our guy was totally free but used his liberty to return to his former behavior, thus costing him his freedom. Hear again Paul's words, "Just make sure that you don't use this freedom as an excuse to do whatever you want to do and destroy your freedom." This exactly describes what this man did; it also describes what some believers do and why they're not living extraordinarily. They, once again, are enslaved to their own flesh. For this reason Paul strongly charges us, "Rather, use your freedom to serve one another in love; that's how freedom grows" (verse 13, MSG).

When we live by love, we cannot be enticed away from godliness. We're in the realm of God, who is love. We're cooperating with His Spirit, and our freedom grows. Without the influence of the Holy Spirit, our flesh will veer toward selfishness, self-preservation, self-love, and other vices. For this reason Paul goes on to say:

> But I say, walk *and* live [habitually] in the [Holy] Spirit [responsive to *and* controlled *and* guided by the Spirit]; then you will certainly not gratify the cravings *and* desires of the flesh (of human nature without God). For the desires of the flesh are opposed to the [Holy] Spirit, and the [desires of the] Spirit are opposed to the flesh (godless human nature). (verses 16–17, AMP)

When we're receiving input from our spirit, inspired by the Holy Spirit, then we'll not gratify the cravings and desires of the "godless human nature." But look closely again at the scripture above: "godless human nature" is also called "human nature without God," yet *we are not without God because He lives in us!* Let me reiterate Paul's declaration to the Romans: when we are spiritually minded— receiving input from our spirit—then the Holy Spirit will "give life to your mortal body." Our body is now infused with life! It's a different scenario than for the one who is "without God" and dominated by his flesh.

At this point allow me to return to the opening statement of this chapter: a good number of believers attribute too much credence to the dominance of their flesh. The reason can only be they've not carefully searched out the Scripture to both discover and implant deeply in their being these truths brought to light by New Testament writers. They've failed to realize that God's Spirit has infused life into their mortal body, giving them the ability to walk in complete freedom.

It again reverts back to faith. If we believe our flesh is dominant, overbearing, powerful, and we're at its mercy, then we will reap accordingly. However, if we believe God's Word, that His Spirit infuses life into our flesh and we're not subject to it any longer, then it will be done according to our faith! Once again we see why Scripture declares, "without faith it is impossible to please God" (Hebrews 11:6, NIV). We must always remember that *right believing produces right living*. The converse is also true; *wrong believing yields wrong living*. Paul concludes:

Since this is the kind of life we have chosen, the life of the Spirit, let us
make sure that we do not just hold it as an idea in our heads or a sentiment
in our hearts, but work out its implications in every detail of our lives.
(Galatians 5:25, MSG)

It couldn't be said any better; this completely summarizes what's been discussed in the past two chapters. We cannot live an extraordinary life by only holding the Word of God as an ideal or carrying it sentimentally in our hearts. It's only
unattainable if we don't believe. That's the hurdle many struggle with, but it's so
simple—simple enough for a child to work out.

In the preceding verse Paul writes, "And those who are Christ's have crucified
the flesh with its passions and desires" (verse 24). Through the power of the Holy
Spirit we crucify ungodly appetites. Now the glory belongs to God, not to us. This
sheds further light on Paul's words: "I have been crucified with Christ; it is no longer
I who live, but Christ lives in me; and the life which I now live in the flesh I live *by
faith* in the Son of God" (2:20). Notice his words "I live *by faith* in the Son of God."
It's faith in the Spirit of Christ living in us that *accesses* the grace to energize our body.
We're no longer under the bondage of *flesh apart from God's life*. We now live by *faith
in the power of the One living in us*. We're free and can live extraordinarily!

WALK IN THE SPIRIT

We are to live proactively, not passively. Extraordinary living flows from an offensive, not a defensive mind-set. Hear Paul's words again: "If by the Spirit you put
to death the deeds of the body, you will live" (Romans 8:13). His words are proactive. If we draw from our spirit, inspired by the Holy Spirit, ungodly desires of the
flesh will automatically become unattractive. We'll be so enamored by true life that
death will lose its appeal.

A good illustration would be a man who proactively protects his thoughts, attitude, and love toward his wife. He doesn't permit any negative or critical thought
to enter his mind. The result: he firmly believes he's married to the most attractive, wise, lovely, and beautiful woman on the face of the earth. If he's enamored

with his wife in this way, if another woman tried to seduce him, he would laugh within himself and think, *I've got no interest in committing adultery with you; I'm married to the best.* This is offensive living.

Religion or legalism is just the opposite. It focuses on what you can't have rather than on the amazing reality of what you do have. The best life available has been freely provided, yet legalism puts your focus on the dirt you came out of. It continually says to a person, "You'd better not sin; you must stay away from all the ungodly things you did before being saved."

Sadly, we're now governed by "thou shall nots" under a law of legalistic Christianity that is not true Christianity at all. If we gravitate back to restrictive laws, we then strengthen the flesh, for the law arouses the desire in our flesh to once again live contrary to God! Paul warns, "Sin gets its power from the Law" (1 Corinthians 15:56, TEV).

Allow me to illustrate. For three years I worked as a tennis teaching professional at a private swim and racquet club. I would spend twenty-five hours a week on the courts instructing both youth and adults. I discovered something interesting while teaching hundreds of tennis players: if I repeatedly told a student *not* to do something, it only strengthened his or her inclination to continue doing it. For example, a beginning tennis player usually has a natural tendency to lean back and put weight on the back foot, especially when receiving strong incoming shots. Inexperience reasons that this tactic gives more time to adjust. However, this approach will always create a weak shot, which most likely will cause a lost point, especially in midlevel to advanced tennis. I discovered that if I repeatedly said to my students, "Don't lean on your back foot," after hitting a weak shot, they'd inevitably continue doing it.

However, if I said to them, "Okay, I want you to get an image in your mind of attacking the ball. Move aggressively into it; don't let it come to you, you go to it." After saying this a few times, then I would simplify my instruction and simply urge, "Move into it," or, "Attack it!" Amazingly, they would stop leaning on their back foot and start stepping into the ball, attacking the shot.

In light of this example, again hear Paul's words:

Let the Spirit direct your lives, and you will not satisfy the desires of the human nature. (Galatians 5:16, TEV)

You can see his words are proactive. We put to death the desires of sin by continuing to receive our input from our spirit, influenced by the Holy Spirit, thus abiding in the law of life. This moves and keeps us in the realm of the extraordinary.

After saying this, let me stress an important point. As a tennis instructor I would tell my students why it was unwise to stay on their back foot. I would warn them it would produce a weak shot that could cost them the point. I did this for the sake of understanding. I usually said this only once or twice. However, I would repeatedly stress the proactive response—"Move into the ball and attack it." That's the image I wanted in their mind.

Paul and other writers of the New Testament do issue warnings of the consequences of reverting back to the flesh. This is done for the sake of understanding, for godly fear is the beginning of wisdom and understanding. However, the same writers put their primary stress on living proactively in the Spirit. Again, hear his proactive words, "For as many as are led by the Spirit of God, these are sons of God" (Romans 8:14).

Paul's Wrap-Up

After the apostle Paul had extensively covered the different facets of salvation, spirit, soul, and body, he then pulled it all together in this manner:

And so, dear brothers and sisters, I plead with you to *give your bodies to God*. Let them be a living and holy sacrifice—the kind he will accept. When you think of what he has done for you, is this too much to ask? Don't copy the behavior and customs of this world, but let God transform you into a new person by *changing the way you think*. Then you will know what God wants you to do, and you will know how good and pleasing and perfect his will really is. (Romans 12:1–2, NLT)

I've highlighted two statements: *"give your bodies to God"* and *"changing the way you think."* In essence, each covers what's been discussed in the past two chapters. Jesus has done it all, the complete work, the price paid in full for our freedom. So now what's our part? It really boils down to these two statements.

First, how do we practically "give [our] bodies to God [as] a living and holy sacrifice?" When a sacrifice is given to God, it's dedicated entirely to Him. In other words, once given, we don't take it back because it's no longer ours to take. If I give a financial gift to God in an offering, I wouldn't dare think of calling the church or ministry and asking for the money to be returned because it no longer belongs to me. This is what we are to do with our body—give it as a sacrifice. But our sacrifice is not a dead one, like money. Rather it's alive, and since such a huge price was paid for our freedom, is this too much to ask? The body we live in should no longer be viewed as ours but His. This means we now *steward* what belongs to someone else and use what belongs to Him to accomplish His desires. But how do we know what He desires? The answer is, "Don't copy the behavior and customs of this world, but let God transform you into a new person by *changing the way you think.* Then you will know what God wants you to do." How can we do what pleases Him if we don't listen to or believe what His Word states? How can we abide in the spirit realm if our mind is still given over to the way natural men think? How can we be spiritually minded if we still think as we did before we were saved?

There must be a total transformation of the way we think and view life. We must study the Word of God to get His view, otherwise we'll still flow with the course of this world.

I've learned through experience that when I read the Bible with a clear mind and heart, it opens up the channel of my spirit's influence to my soul. It's as if the passageway from my spirit to my soul is cleared so I can hear the instruction of the Holy Spirit. I've discovered that I see clearer, think better, and my body seems to have more life and empowerment. If I don't hear the Word of God, whether through simply reading the Bible, praying, listening to inspired messages, reading anointed books, and so on, then it seems as if the influence of the world creeps in, and I find myself conforming more to the customs and ways of this world.

To be quite frank, we underestimate how important it is to hear the Word of

God, and to "make sure that we do not just hold it as an idea in our heads or a sentiment in our hearts, but work out its implications in every detail of our lives" (Galatians 5:25, MSG). In neglecting this we've then wondered, *Why can't I live a successful Christian life? Why is the extraordinary unattainable? Why is my flesh so dominant? Why can't I do the things I long to do? Why did the believers in the book of Acts live so differently from me?* Scripture tells us why: "For as he thinks in his heart, so is he" (Proverbs 23:7). Paul strongly exhorts us:

> Since, then, we do not have the excuse of ignorance, everything—and I do mean everything—connected with that old way of life has to go. It's rotten through and through. Get rid of it! And then take on an entirely new way of life—a God-fashioned life, and a life renewed from the inside and working itself into your conduct as God accurately reproduces his character in you. (Ephesians 4:22–24, MSG)

We put off the old ways by changing our mind-set—the spirit of our mind. The most creative, innovative, powerful, wise Being in the universe is now joined with us. This fact must become more real to us than the ground we walk on and the water we drink. This isn't just mental assent to what He declares over us; it means we literally enter into the way God thinks. We see ourselves as He sees us. We no longer live in our own ability but know for sure the Spirit of Christ lives through us. This is believed to the core of our being. We have "put on the new man."

Having done this, it matters not what circumstances, the world, well-meaning friends, or unsaved persons communicate to you. You know beyond doubt that you are now an extraordinary person and God is glorified in your life.

Reflections for an Extraordinary Journey

The soul—influenced by our spirit or our flesh—is the "decision maker" as to how we live. What's the current state of your decision maker? Is it inclined toward the things of God or the ways of the world?

In what areas of your life do you struggle to escape bondage from sin and experience God's freedom?

What are some ways you can go on the offensive in your life—to be proactive in the Spirit?

17

God's Imperial Rule

I n this final chapter, let's once again turn our attention to the well-known words of the Lord's Prayer:

> Our Father Who is in heaven, hallowed (kept holy) be Your name. Your kingdom come, Your will be done on earth as it is in heaven. (Matthew 6:9–10, AMP)

One day the realization hit me: *Jesus spoke frequently of the kingdom.* As I read the gospels with this thought in mind, it became overwhelming as to how many times He brought up the kingdom. In fact, the phrase appears in over a hundred verses in the gospels.

As I mentioned in chapter 10, when Jesus speaks of the kingdom of God, He's actually referring to the "rule of God." The Greek words most frequently used in the gospels for the kingdom of God are *basileia tou Theos. Theos* refers to God, while *basileia* is defined as "royalty, rule, reign." *Basileia* is derived from the Greek word for "base" or "foundation." Some scholars prefer this root definition because it eliminates confusion with the meaning of "monarchy," and they believe the best translation is "God's imperial rule" or "God's domain."

I love the word *imperial.* One of its definitions is "supremely powerful." Synonyms include *royal, majestic, imposing, grand,* and *magnificent.* Think of these as you continue to see the word *imperial.*

Jesus literally communicates, "Our Father in heaven, God Almighty, Your imperial rule come, Your will be done on earth just as it is in heaven." God's kingdom has come! Not yet physically on the earth, as Isaiah prophesied—that in the future Jesus will rule forever and ever and Satan's influence will be completely removed. Rather the kingdom is within us, His people, and we're to spread its domain wherever we are. In light of this, let's once again look at Paul's words to the Romans:

> All who receive God's *abundant grace* and are freely put right with him will
> *rule in life* through Christ. (Romans 5:17, TEV)

Further understanding of what's communicated in the Lord's Prayer regarding "God's imperial rule" brings Paul's words "rule in life" to another level. The New International Version translates it "reign in life"; Weymouth translates it "reign as kings in Life." Like kings or queens!

How do these two key scriptures interact? We must keep in mind that "the earth is the LORD's" (Psalm 24:1), but He's delegated the authority of ruling it to men. The psalmist writes, "The heaven of heavens is for GOD, but he put us in charge of the earth" (115:16, MSG). Adam messed it up; he gave Satan dominance. However, Jesus, as a man, won it back. Now final authority is back where God originally intended—in the hands of His men and women. However, it's up to us to execute this authority. If we don't, it stays under the sway of the wicked one.

Here's the sobering reality: godly men and women determine whether or not the will of God gets done on this earth! All stories in the gospels illustrate this truth. Let me cite just one: it took Jesus, a man, to stand up in the boat and rebuke a life-threatening storm on the Lake of Galilee. God didn't want Jesus and the other men to die, yet He didn't supernaturally calm the storm while Jesus slept. He needed Jesus, a man, to stand up to it and take dominion over it.

Examples of this principle occur even in the Old Testament. For example, Elisha told the king of Israel to strike the ground with arrows to signify the Lord's deliverance from Syria. The king only struck the ground three times. Elisha was furious and confronted the king: "You should have struck five or six times; then you would have struck Syria till you had destroyed it! But now you will strike Syria only three times" (2 Kings 13:19). God wanted Israel to destroy Syria, but His desire wasn't accomplished because a man limited Him.

Again we read how Israel "limited the Holy One" (Psalm 78:41). It's staggering to think, but because of His integrity, God has limited what He'll do because He won't take back the authority He has delegated. This list of examples is endless.

> The Sovereign LORD *never does anything* without revealing his plan to his
> servants, the prophets. (Amos 3:7, TEV)

Observe the words "never does anything." In Old Testament times, once God revealed His plan, what happened next? Either the prophet, or someone the prophet had delegated responsibility to, would speak out or execute God's will. Keep in mind that in those days prophets were the ones to whom God had revealed His will. However, in the New Testament era, Jesus said John the Baptist was the greatest prophet up to that time. He then went on to say, shockingly, that the one who is *least in the kingdom of heaven* is greater than John (see Matthew 11:11)! How can that be? Because we now have the kingdom within! As God's sons and daughters, each of us can now hear God's plans to execute His will on earth. We are the extraordinary ones who rule in this life in Christ Jesus.

Assimilating all of this together, the Lord's Prayer could now read: "Our Father in heaven, God Almighty, Your imperial rule come, Your sovereign will be done on earth; Your kingdom's domain is established by Your saints reigning through Your abundant grace." Now that's truly *extraordinary*!

MANIFESTING HEAVEN'S DOMAIN

Let's briefly review our journey. Our highest goal is to please God, yet we don't have the capacity to do so in our own strength. But as we've thoroughly discussed, Christians are not to rely on their own ability because we've been given God's abundant grace. Grace is not just forgiveness of sin but encompasses much more. It has delivered us from captivity to our dead sin nature and caused us to be reborn, possessing the exact nature of Jesus Christ. The result: not only can we live pure, godly lives, but we can also produce the same fruit He produced—bringing heaven's imperial rule to this dark world.

Jesus reigned in life. We are to do the same!

Is the full impact of this truth overwhelming you yet? As a man, Jesus Christ took back what Adam had relinquished to Satan in the garden. This will eventually culminate with earth and all its inhabitants restored to perfection. However, prior to this occurrence, the kingdom is already in full force within the hearts and lives of God's people. All we have to do is hear, believe, and operate in God's grace, thus establishing His domain.

Just as Jesus brought heaven's imperial rule into all arenas of life, so we're to do the same. Here are just a few examples:

- Simon struggled in his business of commercial fishing, yet one encounter with Jesus and a day of failure turned into the greatest catch of his career.
- The wedding in Cana was about to fail; Jesus not only saved it but elevated it.
- The state didn't have to care for a helpless woman in Nain after Jesus raised her only son from the dead. Her dignity was held intact, and her legacy would continue.
- Once Zacchaeus faced Jesus, society became safer and more prosperous; the community was spared from theft and poverty because a newly dignified thief would no longer steal from clients. Yet it didn't stop there—400 percent was restored to those defrauded, thus stimulating the economy.
- In another incident, a madman would not waste away in solitary confinement but now would proclaim glorious news, spread the kingdom's domain to ten cities, and live a productive life.

We could go on and on, even beyond what's written in the gospels, for John says that the world of books couldn't contain all the extraordinary works Jesus accomplished. He revealed God's plan to bring heaven's domain to this earth. He showed us how to reign in life.

This is not only our model but our mandate. Not all of us are pastors or teachers because we all have different gifts and callings. But wherever we're located in life's arena, we should manifest the extraordinary. Our businesses should thrive, even when others struggle. Our communities should be safer, more delightful, and prosperous. Our places of employment should boom. Our music should be fresh and original—emulated by secular musicians. The same should be true with our graphic and architectural designs. Our creativity should inspire and be sought after on every level. Our performances, whether in athletics, entertainment, the arts, media, or any other field, should stand out. Our cities, states, and nations should flourish when the righteous govern. Our schools should excel when the righteous teach. Bottom line: when the extraordinary ones are involved, there should be an abundance of creativity, productivity, tranquillity, sensitivity, and ingenuity. All that's found in heaven should be manifest on earth. We truly are to be light in this dark world.

We see snapshots of this in the Old Testament, of course on a much smaller scale. Joseph endured great turmoil due to his brothers' hatred. Yet we learn a great deal about him even as a slave:

> The LORD was with Joseph and blessed him greatly as he served in the home of his Egyptian master. Potiphar noticed this and realized that the LORD was with Joseph, giving him success in everything he did.... Potiphar soon put Joseph in charge of his entire household and entrusted him with all his business dealings. From the day Joseph was put in charge, the LORD *began to bless Potiphar* for Joseph's sake. All his household affairs began to run smoothly, and his crops and livestock flourished. (Genesis 39:2–5, NLT)

Potiphar increased in a magnificent way simply because Joseph worked for him, not as a highly regarded employee, but as a slave!

Even after being falsely accused and thrown into prison, not only did Joseph remain blessed, but again his environment prospered. He was eventually put in charge of the other prisoners, and we read, "The keeper of the prison did not look into anything that was under Joseph's authority, because the LORD was with him; and *whatever he did, the LORD made it prosper*" (verse 23). Extraordinary living accompanied Joseph wherever he was placed, even in a prison cell!

Another Old Testament example would be Daniel and his three friends. They were hired to work for the government of Babylon, the most powerful nation of the world. They were foreign boys with no formal training. Yet upon interviewing each, those in charge realized they were "ten times better" than all the other counselors to the king (see Daniel 1:20). They came up with new methods and operational procedures that were quickly adapted by the realm. They were the extraordinary ones.

I could cite other examples, such as David, Jacob, Ruth, Esther, Jeremiah, and so forth. If this happened on a limited scale in the Old Testament to those who were only near the kingdom, how much more should this be the norm for those who have the kingdom within? We are the hope of the world, the salt of the earth. We are to rule in life through abundance of grace. We are to live extraordinarily!

THE RESTRAINING FORCE

You may ask, "Does God expect us to literally take over the world—the systems of government, education, entertainment, finance, media, and trade—for Jesus to return and step in to what we've prepared for Him?" No, that isn't what Scripture teaches. The New Testament clearly portrays that prior to Jesus' return the world systems will be in darkness, steeped in lawlessness. This is what Paul wrote to the church of Thessalonica concerning the second coming of Jesus:

> Let no one deceive or beguile you in any way, for that day will not come except the apostasy comes first [unless the predicted great falling away of those who have professed to be Christians has come], and the man of lawlessness (sin) is revealed, who is the son of doom (of perdition), who opposes and exalts himself so proudly and insolently against and over all that is called God or that is worshiped, [even to his actually] taking his seat in the temple of God, proclaiming that he himself is God. Do you not recollect that when I was still with you, I told you these things? And now you know what is *restraining* him [from being revealed at this time]. (2 Thessalonians 2:3–6, AMP)

This scripture, as well as others, shows the world's system will be in decay just prior to Jesus' return, after which He'll slay the enemies of God and initiate His physical reign on earth (see Revelation 19:11–20:6). However, we note that something is "restraining" the man who embodies the fullness of rebellion toward God.

In fact, if we keep reading, it is not only the antichrist who's *restrained;* general lawlessness is also held back:

> For the mystery of lawlessness (that hidden principle of rebellion against
> constituted authority) is already at work in the world, [but it is] *restrained*
> only until he who *restrains* is taken out of the way. (verse 7, AMP)

Paul's words don't just indicate the time of the antichrist but encompass all New Testament days, which certainly includes today. So whether the antichrist appears this year or fifty years from today, these words certainly apply now. Someone is holding back lawlessness, but just who is it?

The first logical assumption would be the Holy Spirit. Yet it can't be Him, for during the reign of the "Man of Sin," there will be many who give their lives to Jesus Christ, and Scripture shows that no one can come to Jesus without the wooing of the Holy Spirit or say that "Jesus is Lord except by the Holy Spirit" (1 Corinthians 12:3). Therefore "he who restrains" cannot be the Holy Spirit.

There's only one other possibility, and it's none other than the body of Christ. Once the Lord comes to catch away His true believers—the church (see 1 Thessalonians 4:16–17 and 1 Corinthians 15:51–52)—"he" will have been removed. Jesus Christ has never been referred to as "she," so He is clearly a man. If we're discussing His ruling "body," then it must be referred to in the male gender. On the other hand, in regard to our relationship with Jesus, we are the "bride of Christ" (see Ephesians 5:25–32), thus viewed as feminine. However, in regard to authority, the "body of Christ" is viewed in the male gender.

The ruling body of Christ ("he") can restrain lawlessness as Jesus Himself did by reigning in life. Our Lord said, "As long as I am in the world, I am the light of the world" (John 9:5). Is Jesus Christ still in the world? The answer is yes, but it's not His head, but His body—and *that's us.* Nowhere in Scripture are we told that the Holy Spirit is the light of the world. Jesus says, "I am the light of the world" (John 8:12), but He also says to us, "You are the light of the world" (Matthew 5:14). We're all one—He's the head, and we're His body. As Jesus is, so are we the light of the world.

Light restrains darkness, not the other way around. You've never heard of a "flashdark," only a flashlight, because darkness can't overcome light, but light restrains darkness. If I have an auditorium full of people and give each a lamp containing a sixty-watt bulb, the auditorium would be brightly lit. On the other hand, if only a few people have sixty-watt bulbs, the auditorium would be dimly lit. Even though the darkness could *never* restrain the light, the light would be dim because of a reduced presence.

In the same manner, if only a small portion of the body of Christ realizes who they are in Christ Jesus and walks in the power of grace, then the world is dimly lit. This has been the situation for too long—we've dimly lit the world. But it doesn't have to stay that way! I have a dream! A dream of a light-filled body of Christ comprised of all ages, inclusive of men and women, awakening to what God has hidden within and arising in His glory and power. These believers will live in such an extraordinary manner that multitudes will be drawn to the kingdom of God, not merely by what they preach, but by the compelling demonstration of how they live and their remarkable feats. I believe this dream is God given, for Isaiah prophesied:

> Arise, shine;
> for your light has come!
> And the glory of the LORD is risen upon you.
> For behold, the darkness shall cover the earth,
> and deep darkness the people;
> but the LORD will arise over you,
> and His glory will be seen upon you.
> The Gentiles [unbelievers] shall come to your light,
> and kings to the brightness of your rising.
> (Isaiah 60:1–3)

Notice the world will be in darkness, and the people in deep darkness—however, light will come! Think of that auditorium transitioning from being dimly lit...to brightly lit, as more and more people switch on their sixty-watt bulbs.

Notice how Isaiah prophesies that the glory of the Lord will *arise,* not *descend,* on us. So many Christians are looking for a spectacular outpouring of God's Spirit to come upon the church, thus initiating a great revival. No, I believe God is waiting for us to wake up, to realize who He's made us to be and to activate the power deposited in us. Once we do these things and truly believe, we'll become exceedingly bright and light up the dark auditorium of the world. Unbelievers will be drawn to our extraordinary lives. What exciting days we're living in!

WHAT ABOUT TRIALS?

How do trials and tribulations fit into the scenario I've described? We know we will encounter opposition—the Bible says so. Is opposition potentially a stopping force for an extraordinary life? No, this isn't the way tribulation is to be looked upon by an extraordinary one. Rather it is to be viewed as an opportunity. Joseph's adversity was the path to his great calling. Moses' experience of tending sheep in the desert prepared him to pastor the nation of Israel. He learned strong leadership skills as a son of Pharaoh, but it would also take the heart of a shepherd to care for his nation of battered slaves. David's adversity prepared him and his leaders for his dynasty. I could go on and on.

Paul told the early church, "We must through many tribulations enter the kingdom of God" (Acts 14:22). Let's read his words again, inputting the definitions learned in this chapter: "We must through many tribulations arise and come into the imperial rule of God." In other words, we will not enter into rulership in this life—extraordinary living—without resistance.

If there's no battle, there's no victory. If there's no opposition, there's no new ground to take. For a season Paul had an incorrect view of this area of life. A messenger of Satan was sent to buffet him, and Paul pleaded with the Lord three times to have this problem taken away. God's response to him was, "My grace is sufficient for you, for my power is made perfect in weakness" (2 Corinthians 12:9, NIV). Paul's weakness was his flesh's inability to overcome Satan's opposition. God simply says, "Don't you realize that the extraordinary begins when human ability can't get the job done? That's when My grace [power] fills in the gap. So why should I remove the resistance? You are to overcome and destroy it, through My grace!"

Once this became a reality to him, Paul later said:

Therefore I will boast all the more gladly about my weaknesses [inabilities], so that Christ's power [grace] may rest on me. That is why, for Christ's sake, I *delight in* weaknesses, in insults, in hardships, in persecutions, in difficulties. For when I am weak [in my own human ability], then I am strong [in the grace of God]. (2 Corinthians 12:9–10, NIV)

What an attitude change. He went from "please take it away" to "now I delight in this opposition." He had discovered the power of grace!

This is why a few years later, Paul wrote, "Who shall separate us from the love of Christ? Shall tribulation, or distress, or persecution, or famine, or nakedness, or peril, or sword?… Yet in all these things we are more than conquerors through Him who loved us" (Romans 8:35, 37). We're not just conquerors, but *more* than conquerors! In other words, all opposition becomes an opportunity in the eyes of one who rules in life.

A FINAL WORD

I leave you with a final word of caution, an exhortation. Paul wrote to the Corinthians, "I may have the gift of inspired preaching; I may have all knowledge and understand all secrets; I may have all the faith needed to move mountains— but if I have no love, I am nothing" (1 Corinthians 13:2, TEV). If we discover who we are in the grace of God and the exceeding greatness of the power that's resident within us but are not motivated by compassion and sincere love, then we're no good, not only to ourselves, but also to those we influence.

Jesus was moved with compassion. It was the driving force behind His faith and grace. I challenge you to do a word search through the gospels regarding compassion and how often Jesus was moved by it. We are told in no uncertain terms, "For in Christ Jesus neither circumcision nor uncircumcision avails anything, but *faith working through love*" (Galatians 5:6). Paul was addressing circumcision versus uncircumcision, or living under the law versus living in the Spirit, in this letter. For our purposes we could quote it like this:

> *For in Christ Jesus, neither a common nor an extraordinary life avails anything without love, but what's extremely beneficial is faith working through love.*

For us to try to accomplish the work of God in our own ability is foolishness, which Scripture has made abundantly clear. Yet how many try to please God merely by human strength, apart from faith?

On the other hand, if you fully grasp all the revelation laid out during our journey and attempt to live extraordinarily apart from love, well, that's just as foolish. However, to live in the ability of grace, through faith, motivated by compassion and sincere love, will avail much in the eyes of God and men. May you be one of the extraordinary ones of our generation! You're needed to arise, shine, and reveal His imperial rule and glorious reign.

Now to Him who is able to keep you from stumbling,
And to present you faultless
Before the presence of His glory with exceeding joy,
To God our Savior,
Who alone is wise,
Be glory and majesty,
Dominion and power,
Both now and forever.
Amen. (Jude 1:24–25)

Reflections for an Extraordinary Journey

Consider the statement: "Godly men and women determine whether or not the will of God gets done on this earth!" List examples of how you've observed this play out.

In what areas of your life do you now want to "rule in life through Christ"?

What is keeping you from being extraordinary?

In what ways are you going to enter into an extraordinary life?

We'd love to hear from you. Share your story with us at
www.ExtraordinaryOnline.org.

Appendix

Prayer to Initiate an Extraordinary Life

How does an extraordinary life begin? First and foremost, it has nothing to do with you but with what was done *for you* by Jesus Christ. He gave His royal life, in perfect innocence, for you to be brought back to your Creator, God the Father. His death on the cross is the only price able to purchase your eternal life.

No matter your gender, age, social class, race, background, religion, or anything else favorable or unfavorable in the eyes of men, you are eligible to become a child of God. He desires and longs for you to come into His family. This occurs by simply renouncing your sin of living independently of Him and committing your life to the lordship of Jesus Christ. Once you do that, you'll literally be reborn and no longer a slave to darkness. You're born again as a brand-new son or daughter of God. Scripture declares:

> For if you confess with your mouth that Jesus is Lord and believe in your heart that God raised him from the dead, you will be saved. For it is by believing in your heart that you are made right with God, and it is by confessing with your mouth that you are saved. (Romans 10:9–10, NLT)

So if you believe that Jesus Christ died for you and you are willing to give Him your life—to no longer live for yourself—say this prayer from a sincere heart, and you will become a child of God:

> *God in heaven, I acknowledge that I am a sinner and have fallen short of Your righteous standard. I deserve to be judged for eternity for my sin. Thank You for not leaving me in this state, for I believe that You sent Jesus Christ, Your only begotten Son, who was born of the virgin Mary, to die for me and carry my judgment on the cross. I believe He was raised from the dead on the third day*

and is now seated at Your right hand as my Lord and Savior. So on this day of
_____, 2____, *I give my life entirely to the lordship of Jesus.*

Jesus, I confess You as my Lord, Savior, and King. Come into my life through Your Spirit and change me into a child of God. I renounce the things of darkness I once held on to, and from this day forward I will no longer live for myself but for You, who gave Yourself for me that I may live forever.

Thank You, Lord; my life is now completely in Your hands. And according to Your Word, I will never be ashamed. In Jesus' name I pray. Amen.

Now, you're saved; you're a child of God! All heaven is rejoicing with you at this very moment. Welcome to the family! I'd like to suggest three beneficial steps to take immediately:

1. Share what you've done with someone who is already a believer. Scripture says that one of the ways we defeat darkness is by our testimony (see Revelation 12:11). I invite you to contact our ministry, Messenger International at messengerinternational.org. We'd love to hear from you.

2. Join a good church that teaches the Word of God. Become a member and get involved. Parents do not put babies on the street the day they're born and say, "Survive!" You are now a babe in Christ; God your Father has provided a family to help you grow. It's called the local New Testament church.

3. Get water baptized. Though you are already a child of God, baptism is a public profession to both the spiritual world as well as the natural world that you've given your life to God through Jesus Christ. It is also an act of obedience, for Jesus says we are to baptize new believers "in the name of the Father and of the Son and of the Holy Spirit" (Matthew 28:19).

I wish you the very best in your new life in Christ. Our ministry will pray for you on a regular basis. Welcome to the beginning of an extraordinary life!

OTHER TITLES BY JOHN BEVERE

BEST-SELLING CURRICULUM - Driven by Eternity

It's not only where, but how you'll spend eternity....

We were made for eternity. This life on earth is but a vapor. Yet too many live as though there is nothing on the other side. Scriptural principles may be applied to achieve success on earth, but are we prepared for eternity? Scripture tells us there will be various degrees of rewards, or judgments, for believers which will determine how we spend our eternity.

Curriculum Includes:
* 12 40-Minute Sessions on 4 DVDs
* Hardcover Book
* Hardcover Devotional Workbook
* Also Included: Best-selling
   Hollywood Audio Theater,
   Affabel: Window of Eternity

Messenger International.

life-transforming truth.

UNITED STATES
PO Box 888
Palmer Lake, CO 80133

Phone: 800-648-1477
Email:
Mail@MessengerInternational.org

AUSTRALIA
Rouse Hill Town Centre
PO Box 6444
Rouse Hill NSW 2155

Phone: 1-300-650-577
Outside Australia:
+61 2 9679 4900
Email:
Australia@MessengerInternational.org

UNITED KINGDOM
PO Box 1066
Hemel Hempstead
Hertfordshire,
HP2 7GQ

Phone: 0800-9808-933
Outside UK:
(+44) 1442 288 531
E-mail:
Europe@MessengerInternational.org

www.MessengerInternational.org